Praise for *Competitive Intelligence Advantage*

"Seena Sharp has done it again! This incisive, compact book clears through the clutter that encumbers so many others in the field of competitive intelligence. Seena's no-holds-barred style rings true as she pierces several myths surrounding vaunted business decision making and the holy grail of 'crunching' business data.

"Every executive and aspiring 'high-potential manager' should take to heart Seena's keenly articulated assessment of the many flaws that inhibit truly valuable decision making. Great decisions are a product of insight, experience, and intelligence, which constitute the very heart of the critical thinking skills so eagerly sought by companies.

"Seena correctly underscores how the lack of the latter—solid intelligence input—can handicap a company's thinking processes and help to torpedo strategies. Why is this? As Seena points out, mastering intelligence takes real thinking discipline—the heavy lifting of business analysis. As this book argues cogently, today's shareholders deserve business executives who are willing to get this fundamental skill set under their belts.

"The world is getting more and more complicated, and so is business. Intelligence, as Seena points out, is an avenue to success."

**—Paul Kinsinger, Professor of Business Intelligence,
Thunderbird School of Global Management,
and Managing Consultant of the Thunderbird
Learning Consultant Network**

"Seena Sharp's new book presents a compelling case for the importance of competitive intelligence to decision making. In today's world, where business as usual is no longer the case, executives and line managers alike frequently find themselves without a compass when facing the inherent risk in decisions, whether large or small. Seena Sharp, long an intellectual force in the field of competitive intelligence, provides provocative examples of why both CI and her book are 'must-haves' for all organizational executives that seek advantage and success. And what executive doesn't?"

**—Cyndi Allgaier, Former President of SCIP
(Society of Competitive Intelligence Professionals)**

"Without a doubt *Competitive Intelligence Advantage* provides a clear, comprehensive approach to competitive intelligence for the business executive of today. A delightful read, it demystifies the terminology around CI and clearly educates business readers about this invaluable modern management discipline. As a business consultant, educator, and corporate strategy advisor, I would encourage every one of my clients and colleagues to read this book."

—Babette Bensoussan, Author and Director, The MindShifts Group, Australia, 2006 SCIP Meritorious Recipient

"Seena Sharp presents a 'state-of-the-art' approach to competitive intelligence that is meaningful and actionable to organization executives and managers. It addresses the *why*, the *when*, and the *value* of CI to the company decision-makers from the standpoint of insight, implications, relevancy to organization goals and objectives, early warning triggers, the customer perspective, and the marketplace."

—Bob Margulies, Former President of SCIP

"Savvy business owners and managers must read Seena Sharp's insightful book before making another big decision. The top expert in this field has written a compelling and extremely readable book. Sharp shares a wealth of strategies and practical tips for staying way ahead of your competition."

—Jane Applegate, columnist and author, *201 Great Ideas for Your Small Business*

"Seena Sharp has always provided her clients and fellow professionals a fresh and insightful perspective on the work and subjects she addresses. This book fulfills those expectations, especially with regard to the business men and women who might not know what competitive intelligence is, or why they need it in today's information-overloaded, global marketplace."

—Jan P. Herring, Advisor to Intelligence Professionals, Meritorious Award Recipient, SCIP

"After reading this book, you will see your business differently because you will see the world differently . . . a set of new opportunities to exploit."

—Steve Moya, Consultant and former Senior Vice President and Chief Marketing Officer, Humana, Inc.

COMPETITIVE INTELLIGENCE ADVANTAGE

How to Minimize Risk, Avoid Surprises, and Grow Your Business in a Changing World

Seena Sharp

WILEY

John Wiley & Sons, Inc.

Published by John Wiley & Sons, Inc., Hoboken, New Jersey.
Published simultaneously in Canada.

For general information on our other products and services or for technical support, please contact our Customer Care Department within the United States at (800) 762-2974, outside the United States at (317) 572-3993 or fax (317) 572-4002.

Wiley also publishes its books in a variety of electronic formats. Some content that appears in print may not be available in electronic books. For more information about Wiley products, visit our web site at www.wiley.com.

Library of Congress Cataloging-in-Publication Data:

Sharp, Seena.
Competitive intelligence advantage: how to minimize risk, avoid surprises, and grow your business in a changing world/by Seena Sharp.
    p. cm.
  ISBN 978-0-470-29317-1 (cloth: acid-free paper)
   1. Business intelligence.   2. Risk.   3. Success in business.   I. Title
  HD38.7.S486 2009
  658.4′72–dc22
                                                                    2009016543

Printed in the United States of America

10 9 8 7 6 5 4 3 2 1

Contents

CONTENTS

Introduction: Required Reading (Yes, Really)

It's a whole new day out there in the world of business. Products are sold in odd venues; companies are venturing into totally new markets; customers don't fit the usual profile, and they use products or services in unexpected ways.

What, exactly, is going on? And what does it mean for the decision maker?

Although business has been undergoing dramatic changes for a long time, the changes taking place today are more accelerated, more pronounced—and some even seem downright bizarre. The economic slowdown is part of the reason, of course; but it is not the entire cause, nor even the major portion. More important, expectations have changed, from both businesses and customers.

What's happening outside your business is having more impact on your success than ever before. This external world includes substitute products or services, the economy, industries that are indirectly related, and changes in societal behaviors.

Customers today are smarter; they have access to more information and feedback; and they're more demanding than ever. You may not think so, but this *is* good news—really!

"New" creates opportunities, at least it does for those executives who recognize that *new* or *different* when applied to business is a synonym for "change." And that's where advantages are to be found. Some of the most successful businesses were founded during the Great Depression of 1929 and during other severe economic slumps— Hewlett-Packard, Target, GE, UnitedHealth Group, Wikipedia,

Cargill, FedEx, Microsoft, CNN, MTV, LexisNexis, *Sports Illustrated*, and Hyatt Corp, to name just a few.

In a changing business environment, the past is less and less a guide to what will bring success. More important, following yesterday's path could be even riskier than doing nothing. This is the time to *unlearn* what's no longer true.

The chairman of Saatchi & Saatchi, one of the world's most successful global advertising agencies, wrote in his new book, *Start With the Answer*, about leading in tough times, "When things are not going well, until you get the truth out on the table, no matter how ugly, you are not in a position to deal with it." Competitive intelligence gets at the truth. It objectively details what is happening, much of which may be unknown to most executives. Unless you conduct an analysis of current conditions, the information that you know is only partially current and may be only partially accurate.

How much confidence do you have that your knowledge base is sufficient? That you have much more than half of what you need? That it's accurate? That it reflects this changing world? That it acknowledges what's outdated? How much do you monitor the external environment?

This book is written for management who is unfamiliar with competitive intelligence, but savvy enough to understand that *different* creates an advantage, an opening, and an immediate opportunity to be proactive. It's also for the person who is new to competitive intelligence and needs to get up to speed quickly. Executives strongly believe that they are aware of what's current; most would be surprised to learn that some of their knowledge is no longer true, especially if it concerns anything "really" important. What's the basis for my statement?

First, it takes time to learn what is actually happening. Second, it takes a period of time to accept that changes have occurred. And time is what we're dealing with here. Time is where companies gain and lose (sales, customers, advantage), by missing or recognizing changes and opportunities. Competitive intelligence helps close that gap. It provides the necessary reality and insights sooner.

Any way you slice it, conventional wisdom, experience, and formulas are less and less reliable; they take a beating every day in a world that is changing so rapidly. The old rules may or may not apply. While no one, not even an expert, has a clue what to expect from all this turmoil, the smart thinkers *prepare* themselves for many aspects of business to be different.

If conditions remain the same, then great. If, on the other hand, you're facing multiple changes and unknowns, then consider the significant value that competitive intelligence can yield. How do you know whether competitive intelligence will provide an advantage, whether it will benefit you and your company? Ask yourself these questions:

- Are you planning to expand your line by offering new products or services?
- Have you considered entering a new market or industry?
- Have you been blindsided by loss of sales to a competitor—especially one that is unknown or emerging—or to a substitute (not a direct competitor, but a company outside your industry)?
- Has a competitor introduced a new, unexpected product or service or feature that your customers demanded—and that you didn't know they wanted?
- Has a direct competitor been successful in distributing to a totally new channel—one that's unusual in your industry—or selling to a different customer segment?
- Have you noticed possible signs of an opportunity, but aren't sure if it makes sense for your company?
- Are you hearing conflicting viewpoints from your staff or the industry?
- Do you have a marketing or strategy problem to solve and don't have enough information and insight?
- Are you seeking capital (bank or private equity) and need support for and evidence of the soundness of your decision?
- Are you investigating a possible acquisition and need to supplement the financial due diligence with market due diligence?
- Do you question if your assumptions are still valid (about your industry, competitors, customers, products)?
- Are you unsure that you have sufficient, specific, accurate, and current information to make a strategic decision?

If you're unsure or have answered yes to any of these questions, then you will benefit from competitive intelligence. Good competitive intelligence lays out today's truths. Even if you don't act immediately, at the very least you get a heads-up and a chance to check out these changes for yourself or to monitor these findings until you determine whether they're appropriate for your company. Without a serious investigation, these changes remain unknown—by you and by your competitors.

Changes may be unknown, but only for a time. "Opportunities are never lost. Someone will seize the ones you miss." (Attributed to Andy Rooney, *60 Minutes*.) Another company will figure out the possible advantage in these changes. Competitive intelligence is your partner in getting there before the others.

Recognizing change offers disruptive competitive advantage. Because so few companies actually do CI, the ones that engage in CI disrupt the usual competitor activities and gain an immediate and powerful advantage for themselves. This is how you "un-level" the playing field: by doing what competitors don't recognize or expect and by being proactive.

Unexpected events, unexpected customers, unexpected competitors, and unexpected buying activity are all indicators of some type of shift, some turmoil taking place in the market—your market. And there is no reason to expect this chaos and craziness to stop or slow down. Even if it does decelerate, few companies will respond appropriately to unexpected changes, so opportunities do and will continue to exist. This is an advantage to you if you know what they are.

The greater advantage to your firm exists because companies resist any kind of transformation for a long time before inevitably accepting that specific change (if they don't go out of business). Companies adjust at different rates and at different times along the spectrum; so the benefit to you is realizing that change will work for you, recognizing it as early as possible, and taking appropriate action.

Gaining Control in Uncontrollable Times

The rules of the game have changed. And so must your thinking about your business.

The world economy over the past few years has been in a state of chaos, and the effects on business are being felt far and wide. While hunkering down and riding out this market volatility may seem prudent, the turbulence in today's market will continue (even if to a lesser degree), and companies can no longer afford to sit on the sidelines waiting for the calm to return.

To survive and grow during these turbulent times, a company must gain a measure of control. And, companies who seize control today hold a considerable advantage over those that don't. Yes, there will be some things that are and will remain beyond your control, but competitive intelligence is particularly beneficial during unpredictable and turbulent times. It can bring a measure of control by providing accurate and objective information because that "truth" will reduce uncertainty and the risk of error.

How do you gain control? How do you shift thinking from "change is a threat" to "change is a gift?" This happens when you:

- Become informed and think more broadly and differently than before. The more you know that is true, the better prepared you are to deal with anything that comes your way. Competitive intelligence helps reframe the world as it is changing. It will make you more knowledgeable than your competitors, both known and unknown, by telling you today what all of you will learn... eventually. Proper CI is your early warning sign.

- Understand that looking to past successes makes it very difficult to deal with changing conditions, and may even lead to bad decisions. Use the same critical thinking skills that you used when you first achieved that success, but actively and aggressively temper that with current information.

  A *Harvard Business Review* article titled "When Growth Stalls" stated that 87 percent of Fortune 100 companies over the past half century experienced an "abrupt drop in revenue growth." One reason cited was the companys' failure "to respond effectively to new, low-cost competitive challenges or shifts in customer valuation of product features. . . . the majority of these standstills are preventable." Preventable, had those business entities possessed solid, current, sufficient information and intelligence and then acted on these.

- Focus on insight and customers, not merely on data and competitors. In unsettling times, companies find solace in data, not recognizing that data only reflects the past. If data represents what happened in the past, and the present is different from the past, then it's not logical to expect data to be particularly helpful, except in limited situations. Companies that succeed in these changing and unpredictable times are those led by executives who can pull their heads out of data and move forward with intelligence. Changing times mean moving from comfort to discomfort and to a more accurate view of the competitive landscape and the important factors to monitor.

- Unlearn what's no longer true. It's a given that if change is occurring, then what is true must also be changing—about your customers, your competitors, and the marketplace. Don't guess about what's changing; don't brainstorm about it; just power up your competitive intelligence engine to find out what's really happening in the marketplace.

That outside perspective is one of the most important ideas for keeping up with change and with your customers. The "father of modern management," Peter Drucker, said, "Ninety percent of the information used in organizations is internally focused and only ten percent is about the outside environment. This is exactly backwards." I make this very point throughout this book, substantiated by numerous examples.

Control is increasingly moving to the individual—in all aspects, from business to one's personal life. There was a time, not too long ago, when individuals gave control of their medical care and financial planning to the experts. Now we all expect to be partners, equal or not. And quite often the experts tell *us* to make the decision after discussing the situation with them. They're putting the final control in the hands of their customers, even more reason to be informed.

When it comes to purchasing, customers have increasing influence in the marketplace, as many products, services, and companies are "reviewed" in chat rooms and faux company web sites. Prospects investigate your offerings with the result that control of information is shifting from the salesperson to the buyer. And all this has great implications for you and your company.

What Will We Cover?

This book is based on the premise that all companies want to succeed by gaining, keeping, and serving their customers, the source of revenues. In many instances, they are prevented from doing so by continuing down the same path that worked before and hoping that it will continue to work in the same way. But in these continuously changing times, "doing the same things in the same old way" no longer serves either the company or its customers adequately; it's time for a change.

This book is all about change in business, how it's affecting your business, and how competitive intelligence can make it can work for you. We define what competitive intelligence is and is not (hint: it's not merely information); we passionately argue why fixating on your competition is a misguided approach; we speak to the importance of looking at the entire competitive spectrum and what parts should be of concern to you; we address how you can use competitive intelligence to find new opportunities; we tell you when and why you should conduct CI; and we talk about the next steps and what you can and should expect from competitive intelligence, and more—all supported with more than 70 examples.

We continue to harp on the theme that assumptions are no longer reliable or reasonable. They do not hold up in changing times. They can't. As Michael Porter stated in *Competitive Strategy*, "To be competitive, we have to constantly reexamine our assumptions."

Executives don't seem surprised when changes occur in other industries, yet they don't seem to actively look for changes that are occurring in their own industry. When they don't, they create an opening for competitors to address these gaps and differences.

Or they get blindsided. Competitive intelligence significantly reduces the likelihood of being blindsided. There's no excuse for being taken by surprise, as it indicates a serious defect in the way companies make decisions. They didn't bother to find out what they didn't know; and in a changing world, that question must be asked.

While executives readily accept rapid and constant changes in technology, they often don't recognize how much it applies to other businesses. Those other businesses may not change as quickly or obviously, but they still change, so the same rules for keeping up and keeping customers apply. You may be skeptical about unfamiliar information and inquire whether it's valid and that is absolutely the right thinking. On the other hand, new, different, or strange information is the connection between what you know and what's changing. You have to allow for the possibility that these changes are plausible.

The gap between familiar and unfamiliar is yesterday intersecting with tomorrow. And in the middle is change. You can't get to tomorrow without going through change – big change, little change, weird change, good change.

What is the downside to being smart about your customers and making informed decisions? Companies that don't do competitive intelligence are less prepared and more vulnerable than those that do. How can it be good for your company to have less accurate information and intelligence than your competitors? That's the essence of competitive intelligence; it's a decision input tool whose output is better decisions.

Informed risk is your competitive advantage. Simple. Powerful.

Companies that don't know about or don't engage in competitive intelligence don't understand the return they will get—immediately. The first and most obvious return on investment (ROI) is a better decision, meaning no do-overs, no lost revenue or lost time, no ceding competitive advantage to another company, and no loss of morale over missing the boat. The second, third, and fourth ROIs are more subtle and not evident to others—they result in companies acting sooner, more confidently, and more aggressively.

For the past 40 years, U.S. presidents have received a daily briefing telling them what they need to know—the good, the bad, and the ugly. They understand the need for new and updated information to bridge the gap (sometimes the chasm) between perception and reality. Business, particularly your business, has no less a need.

The hidden bonus of competitive intelligence is that good news is good news and *bad news may be even better news*. How can that be so? It's great to validate and to confirm what you know or believe is true. But it's even more valuable to find out what is not true and needs a serious course correction, and it's more valuable still when it's part of a decision. Knowing what's true today will let you make that course correction.

Why doesn't management think about competitive intelligence? It's not on their radar. It's rarely mentioned in business school, and it's taught in only a limited number of universities, even as a single course. It's almost never a breakout session at conferences, so exposure is close to non-existent. This book introduces you to insights and perspectives about the discipline of CI and what it can do for you, along with tools and techniques, ideas and strategies to reduce risk and seize opportunities.

Perhaps now you're ready to enter the world and advantages of competitive intelligence. If so, fasten your seatbelt, and start to read. CI is an incredible journey, with an even more incredible payoff. As the great American social commentator Will Rogers said, "It ain't what you don't know that gets you into trouble. It's what you know for sure that just ain't so."

1

The Emergence of the Hapless Executive

The mind can only see what it is prepared to see.
—Edward de Bono

Think of all the headlines that you've read over the past few years reporting that this company or that has missed the mark in one way or another. Their shares tumbled furiously, or they closed stores, or they were acquired, or they declared bankruptcy. Merrill Lynch, one of the world's leading financial management and advisory companies, is suddenly sold to Bank of America; Lehman Brothers, an innovator in global finance founded in 1850, is forced to go under and sell a major portion of its assets to Barclay's Bank. Mervyn's, a 59-year-old chain of 175 department stores, most of which are located in California, is liquidated, and the same happens to Linens N' Things and CompUSA. The Big Three auto giants are no longer at the top of the heap, and one or two declared bankruptcy. And how many of the Fortune 500 companies of the 1990s are still on that list?

Where were leaders of these industry giants when the wind was knocked out of their sails? Where was all the collective knowledge and wisdom that guided these companies? Is it possible that all of those executives had a communal lapse in judgment? Could they not have seen the signs?

It is easy for us, in hindsight, to believe we would have seen the warning signs and taken appropriate action. But for those experiencing these setbacks, it's not quite as simple. What about you? What do you do—deliberately—to stay current and aware? Do you hear or even listen to information about your industry that surprises you? Do you learn about events *after* the fact? Is your company more reactive than proactive? These are dead giveaways that you're not getting the information and intelligence that you *must* have to make the best decisions for your business.

Executives Today Know Less about More and More about Less

What is going on? We are, after all, living in the information age, where anyone can know (or learn) everything about anything, anytime they want to know it.

The answer is that while we have increased access to information, most executives are not getting the intelligence they need for strategy or to make better decisions—or worse, they are dismissing or under-estimating it. We receive a plethora of new information on a daily basis, yet it's often ignored. Why is that? Perhaps there is too much information; perhaps the information does not conform to our pre-conceived notions; perhaps there just isn't enough time to take it all in.

Regardless of the reason, however, the result is the same: Company executives and board members are no longer quite as adept in their decision making in a business environment that is increasingly complex and one that requires more information and better intelligence.

These are undoubtedly bright, skilled executives. What then lies behind their failings in judgment? Well, like everyone, they have their blind spots that usually result from one or more of the following:

1. *Success breeds overconfidence and arrogance.*

Successful companies and executives start to believe in their own invincibility and stop doing their due diligence. After all, it's very difficult to relinquish the knowledge and behavior that re-sulted in past successes and brought them to their current lofty positions, even when the present is different. Executives tend to think that they know it all and therefore don't put forth much effort to keep abreast of current trends and changes in their industries.

The problem is *the past*. Author Leslie Poles Hartley said, "The past is a foreign country. They do things differently there." Yesterday's success is only that—yesterday's success. I've never forgotten a reality check comment that I read many years ago and is even more applicable: *Today's success only entitles you to compete tomorrow*. To continue on that same roll of success, you need to constantly monitor your environment to be sure you can repeat those successes.

The domestic auto industry offers the best (or worst) example. For decades the auto companies have consistently claimed that *they* know what customers want. After all, every one of us can recite the testimonial, "What's good for General Motors . . ." Yet when the gas crunch hit in the 1970s, the Japanese gained a significant toehold in the U.S. market by offering the small, well-built, fuel-efficient cars that Detroit said Americans would never buy.

It appears that being blindsided once wasn't sufficient to get the message across. Come the late 1980s, the Japanese scored again by going after the high-end luxury market. Once more,

Detroit miscalculated, relying on its internal knowledge, and the result is that Detroit now "owns" less than 50 percent of the domestic car market. Can this industry finally relinquish its arrogance? Will it?

2. *Executives don't want to hear bad or contrary news.*

Companies that discourage contrary or negative input tend to blame or punish the messenger, or they may underplay or block news the executive needs to hear, thus exposing themselves to a false reality or getting a pasteurized version of the unfavorable news so that it does not appear quite as dire.

Letting only the good news in is a surefire way to keep your company ignorant about the true—and not always pleasant—state of your business. Refusing to acknowledge problems merely · ensures that they won't be solved. The idea of management in denial has been a recurring theme in business, no less so during economic downturns, and one that is likely to continue if they remain closed to all the information, good or bad.

3. *They are unaware of the daily issues that their employees face.*

Higher-level executives are too far removed from day-to-day operations or staff to hear about current, developing problems. Executives tend to be surrounded by human filters whose job seems to be to keep those executives isolated from reality. Sure, some of them report a portion of the intelligence, but most of it just does not get through.

At a conference I attended featuring a panel of three CEOs, one remarked that the same day he received his appointment as CEO, a colleague told him that "today is the last time you will ever hear the truth." Does that ring a bell for you?

Contrast that with the story told about Wal-Mart founder Sam Walton, who established a rigorous management effort to keep his ear to the ground. Walton and his executive team made twice-weekly visits to stores and distribution centers. They talked to customers and staff; they observed merchandise on the shelf and movement across the distribution system; and they discussed their findings at weekly staff meetings.

4. *Executives are not exposed to the same realities their customers face.*

How many times have executives used the company's call center or their own internal help desk? How often have executives personally (and anonymously) served their customers? How many have gone on sales calls in the past few years? How many doctors have actually been patients in the same hospital where they work and experienced the service their patients receive?

The reality is that most managers don't experience quality breakdowns as equipment ages; they don't deal with the frustration of scheduling service calls; they aren't subjected to surly and inconsiderate staff. In fact, in one large company (more than 15,000 employees) with a robust help desk, the executives have their own dedicated technician to take care of every issue they face, so they don't even have to experience what their employees do. And when these issues are reported to executives, they usually defend their company's response.

5. *Executives today may be blindsided by the history, myths, and conventional wisdom related to the industry, competitors, and customers.*

"Managers who have been successful develop a vested interest in maintaining things the way they are," says Robert Sternberg, professor of psychology and dean of Arts and Sciences at Tufts University. He refers to this tendency as "the cost of expertise" in *Inc.* magazine.

It is indeed a phenomenon that has reared its head in recent times. Immediately after the financial meltdown in October 2008, Alan Greenspan, former chairman of the Federal Reserve, stated in his testimony to Congress, "I did not forecast a significant decline because we never had a significant decline." In other words, how could we know something would happen when it's never happened before? At the very least, more and *different* questions need to be asked.

In a changing world, conventional wisdom is not likely to provide the guidance that is needed. Prepare to experience situations that have not previously occurred; that is today's norm.

6. *The premise upon which the decision is based is weak or insufficient.*

Some ideas sound good the first time we hear them. In the excitement of considering the idea based solely its on merits, companies will occasionally skip the due diligence process. It's not uncommon for some of these ideas to gain support and enthusiasm for proceeding without having been fully vetted.

For example, one client had developed a smaller, portable, less expensive version of a business-to-business product that they had been selling successfully for 12 years. Employees suggested, during internal discussions, that a second and different customer base (distribution channel) was viable. Their thinking and strategy appeared reasonable in their presentation to us.

However, it wasn't long into our investigation that we learned why this alternative distribution channel could *never* be successful. The company had never considered those other elements that would preclude success. They relied on a similar strategy for the new distribution channel and they did not realize how different each channel was. It would have been a disastrous decision. As outsiders, we don't rely on a single approach, so we were able to offer plan B, two other viable markets, albeit not as attractive to the client.

Bottom line: Insufficient information or erroneous assumptions can easily put a company on the wrong track. This reality check clearly proved that this particular company needed more information, insight and intelligence. Our experience and readings in the business press reveal that this same mistake is repeated far too frequently.

7. *Executives and their staff become too engaged in or passionate about new offerings, and aren't able to see the flaws. The result is groupthink.*

When a company has invested both time and money into a specific product or service, and there is a lot at stake, the momentum for an idea tends to roll over input that might derail it. As a result, the executive lead and support staff tend to reject the ideas that a reality check may reveal. New information threatens the project and the schedule, so the group marches in lockstep until it's revealed that the emperor has no clothes.

It should come as no surprise that managers will staunchly support an endeavor that brings their company the most money. But what makes money for your company *now* may be short term. Again, the Big Three automakers, General Motors, Ford, and Chrysler, were so committed to their popular SUVs that they did not want to shift production to smaller and less profitable vehicles. They rationalized decreased customer demand for more fuel-efficient cars as a temporary situation. Unfortunately for them, it wasn't.

Similarly, Sony spent billions building and rebuilding its Walkman while consumers were moving on to MP3 players. Sony and so many others simply would not or *could* not abandon their formerly best-selling products in favor of developing a brand-new car, gadget, or whatever might be more efficient or in greater demand from customers.

Executives need to remember the value of the product life cycle and the existence of an arch to sales data. Products don't stay equally hot or profitable forever. There *is* a time to let go.

8. *Executives don't see or hear as much as necessary about the forces operating outside their industry.*

According to Shell's vice president of Global Business Environment, "The big decisions that failed at Shell didn't fail because of our operations or because of project management. They failed because we misunderstood the external world." When outside information is not included in product development, the likelihood of surprise increases, and it's rarely a pleasant surprise.

In the words of famed management consultant Peter Drucker, "Ninety percent of the information used in organizations is internally focused, and only ten percent is about the outside environment. This is exactly backwards." The outside world must be factored into all decisions. After all, that's where your products or services will be sold. Lew Frankfort, CEO of Coach Leatherworks, a high-end leather and accessories company, regularly and deliberately seeks out what he needs to know. "He runs the business on an 'exception basis.' To the extent that there is a significant variation better or worse than expected, we drill in to understand that." That is, he pays attention to what's different from his own beliefs, to find out whether the variation indicates a market change or different customer preference.

9. *Executives narrow their focus to very specific aspects of their industry.*

There is so much information available today, and so little time to digest it all, that some executives focus on only what they *believe* they need to know. They don't look for, and therefore don't see, the bigger picture or the information that may not be obvious. It then becomes much easier to miss problems that are just out of sight.

They focus on the product itself and ignore or underestimate issues relating to packaging or delivery, design or sizing, and attitude or demeanor of those selling or delivering it. A product or service is not simply the end result; it's also what the customer experiences on his or her way to receiving it. Executives need to make themselves aware of the entire buying process, via sufficient due diligence.

10. *Some executives suffer from too much experience.*

Can too much experience hurt your judgment? Occasionally, it can. Familiarity with a particular product or process can blind executives to new, different, or foreign information, which they may dismiss as irrelevant. That can be a very costly mistake. How often have you heard an executive proclaim, "I know what my customers want and need"?

Executives fiercely believe that they know their industry—their customers, competitors, market drivers, how and where the industry is growing, and more. And they truly believe they know it better than anyone else. The reality, however, is that they probably know their industry through a filter, a filter of yesterday's truths and assumptions, and the filter of an insider. Customers, whether B2B or B2C, have a very different view. That's why new companies enter the market—to respond to this alternate view. Competitive intelligence clarifies that filter and accurately reveals what is happening today and what buyers want. Understanding this is the difference between the company's deep knowledge of their product and reality. Reality is where you sell your goods or services.

11. *Executives can experience information overload.*

Executives have the opportunity to know more than ever before and therefore to include better input in their decisions and strategy. The downside to this is that the enormity of available information may result in "closing the door" to protect oneself from being bombarded by the oft-stated sense of information overload. They may prefer to rely on what's known, even if it's outdated or untrue. On the other hand, the mere presence of information does not translate to having the right information. Accurate information may be dwarfed by what's less important but more readily uncovered.

Information benefits companies and executives only when they have the *right* information, *and* analyze it to produce intelligence—insight, understanding, implications, and actions for their company.

Curse of Knowledge

Finally, hapless executives may find themselves trapped by the "curse of knowledge." In other words, once you know something, it becomes hard to imagine not knowing it. These facts appear so obvious to the owners of that knowledge that they cannot even imagine that others don't "get it."

Thus, armed with what we know unquestionably to be true, it becomes even more difficult to make a decision that does not support that knowledge. To quote business journalist Janet Rae-Dupree, "It becomes nearly impossible to look beyond what you know and think outside the box you've built around yourself" ("Innovative Minds Don't Think Alike," *New York Times*). We don't consider information other than what we know because what we know has become word and law. However, if executives can resist this inclination and acknowledge that they live in a changing business environment, it follows logically that they will accept that information of relevance to their business must also be changing. Therefore, what they've come to accept as "facts" may no longer be true, and if they're no longer true, then decisions and strategy going forward must operate from a different knowledge base and point of view:

1. Their customers' positive response to change is their way of declaring a desire for new, improved products or features; smaller or larger sizes; less expensive, lighter-weight, or easier to use products or services.

2. Executives proclaim that they are "keeping up" by responding to customer's desires. If that were true, customers would continue buying from you. Customers hold up a red flag that your company's products or services aren't satisfying them by buying from another. This is how customers tell you that your company is not keeping up. In other words, by not offering customers what they want, you are driving them to a competitor.

3. The shift in mind-set that customers regularly and constantly exhibit must be met with a comparable shift in mind-set from the company.

Curse of Success

The curse of knowledge is comparable to the curse of success. It's very difficult to not feel some degree of complacency when you're successful. However, that outlook results in a decreased ability to recognize change or see how change will impact your company. Success breeds an attitude of continuing to do what you've done and what has brought you success. How can you let go of what worked even if it's not working as well? This is a direct path to being blindsided.

So, should hapless executives trust what they know? Or should they start from scratch at each decision point? The best suggestion is likely to strike a balance between these two: As President Ronald Reagan famously said, "Trust but verify." While Reagan used this phrase in reference to U.S.–Soviet relations in the 1980s, it is equally apt for executives faced with making business decisions upon which the potential success and failure of their business rests.

Be the executive who is prepared and open to input about market changes. It's the key to smarter decisions, better strategy, and greater success.

Moving from Hapless to Happening

How do you move ahead? How do you continue yesterday's success and maintain that momentum? How, when, and what do you or should you verify?

In the chapters that follow, we help you understand the broad differences between information and intelligence and what is available. We cover what every forward-thinking executive should know about better input for strategy and planning. We detail how competitive intelligence offers direct and immediate value to you, along with dozens of examples.

We clarify the differences between market research and competitive intelligence, between competit*or* and competit*ive* intelligence, as well as between scenario planning, knowledge management, and business intelligence. We draw distinctions between data, information, and intelligence and delineate why these differences matter—big-time. We explain what information is useful and address the severe limitations of web searches. And we give you a good list of information resources to start your own intelligence gathering.

Final Thought

Do you still believe you know enough about your market?
Do you know what's new and changing?

Do you know what's no longer true?

Do you know what's changing from the outside that could impact your company?

If you do, what are you doing about it?

If you don't, could you be missing an opportunity?

Have you been surprised when a competitor or new entrant enjoys success with a product or service or improvement that you never considered?

These are all signs that you need to update your knowledge base—with competitive intelligence.

2

Defining and Refining Competitive Intelligence

Competitive intelligence (CI) is not what you think. Competitive intelligence is not all about competitors.

Surprised? You're not alone. Most businesspeople focus on competitors to the exclusion of all else. Consequently, they miss the more important information about opportunities and early warning indicators of change that are included in findings that extend beyond competitors.

Competitive intelligence has unfortunately been too closely linked to competitors, and that limits the benefits and scope of CI. Investigations that focus on a company's competitors will miss the mark. Those who understand that CI embraces so much more than competitors have a distinct competitive and strategic advantage.

Definition of Competitive Intelligence

I define competitive intelligence as follows:

Competitive intelligence is knowledge and foreknowledge about the entire business environment that results in action.

Each word in my definition has been deliberately selected and is critical to achieving the best results from CI.

1. *Knowledge* refers to the past. It's what is known or recognized, and it provides a foundation for understanding the past and connecting to new information.
2. *Foreknowledge* points to the future. It's looking ahead for insights about the near future and encompasses market changes, as well as indications, predictions, forecasts, and estimates for what is to come.
3. *Entire* constitutes the wide range of components or factors that can impact the success of your business. An all-embracing view of the entire landscape is necessary to understand the company's industry or external constituents that contribute to success or failure.
   - Components that affect your business include customers, distributors, suppliers, technology, societal changes, government regulations, competitors, economy, substitutes, other industries, prospects, demographics, and legislation.

- Some of these will have greater priority than others, depending on the purpose, but most will play a part. The best results of CI emanate from this broader understanding. Companies run into trouble when they focus only on competitors. (See Chapter 4 on competitors.)

4. *Action* denotes a decision that must result from this new learning. Without an action based on the results of CI, the information becomes "nice to know." Few people in business today can afford the merely nice to know, unless you are seeking only to be educated.

Competitive intelligence is a management discipline that propels the decision maker to smarter, more successful decisions, thereby minimizing risk, avoiding being blindsided, and getting it right the first time. Executives are always surprised when their decisions or strategy don't produce the desired results. Surprises are rarely good in business. Good CI that includes all the appropriate elements of the marketplace is most likely to uncover information that will minimize surprises.

Surprises in business are often early warning signs of market changes. And every business has surprises. Companies who notice change sooner have the opportunity to determine if those changes are relevant to their business. They can accept them outright or monitor them for broader customer acceptance (i.e., to determine whether the change is gaining momentum.)

The following are typical of changes that occur almost daily:

- American women are the fastest-growing part of the motorcycle business, and they buy more than 100,000 of them annually.
- Women own or co-own 20 percent of all construction firms (housingeconomics.com).
- More than 20 percent of Chinese adults are overweight.
- Salt Lake City is the number one market in the United States for households owning a video game system (Scarborough Research).
- Major league soccer draws the highest percentage of affluent attendees, followed by the PGA.
- Los Angeles County is the largest manufacturing center in the United States.
- Education is more important than income or race for living a long life—and this is true globally (Rand Corporation).

- Pepsi is China's largest potato grower.
- Procter & Gamble has published papers in 40 peer-reviewed journals, although it is a consumer products company with a famously secretive culture.

It might be tempting to think that these facts don't apply to your business because you're not in any of these industries. Yet in our CI assignments in well over 100 different industries, we have found similar, surprising information in each. Are you sure your industry is not hiding some surprises of its own? What are you doing to find out? This is what good due diligence reveals.

Once you learn of these surprises, the next step is to think about what those changes mean for your business, and then conduct additional research and take appropriate action, if warranted. For example, knowing that so many women have purchased motorcycles and that thousands more ride, is there a market for related apparel and gear designed for women? Does Salt Lake City have a dedicated video game store? Does major league soccer provide a possible opportunity for your goods at those stadiums? Knowing that Los Angeles is the largest manufacturing center, is this a good location for other manufacturing companies to tap into their experienced employee pool?

There are, of course, other definitions of competitive intelligence, including one by the Society of Competitive Intelligence Professionals (SCIP www.scip.org), the global organization for competitive intelligence professionals, which defines CI as follows:

> *"Competitive Intelligence is a necessary, ethical business discipline for decision making based on understanding the competitive environment."*

Competitive Intelligence is Strategic

CI is neither simple nor basic. Data and information may be simple and basic, but CI is not. Rather, it requires analysis and human thinking to put the pieces together and to make sense of numerous disparate pieces. It's doing what that famous detective, Sherlock Holmes, did— but applied to the business community, for products, services, companies, and industries. It's having a 360-degree view.

CI is not work that just any employee can do. Both those practitioners who are engaged in CI and those who are using it must have sufficient business experience and maturity in their thinking to assess and determine where and how it fits in with the company's strategy.

Let's add another element to the mix. *Competitive intelligence is both a process and a product.* One *undertakes* competitive intelligence as an activity, and the resulting reports are also referred to as competitive intelligence.

CI is also (or should be) a continuing process—undertaken as part of the overall strategy—as well as an outcome. While it may be requested on an ad hoc basis, the greatest benefits are gained when CI is conducted regularly. New decisions and shifts in strategy are continuous activities that require constant updates from CI insights. After all, data and information are constantly changing. Without new input, current decisions that are based on yesterday's intelligence may be undermined. Or it may reinforce what you're currently doing and indicate that a more aggressive decision may be advantageous.

CI and Leadership

Bad decisions are not characteristics of good leaders, because leaders are expected to think more broadly than their employees and to anticipate outcomes. The bonus is that competitive intelligence is a direct path to good decisions and sound leadership.

Harvard Business Review's article on leadership indicates that 88 percent of senior executives want their leaders to be forward-looking. This requires imagination and macro-thinking along with input from solid information. "The first responsibility of a leader is to define reality" according to Max Depree in his very popular business book, *Leadership Is an Art*, which sold close to a million copies.

Leaders cannot rely on conjuring up the future; their expectations must be balanced with what is currently occurring and what is changing. Depree's article stresses that leaders "must not put too much stock in their own prescience." Instead, leaders must continuously probe, "What's new? What's next? What's better? What's changed?" That means having the right input—external, objective, current information—competitive intelligence.

CI comprises all of the appropriate activities involved in monitoring the business and marketplace for relevant information to help drive the right strategy to move the company forward.

CI Leads to Smarter Decisions

Executives must believe that their decisions are smart decisions, or they would make other choices. But are those decisions truly the smartest ones? You often don't learn how smart they were until you assess the results. Making smarter decisions is an undertaking that requires the foundation of the right information—sound, accurate, reliable, and timely information to enable a company to accomplish its goals. If you don't achieve these results, were your decisions truly the best?

While the purpose of CI is to make the best decisions, the underlying imperative is that the decision connects the product or service with the customer—the one who buys your offering. The decision may be brilliant, but if it doesn't resonate with your customer, then it will not produce the desired results. As Peter Drucker said in his book, *Management Challenges for the 21st Century*, "The purpose of information is not knowledge. It is being able to take the right action."

The right action for your company is preceded by a good decision, and those decisions are preceded by good information. That's why information is not useful by itself in making decisions; good decisions require understanding and analysis to move them ahead to intelligence and then to action.

Competitive intelligence is another way to test, test, test your decision. And the bonus is that CI is probably far less expensive than implementing a decision—or redoing a bad one.

CI Minimizes Risk

This is one of the major benefits of competitive intelligence. It minimizes risks and therefore enables you to manage risk—to your benefit. When you buy a car, chances are good that you read all you can about your choice, talk to your friends, and check out web sites and chat rooms. No doubt you do this to minimize your risk and learn about other buyers' disappointments or problems or other hidden information *before* you make the purchase.

The real question is, "Do you do as much research when you're making a strategic or marketing decision?" Be honest. If not, what is your risk of making a mistake? And, can you afford that mistake? Most large companies often have a cushion and can absorb mistakes; small ones can't. Large or small, mistakes are not desirable in business—and the risks can be minimized.

Change Is Here; Change Is Now; Change Is the New Normal

"It is not the strongest of the species that survive, nor the most intelligent, but the one most responsive to change." Charles Darwin said this about biological evolution, but it also applies to business evolution.

If nothing else, the past few years should have seared the idea in our brains that the rules of business today do not match anything we're familiar with. This is an opportunity, as so few businesses will take the time to investigate what changes are occurring and how to adapt their businesses to this new reality.

The overriding issues that will impact your business are the changes taking place, not what's happening with your competitors. Businesses will be far better served and more successful when they focus on those segments related to change. There will always be competitors and they are far less likely to define and be the cause of challenges in your business. This is discussed in more detail in Chapters 3 and 4.

Change is the elephant in the room. Change is also where the opportunities lie. Change means being *different*, but not just for the sake of being different. Change speaks to truth—the truth of shifting desires, shifting offerings, giving customers what they want, and more options, even when they don't articulate it. Change is the clue, the indicator, and the signal to what's developing today and what will likely be the face of the near future.

This holds true regardless of the industry. Southwest Airlines developed a different model in an industry with dozens of competitors. Southwest recognized that air travel was attracting a different demographic and that a different focus could be successful. Nordstrom created a totally different model for the department store built on customer service—not an unknown concept, just one that hadn't been performed properly.

Las Vegas was a small, desert city with a (dare we say?) squalid reputation. Talk about change! Vegas first changed to an adult fantasy travel destination for singles and couples—mega-entertainment for all income groups. Then it shifted focus to a family-oriented site. Now it's back to targeting adults, but with a changed focus from previous campaigns—change that reflects societal changes.

Similarly for Red Bull, PT Cruiser (didn't we have enough car choices?), newspapers in color (*USA Today*), Target (high-end designers creating low-cost options), and CNN. These are all examples of offering customers a product or service that resonates with customers. Competitors had not recognized these changes or didn't think they were important. In a business context, change is synonymous with opportunity.

Yves Saint Laurent, the great fashion designer, was noted for one of his greatest contributions—the pantsuit. He didn't invent it. What he did was refine it and make it respectable for women to wear pantsuits. His competitors didn't figure this out; he looked to his customers and understood what else they wanted, beyond the traditional dresses, skirts, and suits.

Competitive intelligence provides the foundation of information to help you determine whether an idea is a good opportunity for your company. Does your new idea fit with your current distribution channels, or will you have to develop new ones? Same for suppliers—can your current suppliers provide the materials, or do you need to develop new resources? Does it fit with your pricing strategy, your revenue goals? How long will it take to see the ROI that's necessary for your firm?

Let's Talk Intelligence

When we talk "intelligence" in the context of competitive intelligence, we find that it is often confused with related fields like business intelligence, market intelligence, market research, knowledge management, and environmental scanning. These are all used interchangeably, even if inappropriately. It might be useful, therefore, to touch upon some of these.

Business Intelligence

Business intelligence is *not* the same as competitive intelligence.

BI currently refers primarily to data mining, a practice that is heavily driven by information technology. It gathers enormous amounts of unstructured data to slice, dice, and otherwise process it via specialized software. The purpose is to produce historical and current views of internal business operations (i.e., production metrics), sales statistics, customer satisfaction, and project assessments. This information can yield very useful information for uncovering patterns, learning details about regional preferences, and optimizing marketing efforts, as exemplified by Amazon in the United States and Tesco in the United Kingdom.

The term *business intelligence* was frequently used as a synonym for competitive intelligence until the late 1990s, when the term was usurped by data mining activities. BI is currently and mostly used within the IT community and requires software that analyzes data rather than providing a broader understanding of quantitative and non-quantitative issues.

Market Intelligence

Market intelligence is a newer term that is becoming synonymous with competitive intelligence, as differentiated from competitor intelligence, and indicates a focus on the market (rather than on financial intelligence, technical intelligence, etc.).

Some think it refers to intelligence about consumer products and services. Others, in market research firms, use the term to "up" the value of market research—to indicate the inclusion of analysis. It's also used in the financial arena to refer to data about stocks and similar markets.

Open Source Intelligence

Open source intelligence, sometimes referred to as OSINT, is a term that is and was used in government and the military, but is now creeping into the business lexicon. It generally refers to intelligence that is derived from unclassified, legally accessible information sources.

Market Research

Market research and competitive intelligence are both forms of research and provide complementary information and insights. That's where the similarity ends, as detailed later in this chapter.

Knowledge Management

Sometimes referred to as KM, this is sharing of information, usually internally within an organization. Both CI and KM rely on information, with KM focusing mostly on resources from within the firm, while CI obtains information from sources both internal and external. KM is similar to CI in that each is a product or result, as well as a system or process, but KM is not research. And KM does not replace CI.

Part of the interest in knowledge management within a company is the belief that 80 percent of the information the company needs to know is located inside the company. That statement belies the fact that much of what is known within a firm is not shared, or rarely shared, because there's no easy way for employees to do so. Then, too, there's the deeply rooted belief that knowledge is power, and giving away one's knowledge reduces one's influence and respect. From our vantage point, much of what a company already "knows" is familiar; it's often dated, contains industry or company assumptions, and cannot include that external view produced by "proper" CI.

Having said that, there is a place for KM in the CI community, but it must be part of an overall system or attitude of capturing and sharing relevant and current information. If KM could accomplish its stated mission (i.e., to capture relevant information about customers, competitors, suppliers, distributors, market changes, regulations, etc.), then it would be an absolute gold mine. To date, we rarely hear about success in this arena.

We were impressed with how one of our clients had set up a very rudimentary KM system that garnered a substantial amount of important information and was as low tech as the suggestion box. The company placed a large whiteboard in a corridor that most employees passed by during the course of a week and asked people to scribble a few words about any information that might be of interest to the company (ideas for new features, competitor information, complaints, random comments, etc.).

The company sponsored a pizza lunch one Friday each month to talk about items on the whiteboard, and it was open to all - even if they had not contributed anything. During lunch, the people who scribbled comments had the opportunity to provide greater details and better explain their shorthand. As a result:

1. For many of the comments, at least one other person remembered hearing or seeing the same or similar information, but either didn't

think it was important or forgot to write it down. Accordingly it validated the speaker's statement, and the executives had the opportunity to decide if this was information worth monitoring or investigating further.

2. It was a teaching tool for those who didn't fully understand what was important. It clearly relayed what information was of value to the company.

3. People met other employees, from a wide range of functions and levels, many for the first time.

4. Those who made the comments received positive feedback and respect, thereby encouraging them and others to pay more attention to information that is in their space on a daily basis but goes unrecognized for its value or has nowhere to go. Many recognized this as an opportunity to gain awareness or recognition for themselves, especially with those in senior positions.

5. It created a positive and fun atmosphere that gained buzz in the company and created lots of goodwill for the firm.

As word spread about the lunch, more people attended, more comments appeared on the whiteboard, and the lunches became weekly events.

Sometimes the most basic ideas produce awesome results. The old-fashioned suggestion box is still a viable and successful way to receive input from employees and customers.

For more reading about knowledge management, check out www.kmworld.com.

Environmental Scanning

This refers to gathering and monitoring information from a wide variety of sources that impact your business both directly and indirectly. It's seeking internal and external information to keep a company aware of opportunities and threats, as well as overall issues that are considered useful and important for that industry and company. Sources are not limited to electronic ones; this is macro-scanning in its broadest context.

The Term *Intelligence*

The word *intelligence* is problematic for some companies and individuals, especially those who have previously worked in or with government. It conjures up thoughts of illegal or unethical activities. For others, it bears resemblance to the work done by spy agencies or by detectives in the classic dime-store novels. To the extent that each probes the environment for information, the terms *intelligence* and *competitive intelligence* are similar, but that's where the similarity ends. Competitive intelligence is good, old-fashioned investigation to gather and analyze business information and turn it into usable intelligence. We liken it to Sherlock Holmes, who gathered a wide array of information, figured out what was relevant, looked for patterns or relationships, and put the pieces together to solve a problem.

The bottom line to this discussion is that there are many terms to describe CI activities, some of which use the word *intelligence* and some of which use other terms, which change in popularity every few years. Currently, some companies are using the term *insight* (rather than intelligence) to indicate learning from CI activities, such as *business insight, consumer insight,* or *market insight.* Some market research people are using the term *market intelligence* to raise the profile of market research and to make it appear more current and strategic. We list several dozen terms and department titles in Chapter 13.

Types of Intelligence

There are subsets of competitive intelligence that focus on specific areas, including technical intelligence, financial intelligence, conference and trade show intelligence, and executive profiling. Articles on these specific categories can be found in the archives of *Competitive Intelligence Magazine*, published by SCIP and found on its web site, which also includes books on some of these topics (www.scip.org).

Due Diligence

Due diligence, a phrase that refers to gathering the necessary information to make a decision, is better known and more commonly used in both the financial and legal communities.

1. Financial due diligence is used by financial investors when considering mergers and acquisitions, loaning funds, or investing in a company. It usually details sales, profits, return on investment (ROI), cash flow, liabilities, market risks, cost of goods, inventory turnover, and the like.

2. Legal due diligence is used for researching briefs and vetting witnesses. It's being used more and more to learn about current clients (companies and people) and to profile prospective clients, industries, events, and litigation that might be ripe for pitches. By staying on top of current clients' industries, law firms can learn about new areas under consideration, which creates opportunities to cross-sell. It's being used increasingly for business development. A firm that specializes in trial work, for example, may want to expand into political or environmental sectors.

Similarly, competitive intelligence is synonymous with *market due diligence*. In the context used here, it refers to having all the information necessary to make a strategic decision about the marketplace—targeting a different customer group, exploring a previously unused distribution channel, or leveraging existing capabilities for an alternative use, likelihood of success, and so on.

Competitive Intelligence Is *Not* . . .

Having defined competitive intelligence and provided explanations of other types of intelligence, we face, once again, the idea of what competitive intelligence is and is not.

Competitive intelligence is *not* merely data and information. The way it's practiced in many firms, it sometimes appears as though that's all it is.

Competitive intelligence is *built* on data and information, but there is much more to it. Understanding the full scope of CI will provide significant competitive advantage. It's the difference between thinking a bank is merely for processing checks and exchanging accumulated pennies and dimes for bills versus an understanding of its loan and investment capabilities.

Competitive intelligence must include thoughtful and deliberate analysis in addition to gathering a wide-ranging array of data and information. Analysis can refer to formal or informal techniques. Analysis does not refer to comparing last year's sales to the current year's sales and noting a 12.3 percent increase. It's noting the change and finding out the cause: sales of a new product, acquisition of a company, increasing price, adding a new distribution channel, and so on.

Analysis results in insight *and* thinking as to what it means for your company. It results in a full understanding of all the forces at play in the marketplace—the customers, distribution channels, competition. Depending on the purpose, it may include competitor capabilities and weaknesses, industry gaps or growth areas, and the economic indicators. This is much broader than mere data and information.

CI is not rumors; it's not data mining; it's not competitors' secrets; it's not newspaper articles or talking to sales staff or doing market research. Yes, except for uncovering competitors' secrets, all of these are parts of CI.

While some may consider the various parts to be CI, at best each provides only rudimentary information, falling woefully short of good CI. It's far more valuable to see competitive intelligence as an integral part of strategy formulation. How can you develop strategy and direction if you don't have a firm grasp on the full picture of today's reality—delivered from accurate, current, logical resources—and sufficient information that is analyzed for implication and insights? Unless information is understood as a value enhancer for the company, it's merely interesting information. Used in the way it was intended, it's a powerful and little-used strategic tool. (See Chapter 5 for an in-depth discussion of the differences between data, information, and intelligence.)

The Difference between Competitive Intelligence and Market Research

Competitive intelligence and market research are often mistakenly thought to be the same discipline. They are both serious professions that enhance decision makers' understanding of their market, and they often complement each other. Both research and focus on learning about the market, but that's where the similarity ends. They differ in methodology and results.

Market research tends to focus on consumers, is mostly quantitative, measures opinions, and mostly reflects what has occurred. Competitive intelligence is more qualitative and future-focused, looking at what is emerging in a market or industry, and has a broader scope, including many more external factors.

Competitive intelligence uncovers discoverable issues that are as yet unknown, especially external forces. We recommend conducting CI prior to market research, to incorporate these emerging areas into market research surveys or focus groups. Unfortunately, it seldom is. CI uncovers additional information that supplements and improves market research, as it doesn't rely on the respondent's experience base or opinions.

Market research is a *component* of competitive intelligence that adds an important view and an additional layer about the customer's perspective. It clearly and quantitatively identifies the current thinking of customers and adds to deeper understanding of the market.

CI uses different methodology and provides a different perspective on the marketplace than market research does. Market research is statistically oriented (regression analysis, significance levels, probability dispersion, market segmentation) and relies on surveys, questionnaires, and focus groups, which are not part of competitive intelligence methodology. CI should include the customer's perspective, but may not. The challenge is to determine which research method is most appropriate. In many cases, both are. We frequently include market research results in our CI investigations to provide an additional component about the user. Market research may include a qualitative component (interviews) and is being used increasingly business-to-business.

Market research does have its limitations. For example, during the 2008 California Democratic primaries, Zogby, the highly regarded political pollster admitted, "We blew it." Zogby explained that despite its careful market research techniques, it "underestimated Hispanic turnout and overestimated the importance of younger Hispanic voters. . . . And African American turnout was 'overestimated'" (*Los Angeles Times*). It's hard to believe this could occur today, but it does, and this is not an isolated incident.

It is much more difficult to gauge whether responses to market research questions are accurate, as the consumer's input is accepted as valid, yet a survey by Marketing Sherpa and KnowledgeStorm on how technology buyers fill out registration forms revealed that responders frequently do not provide truthful responses. Only 38 percent provide correct phone numbers all the time; 60 percent do not always provide accurate information about their company's size, and 45 percent do not always provide their company's true name. And this is not even crucial input. Competitive intelligence can provide a good counter to ferret out misleading information.

An article in *Inc.* magazine by David H. Freedman captures this challenge: "Customers can tell you a lot. But sometimes they don't know what they're talking about." And there's always the issue of denial. When people are asked questions in a survey or during a focus group, there's often a reality disconnect, such as feedback on the number of hours spent exercising, the number of fruits and vegetables consumed daily, hours spent on the computer, or issues related to driving. It's not a matter of lying; our recall is closer to what we want to believe than what we are actually doing.

Table 2.1 offers a quick look at the differences between the two disciplines.

Table 2.1

Comparison between Market Research and
Competitive Intelligence

Market Research	Competitive Intelligence
Reflects customers' current thinking and beliefs, which may be different from reality.	Uncovers the reality of the marketplace (what is *actually* occurring) and what is emerging but generally unknown.
Captures pronouncements.	Captures actions.
Snapshot of a particular time (past or anticipated). Often ad hoc; may be repeated for comparative purposes. Focus groups always in multiples.	A dynamic view of a changing marketplace, focused on growth opportunities for the near future. Usually ad hoc.
Tactical and methods-driven.	Strategic and results-driven.
Mathematically based; heavy use of rigorous statistical formulas. Data is static; clearly identifies and compares differences among segments. Uncovers mostly behavioral activity and demographics, such as details of light, medium, and heavy users.	Results more likely to reflect consensus, rather than mathematical accuracy, and therefore more fluid. Uncovers marketing, financial, operational, and management information, as well as gaps, opportunities, market drivers, alternative uses, potential problems, unknown customers, emerging competitors, substitutes, etc.

(continued)

Table 2.1
Continued

Market Research	Competitive Intelligence
Draws mostly from consumers and used primarily for consumer products, although it is increasingly used for industrial products, and by business-to-business (B2B) firms.	Taps a wide range of constituencies, including suppliers, distributors, customers, competitors, experts. Includes entire supply chain, from raw materials to market. Used for both business-to-consumer (B2C) as well as business-to-business (B2B), including industrial, institutional, commercial, and nonprofit organizations.
Source: Primary research. A large proportion of market research (surveys and focus groups) is now conducted on the Web. Heavy reliance on questions, both open- and closed-ended (yes/no, range, any response).	Source: Direct contact, sometimes referred to as human intelligence and secondary sources (published and printed documents); may include market research studies. Primary sources more engaged in conversation than in answering questions to uncover information not directly revealed by the issues as well as nuances.
Results are usually quantitative; may include a qualitative component.	Results are mostly qualitative and will likely include a (smaller) quantitative component.
Objective: Answer questions.	Objective: Answer questions and raise questions about unknown customers, current and emerging competitors, market shifts, external forces (outside the industry, such as the economy or substitute competitors).
Software widely used.	Software can gather and organize information but cannot produce intelligence.
Widely recognized and used. Often repeated for comparative purposes.	Not well known or familiar to most business people; primarily used ad hoc or occasionally.

Market Research	Competitive Intelligence
Better for capturing yesterday and today.	Better for capturing today and tomorrow.
Usually narrow in scope; may include broad inquiry.	Usually broader in scope; may include narrow component.
Primarily used for product planning, marketing, and consumer messaging.	Used for strategy, M&A, entering new markets, expanding current line, product launch, identifying threats and opportunities, R&D, profiling.
Need a large number of respondents to generate statistically reliable results.	No minimum number of contacts. The number may be limited, as the results hinge on speaking to the right people.

Market Research and Its Limitations

As a proponent of market research, I also have to be realistic about the limitations, and there are a few. However, when combined with CI, those limitations can be reduced.

1. The answers from surveys or focus groups may not be the most important or the most valuable. The best results come from taking sufficient time to flesh out what the customer actually means rather than settling for the limitations of a one-word answer or selecting from a range. How often have you been frustrated by the options available for answering when your response is not included?

2. It's not unusual for market research respondents to say one thing and actually do another.

3. Respondent statements include an emotional component, whereas behaviors (e.g., purchases) reflect what actually occurs. You can take behavior to the bank.

4. To overcome what has been learned about what consumers say and do, market research is increasingly using a technique of observation—actually watching what consumers do. Researchers may visit consumers' homes and/or offices to monitor how closely their statements about what they buy or do match what they have

in their pantries. And it fleshes out areas that weren't included in the original survey design.

5. Market research is an important *complement* to competitive intelligence, as it reveals what consumers believe or want to believe, but CI is rarely included as part of the market research process.

An example of the mismatch between response and action occurred when gas prices began rising significantly a few years ago. Respondents to market research surveys clearly indicated that they would move to smaller cars and hybrids and that they definitely would not buy gas-guzzling SUVs. Much to the surprise of almost everyone, sales of larger vehicles (trucks, SUVs, and crossovers) increased 3.5 million units, while car sales overall declined 3.3 million. The massive Ford Expedition actually saw a 20 percent sales increase in the first five months of 2007, while Honda announced it was dropping its Accord hybrid (*Brandweek*, June 11, 2007). Behavior did not match stated intentions.

Conversely, during the recession beginning in 2008, a surprising number of reports and articles indicated that behavior this time would be different than in previous recessions. This information was revealed by both competitive intelligence and market research techniques. Stay tuned for long-term results.

Competitive intelligence and market research are separate professions, requiring different skills, with the same bottom line: to discover what customers want. The best competitive intelligence embraces all the relevant information and issues that affect market success.

Scenario Planning

Scenario planning is considered by some to be part of competitive intelligence and is a hot topic at CI conferences. Since competitive intelligence has a future-focused component, looking at what is emerging in a market or industry is part of the investigation. After all, to ensure survival, businesses need to anticipate the future and prepare for events that could happen. Included among commonly used approaches to forecasting and predicting is trend analysis, which may not be as accurate in a fast-moving industry, and thus the interest in scenario planning.

Scenario planning is a tool that some companies use to look at the factors that might impact their business, especially their competitors.

The challenge is to construct scenarios of possible and plausible futures, and then consider how competitors or your company would react. Some companies use scenario planning as a substitute for all or part of competitive intelligence. The idea is that the exercise will develop that much-sought-after insight and foresight about the future. If only it were that easy.

Scenario planning has benefits and specific applications, but it does not produce the same results as competitive intelligence. Scenario planning is useful for:

1. Thinking more broadly and deeply about your company or industry.
2. Identifying the company's vulnerabilities.
3. Opening up a dialogue within the company.
4. Creating a safer place for wild and unexpected ideas to flow (ideas that should be captured and monitored to determine whether some actually develop and are early signs of market change).

Scenario planning also has limitations:

1. Developing effective scenarios requires considerable knowledge, discipline, and a broad objective outlook. Companies doing scenario planning often attack only a few (three or four) scenarios, and they are not necessarily objective.
2. Many scenarios are subjective and reflect the quirks of their creators. The scenarios are then laden with assumptions about hypothetical events and a plan is created to handle the outcome. However, reality often has a way of interfering, and, unless the plan is open to the unexpected, one has to question the realism of both the scenario and outcome. For example, one company's disaster recovery plan included an earthquake scenario in which the quake struck at 2:00 a.m., a time when none of the company's personnel were at work. The plan then further assumed that all personnel would be available to respond—an unrealistic expectation, which can blindside a company.
3. Ideas frequently are extrapolations of what is currently happening in the company or industry (i.e., using more technology, better customer service, doing the work faster, etc.).
4. There is often lack of inclusion of ideas that are unexpected or unknown, as few people can think of such ideas that seem logical.

Much of today's reality is surprising and unexpected and would not become part of possible scenarios.

5. Suggestions that are outside the familiar are easily dismissed as silly or ludicrous or highly unlikely to occur; therefore, companies are more likely to under-react when they hear early rumblings from the marketplace.

6. Interpersonal interactions hinder free and open discussions of select issues, and hierarchy/status may well play a part.

Last Word on "What Is CI?"

The most important message here is not the descriptions or definitions. Rather, it's the understanding of the benefit derived from competitive intelligence in contrast to other disciplines and the increased value to your company and clients.

Language and terminology are dynamic. They reflect the growth and changes within a profession, and it certainly has been the case for competitive intelligence. Add to that the understanding that terms may have different meanings for the professional, for the non-CI practitioner, and in the dictionary.

Regardless of what term you use, the results garnered from doing competitive intelligence are invaluable and far better than not doing CI. After all, the value of research (market intelligence or market research) is not the data or information that's gathered, and it's not undermining or beating your competitors. It's having the right information to make the smartest decisions to move your company forward.

3

Competitive Intelligence

What You Don't Know Will *Hurt You*

Are we serious when we ask, "Is there a difference between competit*ive* and competit*or*?"

For most businesspeople, these terms are one and the same. *They are not*, and those who understand the difference will always have a significant advantage. It's similar to believing that selling and marketing are identical disciplines. They are not. And when you don't understand the difference, you miss the value of both.

Competit*ive* intelligence and competit*or* intelligence are *not* synonymous, and knowing the difference between them is more than mere semantics. In fact, the distinction is so significant that it will have consequences for the prosperity of your company or product. If that sounds like hype, take the measure of your attitude after you finish reading the chapters on competitive and competitor intelligence (Chapters 3 and 4).

What *is* the difference between these two? *Competitor* intelligence has a narrow focus that excludes critical information; *competitive* intelligence takes a broader, more objective and more accurate view of what business faces and what can derail or challenge your company.

The puzzle shown in Figure 3.1 graphically and deliberately demonstrates that competitor intelligence is merely one element in the business environment. Competitive intelligence is more expansive in that it considers *all the elements that impact the company's success—*customers, suppliers, distributors, substitutes, regulations, technology, the economy, other industries, demographics, culture/societal issues—and competitors. Ignore these other elements and you're setting yourself up to be blindsided.

Competitive Intelligence: The Larger View

The two examples that follow should shift your thinking about the value of the entire business environment beyond the notion of competitors and turn you into an ardent believer in the value of competitive intelligence.

Imagine that you are buying a home or renting an apartment. If you were doing the equivalent of *competitor* intelligence, you would compare house A to house B to house C and so on. You would evaluate the number of bedrooms and bathrooms, the square footage, number

Competitive Environment

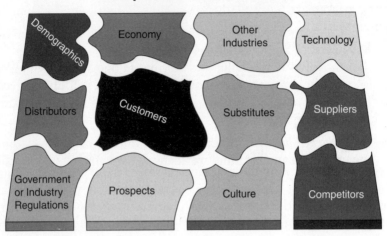

FIGURE 3.1 The Entire Competitive Environment

of floors, kitchen space and appliances, fireplaces, style of the house (traditional, Tudor, contemporary), size of property and amenities (pool, deck, grassy area), and so on.

Even a renter, however, looks at *far* more data points than these. They consider the neighborhood: What does it look like? How well is the area maintained? How noisy is the location? How far apart are the homes? They also consider the commute to work, quality of schools, presence of the venues for things they like to do or that they consider important such as movies, sports, restaurants, parks, gourmet supermarkets, and specialty shops.

The latter would comprise the *competitive landscape*, which includes those elements that are important in making this decision, even if you're planning a short-term stay. I doubt that you would choose a place to live based strictly on the number of rooms, without considering the other details.

This applies equally to business decisions. For example, one of my clients manufactured metal frames that supported handles of plastic bags used in the supermarket or drugstore. The company was performing well, and in looking to expand, the executives wrote a business plan and submitted it to the bank. The bank was sufficiently impressed and agreed to give them the loan, provided they would improve the market section. They asked us to provide sufficient market intelligence to satisfy the bank's demand to determine how viable the market was, going forward.

We first performed an industry assessment with the usual elements: market size (current and growth trends), distribution channels, competitors and comparable product information for each, and a summary on the industry and how it's changing. That was step one, and even that included far more than only addressing competitors.

Next we reviewed and analyzed all the *other* industries that could impact our client's success, which led us to look at five other industries, the entire business environment as it applied to this client:

1. *Supermarket business.* Since most of the frames were sold in supermarkets at that time, we focused here first. We compared the number of plastic and paper bags that supermarkets purchase, as well as the costs of storing and shipping for plastic versus paper. The differences in weight, storage space, and costs for each type were quite significant.

2. *Packaging industry.* There was a time when the only option was paper bags. Then plastic bags began to replace them. Now there are paper bags with handles and customers using their own bags. Is there another option on the horizon?

3. *Plastics industry.* Plastic is the raw material of these bags, so they needed to understand what is happening in this industry regarding price or availability. Are any manufacturers switching to plastic frames?

4. *Petroleum industry.* Plastic is made from petroleum, and petroleum prices have been extremely volatile over the years. This will impact the price and availability of plastic bags, so this industry was relevant and deserved inclusion.

5. *Environment.* Consumers continue to be concerned about the biodegradability of products made from plastic. Although this concern has ebbed and gained momentum over the years, it had to be factored into the outlook. There are biodegradable bags made from corn that look like plastic, but since the customer doesn't know which ones are "green," environmental concerns continue.

After evaluating all these additional industries, our client had a comprehensive and realistic overview of the *entire* competitive environment, a conclusion that gave the bank the confidence to approve the loan.

The bonus was that the company also used this information for strategic and marketing purposes. Further, because of the thorough intelligence they now had, they gained even more confidence about expanding, moving faster and more aggressively, thereby increasing sales sooner and at a greater pace than previously.

If we had only looked at competitors, would that have been sufficient? We are certain it would not, and the client and bank obviously agreed that a broader, macroview was more advantageous. Excluding any one of these industries could have posed a serious challenge to a realistic understanding of what the company might face. After all, the purpose of competitive intelligence is to support the development of more resilient, more robust strategies and tactics and to minimize risk. A narrower focus will not help achieve that purpose.

External Perspective

As noted elsewhere, I attended a conference in Europe where Shell's vice president of Global Business Environment informed the attendees, "The big decisions that failed at Shell didn't fail because of our operations or because of project management. They failed because we misunderstood the external world." When a company focuses on the entire competitive landscape, it includes the changing marketplace, which every business *must* do. The marketplace is not merely about the actions of competitors. Rather, it is about client demands.

McDonald's is famous for constantly re-examining the market and exploring its customer's preferences. The company regularly changes its offerings and experiments with new products—breakfast foods, chicken products, salads, and now high-quality coffee. It's ironic that McDonald's is frequently mocked for its latest product du jour, because that is exactly what we in marketing applaud—test, test, test. It's the only way to know what customers will buy versus what they say they want.

How did McDonald's make the seemingly absurd decision to compete against coffee giant Starbucks? The fast-food chain noticed that customers were buying their food at McDonald's, then going to convenience stores for water and other bottled drinks, and then to Starbucks for coffee. McDonald's started adding these beverages because its customers wanted them, and they could now find them all in one place. The company was responding to its customers. It was not going after Starbucks. Neither Starbucks nor McDonald's ever thought the other was in its circle of competitors. That's how business is changing today; and that's what competitive intelligence reveals. To put the competitive-versus-competitor discussion into perspective, a competitor analysis of Starbucks would not have included McDonald's, nor vice versa.

This need for a broader approach and external view was made patently plain to our major credit card company client (an example we use in other parts of this book), which made a decision to enter the campus card market. This company believed that its competition consisted of other credit card issuers, companies in the same category. The reality of the marketplace painted a much different picture. The big surprise was that several other industries were also competing in that market space; in addition, there were threats from alliances among these different industries and from systems integrators. For this client, competitors included industries it had never considered—banks, telecom, hardware and software providers, and a university that had been successful in this market and in mentoring newcomers.

At first blush, our client could easily compete in this market segment, provided that its competitors were *only* other credit card providers or financial services providers. Our client had the advantage of being one of the largest and most highly respected members in its field. When it decided to enter this new market, however, it hadn't considered that the playing field included a completely different set of competitors, which meant that our client had no idea of the unexpected risk.

Our competitive intelligence investigation detailed the other forces that were at play, which the credit card company hadn't spotted on its radar and hadn't factored into their marketing equation. The complexities of dealing with the university system are very different, and not in a good way, from other business customers, and they are likely to create additional demands and barriers. Further, our client didn't realize that it would be serving *two* customer segments within the university: the administrators and the students. We detailed what each expected from this campus card and explained why the two groups' priorities were totally opposite.

The issue of different priorities can be dealt with if you're aware of them and accept this unexpected challenge. The company ultimately pulled out of that arena after unsuccessfully spending tens of millions of dollars. Its focus on competitors had been too narrow, and it hadn't understood the marketplace. As a large firm, it had the cushion to absorb such a colossal failure. But could your company do the same?

There is a belief that the most successful companies know their market. But *do* they? The firms that understand the difference between the competitor and competitive landscapes and that monitor the latter are the most likely to succeed. The best competitive advantage and least risky strategy is to know your industry broadly, narrowly, and deeply and to be aware of all the external forces that affect your ability to succeed. Even if you believe that your competitors are the most important focus, that doesn't make it so. In extremely competitive times and declining economic periods, reducing risk is even more critical.

By limiting your efforts to that single element—competitors—you are similarly limiting understanding of your market. After all, "To be master of any branch of knowledge, you must master those which lie next to it. And, to know anything, you must know all." (Oliver Wendell Holmes)

Start with the Customer, Not the Competitors

Although it seems perfectly clear, the following is a truism worth repeating, especially since so many companies put more time and effort into monitoring their competitors than their customers. Management guru Peter Drucker said, "The purpose of business is to create and keep a customer." Obvious, right? Companies that provide prospects with what they want are rewarded with sales, customers, and market share. Simple!

Why is this so difficult for so many companies to understand?

It's hard to give your customers what they want (whether or not they know what that is or can verbalize it) without having an objective, external, broad understanding of what is happening in the entire marketplace and not just in your industry. The key to discovering that landscape lies in having the right knowledge, insight, and under-standing, and that means getting the right intelligence, supplemented with observations, broad reading, and traditional market research.

In their book, *The New Age of Innovation: Driving Co-Created Value Through Global Networks*, renowned strategist C. K. Prahalad and coauthor M. S. Krishnan emphasize the importance of building cus-tomer relationships. This, they say, requires doing due diligence to understand customer needs. It's not technology; it's not software; it's taking the time and effort to find out how customers are changing and how you can serve them better and sooner than your competitors.

"Consumers are more knowledgeable and more powerful than competitors," says Bruce Nussbaum in *BusinessWeek*'s "Innovation Predictions 2008." In one of these predictions ("The Customer Is King"), he explained that "Consumers replace competitors as the key reference point for corporate strategy." And, as pointed out in Trend-watching.com, "Consumer expectations are often set outside your own industry. Limiting yourself to your own industry will make you miss important changes in consumer expectations, and will thus put you at risk of disappointing or even annoying consumers."

Some B2B (business-to-business) companies have begun eliminating the intermediary (distributor) and going directly to the consumer. Pharmaceutical companies are the most blatant and successful in terms of marketing directly to the consumer (D2C), even though their prescription drugs can be obtained only via doctors (B2B). Direct-to-consumer has changed the distribution channel for marketing these companies' products. In 1995, five percent of marketing budgets for pharmaceuticals were D2C. Just 10 years later, that percentage had increased to 30 percent.

Companies in other industries have and are marketing their B2B products directly to consumers, even though the consumer can't buy the product directly. Examples include Intel, Dolby, and Nutra-Sweet—companies whose products are embedded *in* the products that consumers buy and that the customer asks for by name. Small-scale organic farmers and food manufacturers are selling directly to the consumer, online, at farmers' markets, or at community-supported farms or food clubs (in which produce is trucked to a distribution center where the customer picks up their order).

Wal-Mart is one of the most successful retailers of the twentieth (and, so far, of the twenty-first) century. Sam Walton built his company by focusing on small communities that were underserved and over-charged. He recognized that delivering what the customer wants was one of the keys to success. Walton reportedly said, "You guys [manufacturers] are always trying to sell me more Tide. I really don't care if I sell Tide or Fab. I just want to sell what the consumer wants." The focus has to be on the consumer, who can fire his or her provider, at will.

The Customer Is King

The customer is the single most important aspect of a company's marketing strategy, as noted in a spate of books on the subject of consumer-driven marketing, including *The Game-Changer: How You Can Drive Revenue and Profit Growth with Innovation*, by A. G. Lafley and Ram Charan. Lafley, who became CEO of Procter & Gamble in 2000, has often acknowledged that "the customer is boss." Under his successful leadership, P&G "made a seminal change in the psyche and working of the organization, changing from a technology-push innovation model to a customer-pull one."

According to the authors, placing the consumer at the center "delivers sustained organic growth and profits, no matter whether your business is consumer products, services, or business-to-business industrial products." Lafley continues, "The most important part of the system is the one in the middle: the consumer. . . . Everything begins and ends with the consumer. We have created new products that serve our consumers in new ways, such as Swiffer, Crest Whitestrips, and Tide Coldwater detergent."

Unlike the past, the customer is no longer passive. With so much information, including product and service reviews available online, the customer is almost as knowledgeable as the producer about the company's products and/or services. Most Gen Y, Gen X, and even baby boomers consult online reviews for everything from international travel to neighborhood restaurants to the latest products they want to buy to where to get good (or bad) customer service and better pricing.

In this new century, the customer is king, and that fact trumps anything a company can say about itself. This is primarily due to the considerable number of options customers have for your product or service (including substitutes), along with other customers' feedback, reviews, and videos that they can access via the Web. Customers are no longer willing to wait for you to improve your offering or to change your pricing. You have to earn their interest and their votes (i.e. dollars), which are often lost faster than they are gained.

This is no longer about customer loyalty to a company. Patrons are loyal to those products that satisfy their needs, not to the manufacturer's opinion of their customers' needs. There wouldn't be such a large disconnect between auto manufacturers and consumers if the industry truly focused on the automobile buyer. Yet decade after decade, American automakers proclaimed that they knew what their customers wanted. And all the while, market share kept shrinking.

As its clientele changes, a company has to be equally nimble in its mind-set to acknowledge reality and in the way it responds to these changes. This is how you show the customer that you understand the conversation. Certain select retailers, who are thinking externally and are aware of more than changing fashions, have incorporated restaurants into their stores to increase the time spent there.

1. Ralph Lauren's RL restaurant in Chicago has increased sales from $1.4 million to $7 million in just six years, thereby taking revenues from restaurants nearby on tony Michigan Avenue.
2. IKEA has restaurants in all 34 of its U.S. stores; Bloomingdale's, Nordstrom, Bass Pro Shops, and Tommy Bahama sportswear stores also include restaurants.
3. Borders and other booksellers have added coffee bars to keep customers just a little longer.

What about the Competitor?

Obviously, we cannot ignore the competitor. We agree that there is value in doing competitor intelligence, a subject we detail separately in Chapter 4. There absolutely is a place for competitor intelligence when used appropriately. However, the balance between competitive and competitor intelligence generally should be weighted overwhelmingly in favor of the former.

A focus on competitors is shortsighted, because competitors don't buy your products—customers do. While this may appear to be obvious, if companies understood this, they would focus more on customers. Customers not only buy your product or service, they provide the most useful information if you listen. They will tell you and they want to tell you how to serve them better. They offer ideas for new products, features, or improvements; they tell you about problems with the existing offering; and they suggest alternative uses. A decision to focus more on customers than on competitors will yield far greater benefits to the company.

Why do so many companies focus most of their attention on their competitors? They think they will take away a competitor's customers and gain revenue. This approach might make sense if business were a zero-sum endeavor, where in order for one company to gain customers, another company had to lose them. The more likely scenario is that a new entrant will expand the industry—*if* it offers what customers want.

For example, the $7.9 billion salty snack-food industry grew almost 3 percent in 2007, selling familiar products such as Frito-Lay. Robert's American Gourmet, an all-natural snack made with real food (i.e., cheddar cheese), grew 20 percent, the same growth rate as sales for the entire category of all-natural snacks. All-natural snacks, a small sub-segment of the industry, appeals to a growing customer segment that wants healthier snacks made with natural ingredients and no trans fats. Robert's successfully *expanded* the snack category. It created a profitable company by not following competitors and by providing customers with a product that existing manufacturers were not providing. Producing products or services that customers want enlarges the market. This is proven by the fact that purchasers will spend their money on some other product or service that better satisfies their needs, regardless of whether your company agrees, according to Brandweek.com

Cirque du Soleil expanded the market for circus-like entertainment by offering a show that didn't appeal to the Ringling Bros. and Barnum & Bailey Circus crowd. Curves Women's Only Health Clubs attracted customers that wanted a different workout experience.

And whatever you believe is the reality, dismiss outright the idea that your company or your product does not have *any* competition. We hear this constantly from both large and small companies, and it is simply not the case. We have yet to find an industry in which competitors do not exist. The reality is that there is *always* competition. It's either unknown, or customers are using an alternative product or service, or waiting for a better offering. If there really is no competition, then you have to investigate if anyone other than you is interested. It matters little how important or good your product or service is if your target market is not curious or attracted.

The Supplier Aspect

An example earlier in this chapter detailed a market analysis of the supporting frames for plastic bags for a growing company. While we looked at the usual forces operating in the marketplace, including competitors, competitive products, substitutes (paper bags), and legal and environmental issues, we also considered the impact of plastic and petroleum industries as the major suppliers to the plastic bag manufacturers.

These suppliers have a stake in plastic bags, and they have a broader view of the market for their products in general. Paying attention to what is happening to them and to their industry provides a better picture of how your raw materials may be impacted and whether others are starting to encroach on your playing field. Your suppliers have an interest in the direction of your industry, and that makes them a good source of information for any trends or threats. Suppliers include raw materials and packaging.

Distributors

Aside from learning the obvious—the preferred channels and why they're preferred—distributor analysis can show you how the buyers are reached and from whom they buy (i.e., direct sales people, distributors, value added resellers, etc.). If you're considering entering a new industry or market, you will learn how open distributors are to a new vendor, how they operate, and what the business drivers are. Understanding how this part of the food chain operates gives you the background necessary to establish your own distribution channel strategy. But . . . there is more.

Distributors offer much more than a channel. For many industries, distributors *are* the buyers; they are the portal to other customers. They know what works in the marketplace and can identify the barriers to market entry. They know what the competitive strategies are, and they have an even better understanding of the customers' wants and needs, as we have found in so many of the projects we have undertaken for our clients.

Why do they share this information? Because they are ever hopeful that someone, some company out there, will be a valuable new addition to their stable. They don't want to miss out on what might be the next hot company.

Even more significant, distributors can help you assess, almost better than anyone else, the marketplace. They do so by aiding in SWOT analysis: the *strengths* and *weaknesses* of the company (internal perspective) and the *opportunities* and *threats* in the marketplace (external perspective). This information will allow you to adjust your marketing and sales strategies to become even more successful, or to completely transform your market offering from failure to success. (Note: SWOT is not exclusive to input from distributors.)

For example, a nonprofit organization with whom we worked had created a videotape targeted toward preventing drug use among tweens (i.e., preteens). The organization, pleased with its idea to market this through a particular distribution channel that no competitors were using, was certain this was a fabulous new discovery—its *aha!* moment. A few key members raised concerns about why no one else had discovered this gem. Our research showed that others had considered it and had tried it, only to find that it didn't and wouldn't work. This was information that had not been factored into their "discovery." The nonprofit executives got their *aha!* moment. It was not the one they wanted, but the one they needed.

The Competitor Landscape: Direct, Indirect, and Substitute Competitors

As Figure 3.2 illustrates, competitors are no longer defined merely as *direct* competitors, as discussed in detail in Chapter 4. Competitors are *any* business that attracts your customers or potential customers. Consider the challengers shown in Table 3.1 and how they relate to your business.

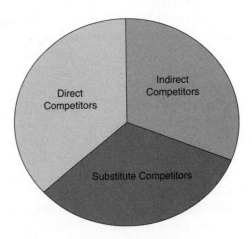

FIGURE 3.2   Types of Competitors

Table 3.1
Types of Competitors

Type of Competitors	Description
Direct	Companies offering the same or similar products or services to the same or similar customers
Indirect	Companies in *related* industries or with related capabilities (primary or secondary) who are selling the same or similar products and services
Substitute	Companies in *different* industries offering the same or similar products and services

Substitutes

Management easily and constantly dismisses substitutes. After all, they think they're the experts; their product or service is authentic; it's the real thing. Why would anyone buy a substitute?

But customers do, and so it's important that you understand who and what they are and why they matter.

Substitutes are any offering that your customers or users view as alternatives for your product or service. Granted, the substitute may not be perfect and it may not rival or even come close to the quality of your offering. But to the customer, the substitute has enough of the characteristics and utilities in common with your offering to warrant purchasing and using that product or service instead of yours.

The more important point to realize is that every substitute purchased is a sale that your company *did not get*. It broadcasts that the differentiators or advantages of your product or service were not conveyed or were not sufficient.

Southwest Airlines built its company by understanding that it was not competing against other airlines, but competing instead against cars and buses—hence the short hauls and cheap seats. Although Southwest's direct competitors today may well be other airlines, in the early days its quick flights substituted for long car and bus rides. Unlike traditional airlines, Southwest did not offer assigned seating, and the company made it easy for customers to return unused tickets.

Michael Porter, Harvard Business School professor and the leading authority on competitive strategy, wrote that "All firms in an industry are competing, in a broad sense, with industries producing substitute products. . . . Identifying substitute products is a matter of searching for other products that can perform the same function as the product of the industry" ("How Competitive Forces Shape Strategy," *Harvard Business Review*).

MinuteClinics are substitutes for doctors' offices, and usually located in retail spaces, such as Target or large drug store chains. They offer inexpensive, quick attention to common ailments such as strep throat, ear infections, and immunizations. When they first opened in 2000, these "ATMs of health care" were ridiculed and dismissed as inferior to traditional clinics and doctors' offices. In early 2009, the prestigious Cleveland Clinic entered into a collaboration agreement with MinuteClinic, which now has more than 500 U.S. locations. Other industries and substitutes that were once dismissed include plastic used in place of steel, fax copies of legal documents in place of originals delivered by FedEx, fine jewelry sold on QVC or HSN rather than in jewelry stores, and cable stations in place of broadcast TV.

When it comes to the use of substitute products, it matters little what *you* think. It only matters what the customer thinks. Therefore, when you study the competitive landscape, it is a good idea to find out if there is a substitute product or service that will impact your strategy. Then figure out why it appeals to customers who could/should be yours but are spending their dollars elsewhere. This is the real value, determining their attraction, and weighing the option of adapting the substitute idea to your business.

Technology

Technology often introduces new and sometimes unexpected competitors. The advent of the Internet, for example, actually opened the marketplace for a California-based T-shirt designer, who suddenly was able to provide his design services to a pub in Amsterdam. That same technology allows me to order my "just desserts" from my favorite chocolatier in Bruges, Belgium. Suddenly, my local Godiva shop has lost my business.

Technology allowed FedEx to "steal" the package business from the U.S. Postal Service. MapQuest, Google maps, and other online mapping firms have done away with most paper maps that used to be available from your local garage or gas station as a source of additional revenue; and the nearly ubiquitous GPS that is becoming available on many telephones may do away with even that source. Then there are the electronic books available through Amazon's Kindle and Sony's digital e-reader. Will the book publishing business as we know it survive in the era of downloads?

Unquestionably, technology is having quite an impact, and it makes the competitive landscape much more uncertain. When looking at the broader competitive landscape, it is increasingly difficult to ignore the new technological trends that may impact your product, service, or industry, either directly or indirectly.

Demographics

There is little question that changing demographics can and will affect your business. On one hand, for example, an aging population will impact health care, housing and housing construction, and many areas of the retail sector. In fact, a friend joked about a department store chain that went out of business in Southern California because its last customer had died. (Its merchandise mix did not seem to have changed much from the time it started back in 1904.) On the other hand, population growth (from both migration and increasing fertility rates) is equally likely to affect your market. And these are not the only demographic factors.

What's important here is to constantly monitor your market. Both market research and competitive intelligence will uncover the appropriate details. Who's buying? What are their attitudes? What drives them? What are the complaints and frustrations? Are they changing? If so, how? And can *you* change to meet their needs and wants?

Appliance manufacturers are finally retooling their goods for an aging population by offering easier-to-open refrigerator and oven doors, raising the height of washer and dryers so bending is not required, adding automatic shutoff burners, and implementing brighter LED lighting. More and more bathrooms are adding grab bars and installing easier-to-handle faucet levers. OXO small hand tools (e.g., can openers, garlic presses) grew to become a very successful company by offering commonly used products housed in great design. The company attracted much younger buyers who were not part of its target market. These appliance improvements may have a similar story, as design is increasingly recognized as a desirable feature.

Women and those over 55 years of age are often invisible to marketers, even though women account for approximately 80 percent of the gross domestic product (GDP). Until the recession, those over 55 were the group with the most disposable income and the least financial obligations (no children, house paid off, etc.). Does your company have a plan to attract these moneyed consumers?

We conducted two investigations of Gen Y, which clearly delineated the significant impact of this age group, now and in the future. They are almost as large as the boomer population and as different in their attitudes and behavior as boomers were when compared with their previous generations. They are expected to impact the market in the same unpredictable way. How much do you know about them?

Demographics are part of the competitive environment. Include these if you want to avoid suffering the same fate as that department store that is missed only by its customers who are now shopping on another plane.

Culture

I use this term to refer to a wide range of macrosegments, including society, lifestyles, and attitudes—broad areas that are constantly changing. Issues that appear to dominate the news change regularly, from rampant conservatism to uncontrollable spending to fear of germs. Cultural analysis provides an opportunity to determine whether your products or services match up with current prominent concerns and, if so, to reconfigure your marketing and advertising to fit with these shifts, if it makes sense for your company.

The Color Marketing Group and the Color Association of the United States are the primary groups that determine colors for the next year or two. While this may appear frivolous, their pronouncements are critical for their members, which include auto manufacturers, home decor firms, branding and logo consultants, and fashion designers, all of whom want to get their production schedules in sync with consumer tastes. Color differences may be too subtle for most to recognize, but they reflect the times and impact purchasing behavior.

In fact, Google's multicolor design has been so significant that there's actually a name for it: the Google effect, which includes not only the group of colors that the company uses, but also its flexibility to tweak its logo for various holidays. Look at Kraft Foods, Wal-Mart, and Stop & Shop logos for the Google influence.

Social trends affect a lot more than color. They can help your sales by determining what colors will resonate with customers based on societal and economic changes, from the color of your product to the color of the walls of your store or restaurant. Social trends affect your product or service every bit as much as all the other elements that impact your business. Even if it's not important to you, it doesn't mean it isn't important.

We want and buy products and services that were unthinkable just a few years ago. What would have seemed ludicrous in 2000 now is viewed by some customers as welcome. Have you heard about "death midwives"? There are increasing options for burial, even among traditional choices, such as ecological burials, motorcycle hearses, and artistically customized urns. And many people welcome assistance with all the paperwork, especially those who may not have family nearby to help.

Similar to this is the entrance of retirement coaches, the latest in the growing coaching industry. People are living longer, and many don't know what they want to do. For those who seek assistance, retirement coaches help explore areas previously unconsidered, set goals, and create second careers (if desired) that fit flexible schedules and new interests. Additionally, an estimated 20 million drivers over 70 years of age are just not giving up their keys. There is a small but growing niche for driving coaches that cater to this specific demographic, which is expected to reach 30 million by 2020.

Economy

During a previous recession, an ad agency client commissioned us to find out how consumers behave in a down economy. The agency's idea was to give its clients a heads-up about what changes are likely to take place when the economy spins in a downward spiral. As a result, the agency's clients adjusted their marketing and promotional materials, maintained sales while competitors' sales were declining, and were in a strong position when the recession ended, due to their constant communications strategy. The bonus was that the advertising agency was rewarded with more business due to their clients' new marketing campaigns.

In the recent economic downturn, consumer spending was clearly in retreat, driving the economy down even further. But even in a bad economy—in the midst of a housing crisis, a credit crisis, an auto industry crisis, a crisis of confidence in the ability of government to fix the problems quickly, and one in which jobs are being lost at an unprecedented rate—people are still eating and buying. Yes, they are adjusting their budgets and rethinking their spending habits, but they still have to spend, because we no longer till our own lands for food, sew our own clothes, or do all those other things needed to create what we now purchase.

In down times, there is an increased consumer focus on ways to *save* money. Many people respond in anticipated ways, by clipping more coupons, transitioning to less expensive brands or products, buying more promotional goods, and limiting purchases to what they need now. Others take more drastic action, such as growing their own food in today's "victory gardens" to cut expenses as well as to eat local—very local.

Smart companies who spend the time to understand changing times figure out what customers are doing and then adjust their products or services to serve that changed marketplace for the current economic climate. The Hyundai car company did just that and enjoyed increased car sales when the rest of the industry was in free fall. With auto sales and jobs declining rapidly, the company developed a strategy and advertising campaign offering its cars with a guarantee: Lose your job, and we help with car payments, or return the car with no adverse impact on your credit rating. Hyundai's plan reduced the customer's risk, just as competitive intelligence reduces your risk.

Industry and Government Regulations

Regulatory policy in many countries increasingly shapes the structure and conduct of industries. This is happening in banking, pharmaceuticals, transportation, and many other businesses. Unquestionably, regulation (by government or industry) is the single biggest uncertainty that can affect market decisions.

Legislation for higher-mileage vehicles means a big change in investment; legislation in the financial markets will contract or expand the availability of capital; legislation affects energy (electricity) pricing; regulatory requirements affect which drugs are introduced and how. Increasingly, legislation has a major impact on such things as plastic bags, lightbulbs, battery disposal, and many other areas. It has changed the paint industry and has created new opportunities for recycling companies. It regulates land use, work environments, minimum wages, and more. Companies that do not do their due diligence on pending or likely legislation that may impact their new products or services or that choose to ignore those regulations, may well find themselves in trouble, if not out of business.

Other Industries

All businesses are impacted to some degree by neighbor industries that are indirectly related to their own. The example about metal frames for plastic bags discussed earlier in this chapter clearly identified the value of being aware of other industries that are indirectly related to yours and could impact your business. Those other industries included the supermarket industry, plastic industry, packaging industry, petroleum industry, and environmental concerns.

Thorlo socks became very successful by offering different socks for different sports or needs (more padding in the toe or heel). This all came about because the sneaker market was diversifying into different models for different sports. If people were buying shoes constructed differently by type of activity, then perhaps this would translate into socks also. It may be hard to remember, but at that time, companies offered one basic sock model. Thorlo paid attention to an indirect market, sneakers and athletic shoes, that was successful in understanding customer needs, and used this to its advantage and subsequent success. Offering socks, customized to match the sneaker, may appear obvious, but no other company thought of it. Thorlo came to this recognition by following a related industry.

Market Puzzle: The Last Word

Review the puzzle at the start of this chapter (Figure 3.1) and see if you have a different view of your industry, as well as opportunities and areas to monitor. Depending on the market, the customer, and the competitive landscape, the picture and the boundaries are always changing.

Some pieces may loom larger and some smaller. Next year your puzzle may show different large or small pieces. There may even be some new pieces added to the puzzle, while the old pieces may have morphed into something either similar or different.

The forces that impact your industry and your product or service include customers/buyers, competitors, suppliers, distributors, government or industry regulations, demographics, substitutes, technology, economy, trends, related industries, prospects, and more. An early clue to the growing importance of external forces is evident when changes in the overall competitive landscape emerge and, even more obviously, when they begin to gain traction. This may come in the form of new or different competitors, new ways of buying the product or service (distribution channels), new features, changes in sizing of the product or bundling/grouping (e.g., selling only multipacks).

You cannot know the whole truth if you cannot see the entire picture, and you cannot see the entire picture if you focus on only one or two elements.

Executives need to gain greater insight into the areas in which their level of awareness is not complete so that they can quickly respond to them. Competitive intelligence findings explicitly describe areas that haven't previously been known to the executive team. The next step is to develop a plan that includes all factors of the business. Know all the forces that affect your industry and customers; question whether they're still relevant; change what needs to be changed;

validate what you think is true; and learn what is no longer true and what's new.

Without an external view, you are relying on experience and assumptions that may or may not be correct and excluding input on what has changed. It's a good idea to remember *Sesame Street*'s popular song: "One of these things is not like the others . . . " Notice what isn't, and try to figure out why. This is how you become aware of the first stirrings of change. The idea is to keep up with your customers and markets, even as they shift.

This applies to all aspects of decision making, even the U.S. Supreme Court. This discussion between U.S. Supreme Court Justices Antonin Scalia and Stephen Breyer on the constitutional relevance of foreign court decisions reminds us of the widespread value of paying attention to external events, regardless of your business.

> **Justice Scalia:** *Why is it that foreign law would be relevant to what an American judge does when he interprets—interprets, not writes? The Founders used a lot of foreign law. If you read the Federalist Papers, it's full of discussions of the Swiss system, German system. It's full of that. It is very useful in devising a constitution.*
>
> **Justice Stephen Breyer:** *There are so many ways, so many ways, in which Justice Scalia and I absolutely agree, so many ways in which foreign law influences law in the United States Supreme Court and the other courts as well. We read what judges in other countries say on the issues we're considering because how do we know we looked for everything? I mean, what I see in doing this is what I call opening your eyes, opening your eyes to things that are going on elsewhere, use it for what it's worth.*
> —Source: AU Washington College of Law, Jan. 13, 2005,
> American University Washington College of Law,
> U.S. Association of Constitutional Law Discussion

That's not a bad concept to remember: Open your eyes to what else is happening. Look at the broad picture both inside and outside your industry. Success depends on monitoring *all* factors that have the potential to impact your business.

4

Why Fixating on Competitors Is Misguided

Most people confuse *competitive* intelligence with *competitor* intelligence, as discussed in Chapter 3. In the previous chapter, we hammered home the concept that competi*tive* intelligence efforts cannot be limited to a mere analysis of competit*ors*. Competitors are but one element, a subcategory, in the entire competitive landscape. Focusing on the one element is like studying one ingredient in an entrée and assuming that you can deduce everything else about that dish. That said, this chapter discusses the "Competitors" piece of the puzzle (see Figure 4.1).

Think about the surprises you've had when eating a familiar entrée in various places and why one restaurant is well known for the very same, yet less stellar, dish that is offered in so many other restaurants. Think of the various ingredients included in that meal; a "secret ingredient" may be the reason. In-N-Out Burger is a privately held chain of take-out locations (mostly in California) that serves an extremely limited menu—only three choices of burgers, as well as fries and shakes. Suffice it to say that burgers are not a unique product, and the number of competitors is staggering. Yet In-N-Out is a destination place as well as an enviably profitable company. Its competitors are irrelevant to its success.

And that's because business is rarely a zero-sum game. That is, it's not necessarily true that for one company to succeed, another must fail. Among the very few business examples of this extremely limited playing field are aerospace giants Boeing and Airbus and also the world of sports. In sports, only one team can win, so the individual players and the teams have to study and analyze their opponents and their strategy. But even they cannot ignore the other elements at play in their game. Many sports analysts believe that coaches are actually more important than talent. For any specific matchup, coaches must also pay

FIGURE 4.1 Just *One* Piece of the Puzzle

attention to weather, field conditions, equipment, travel, timing, the attitudes of sportswriters and fans, and the specifics of their players and how best to use them.

The reality is that there are many successful companies in the same industry. Yet most competitive intelligence investigations are designed around competitors and how to beat them. These firms operate under the erroneous assumption that company sales will increase if they take away market share from competitors. If that were true, then focusing on competitors and studying their every move would have greater validity. While there is no question that it is important to know about competitors, since they are part of the entire business environment, it's important to remember that they are only *one* part.

The American automotive industry, along with IBM, Sears, and even that venerable food giant McDonalds, all got it wrong when they merely looked at the competition. It was only when they refocused on their customers and what had made them successful at the start that they regained their bearings.

Still, there are other good reasons to know what the competition is up to. Discovering what your competition is doing, and then doing something different, can serve as the foundation for success. Rather than copy what other purveyors of coffee were doing, Starbucks expanded the market for coffee drinks by serving high-quality coffee and unique beverages in an appealing environment. The company focused on customers, not competitors. One could argue that Starbucks was successful because it ignored its competitors. Regardless of the approach, it is useful to know what your competitors are doing. But before you undertake a look at how they are operating, you need to know exactly who they are. And you may be surprised at how some executives define their competitors.

As keynote speaker at an annual conference for financial planners, I asked my audience whether they could identify their competitors. Their immediate and universal answer was "other financial planners." Probing further, they narrowed their competitors to those financial planners in a similar-size organization, so that a small company of financial planners viewed other small companies offering financial planning services as its only competition.

Pushed further for a clearer answer, the silence was deafening. The reality, as I pointed out to them, is that many other professionals provide financial planning services, and they account for a significant part of the business. Who are these providers? Attorneys, banks, CPAs and other accountants, brokerage houses, and insurance firms. Then there are do-it-yourself software tools and self-help books. Faced with this response, the financial planners at this conference laughed and assured me that they didn't consider these others to be competitors. "They're not as good as we are. They don't have the same expertise and experience. They don't offer the full range of services." That may well be, but for customers who get their financial help from those "lesser" venues, that rebuttal is totally irrelevant.

The financial planners didn't quite grasp the notion that a competitor is *any other company, individual, or tool offering a similar product or service that solves the customer's problem*. My audience needed to recognize that all entities offering financial services, regardless of their actual business (e.g., lawyers), are competitors. They may be indirect competitors; they may be substitute competitors; but they are *competitors* nonetheless.

It doesn't make much difference to the customer how financial planning firms view these others or that the alternative providers don't offer the same services or have other "failings." Their customers knew they could go to a financial planner, but they chose not to. They became someone else's customer because you, the financial planner, did not attract them. And neither did your direct competitors.

Why Competitor Information Is Least Useful and Least Important

Yes, it *is* important to know about competitors and to be aware of their moves. We've said that. So why is that information less than totally useful? First, it's a mistake to assume that your competitor's strategy or company is similar to yours. It likely is not, so the elements of its strategy must also be different, as well as the importance of the specific data element you're seeking. For example, Apple, Dell, and Hewlett-Packard all are major computer manufacturers, but their strategies are very different.

Even if you're aware of specific information (profits, number of employees, locations, importance of driving business to the Web, web pages viewed, etc.), can you really make a direct comparison with your own data points? Metrics, data, and other information may be more important to your competitor than to your firm.

The important question to ask is then, "How does detailed information about a competitor's company help you?" For instance, suppose one of your competitors discovered an opportunity. Would you emulate its offering with a "me too" product or service? Would its customers buy from you? And, if you think they would, why? Do you know whether your direct competitor is planning to be more aggressive in products competing with yours? Is it planning to exit this segment in the near future? Is it planning to focus on low-end offerings?

Do not delude yourself into believing that your adaptation is or may be better. That determination will be made by the customer and the marketplace, not by you. Customers don't like change, and if they don't perceive any reason to change, then your allegedly superior product has no merit. Also, keep in mind that the differences and advantages that companies cite in their adaptations are often not viewed the same way by customers. We are repeatedly told by clients how and why the client's product or service is superior. Yet when we speak with customers or distributors, they are either not aware of those differences or do not consider them to be important.

If you're going to "adapt" your product to a competitor's, you are best served to undertake an investigation to arrive at your decision independently. And this is where a dose of self-honesty is absolutely crucial. It's far too easy to get caught up in the excitement of a new offering and competition. A better alternative is to create or find your own opportunity, claim it, and then run to the bank with it.

What information do you really need to know, and what can you disregard? The specifics of what you want to know about each competitor will vary depending on your company, the industry, and your purpose in doing CI. These are some of the more relevant things to know about existing competitors.

1. Who are your primary competitors, and on what basis do you compete?
2. What are their strengths and weaknesses? How do these compare to yours?
3. What advantages, if any, do you have over them—and they over you?
4. Are they a threat to your venture and, if so, how?
5. Are they offering something you are not?

6. How do their products or services compare with yours?
7. Identify what specific competitors are doing successfully that is different.

The most useful question when investigating your competitors is "What do they know that you don't?" This tells you what they have figured out about the marketplace that you haven't yet discovered.

Emerging Competitors

Smaller and emerging competitors may be more important than even the most successful existing major competitors. New entrants to the industry are often the missing link in the evolving marketplace, as they have figured out what customers want but are not receiving from established providers.

Remember, a competitor is any other company that solves the customer's problem. Customers care less about the company size or longevity than they do about simply getting what they want. They prefer to buy from someone they know, or a known brand name, but in the absence of that, they will buy from unknown companies.

One more point: Remember that all successful companies started off small.

Strengths and Weaknesses

Performing SWOT (*strengths, weaknesses, opportunities,* and *threats*) analysis of the competition and your company is quite valuable, as it helps explain the challenges that your company faces. Ideally, you want to capitalize on your strengths, improve the identified weaknesses of your offerings, capitalize on your competitor's weaknesses, benefit from the identified opportunities, and mitigate each actual and potential threat. SWOT is one analytical tool that will reveal some of this.

This is where the other puzzle pieces will be particularly useful. Distributors, suppliers, and competitors add an important external perspective on how your company is viewed and its reputation.

Differences Worth Noting

Companies market their products or services fervently believing that what they offer is of great value. When customers don't respond quite as enthusiastically, it's time to look at the competitors to determine whether they are offering something more or better. After all, there must be a compelling reason to motivate someone to switch to a different supplier. This means you need to know what your competitors offer. These are differences worth noting, especially if the competition attracts your customers. It's easy to ridicule or underestimate a competitor, especially when defending your company's offerings.

Anything competitors do that contributes to their success is important to recognize and analyze. More often than not, however, it is *not* the price, as has been revealed in numerous surveys over the years. Rather, customer service is still not practiced, at least to the level that customers want, and ranks at the top of what business-to-business (B2B) and business-to-consumer (B2C) customers crave.

One of our clients produced *the* most commodity-type of product: zinc fittings. There is no way to differentiate one company's products from another. You cannot offer these fittings in various colors or materials, so there's little opportunity to create a better product. When probing the distributors for the possibility of a new vendor and asking what is most important in considering a new line, price ranked third or fourth for all our contacts.

The distributors were more amenable to a new supplier than might be expected. Existing competitors understood that customer service was important, but they still didn't practice it in a manner that sufficiently satisfied the distributors. For this product category, customer service included delivery when promised, ease of working with the company, and quick responses to inquiries. As a result of our competitive intelligence efforts, our client learned what was important to the distributor and what they needed to do to become a vendor.

Customer service is often a company's secret weapon, because so few understand it or practice it well. It's not uncommon for great customer service to trump all else that is learned from an in-depth investigation of competitors. It may indeed be a bigger differentiator than the minutiae of competitor intelligence.

Still not convinced? Think of the times when you, as a customer, complain about a product or service and can't imagine why the company just doesn't get it.

Gaps You Can Fill

In any number of instances, businesses have grown by serving the unmet needs of customers. This is what creates a vacuum for a new company to enter a seemingly saturated industry. The existing competitors are blind to these openings that they could fill. How often do you view chat rooms or listen to complaints from your customers? These tell you what customers want improved, what the hassles are, and where the opportunities lie to be the company that pays attention.

The Case Against Competitor Intelligence

If we can find value in doing competitor intelligence, why do we seem to be down on it? Here are some of the reasons why competitors cannot be the focus of your CI activities:

1. The competitor's focus may not be the same as yours. Even if you categorize specific companies as direct competitors, they're still *not likely to be in the exact same business as you* in terms of features, SKUs, customers, regional or global territories, and so forth. This is easily forgotten in the passion of learning about the competition, especially in areas where they may be (or appear to be) stronger. You don't know their strategies or priorities (no matter how much research you do), so their decisions may be irrelevant to your strategy.

2. You don't know, and likely cannot uncover, competitors' new strategies until they are already in place. A new CEO or head of strategy or marketing may shift away from known strategies, in which case, you'll be dealing with outdated and erroneous information.

3. The more time you spend dissecting the competition, the more credit you ascribe to them for their acumen. You believe they know something you don't. You think they have figured out something before you have. This is a subtle way to undermine your managers' and executives' contributions and willingness to suggest other paths.

4. Competitors make mistakes, and you won't know what they are until time passes and their decision is in force. If you replicate or

adapt a competitor move before the results are clear, you may be repeating a bad decision. Competitors' flashy or novel moves may be attractive and compelling, but that doesn't always translate to success.

5. If you want to be the leader or get ahead of the leader, you cannot be following the leader. Taking all of your cues from competitors' actions suggests a lack of confidence in yourself and laziness in conducting your own objective investigation.

6. A focus on competitors creates a situation where your company puts disproportionate attention on one aspect of a competitor's business, when it may not even be a differentiator.

7. Even leading companies eventually fall in ranking. Few could imagine, not many years ago, that such giants as Sears, Disney, FAO Schwarz, Marlboro, Andersen Consulting, Jack Welch, Starbucks, Disney, Sumner Redstone, Krispy Kreme, Rubbermaid, Enron, GM, and countless others would lose their significant leadership positions.

The Case *for* Competitor Intelligence

We agree that there is a place for competitor intelligence, but not as the sole or major focus of competitive information. Here are some instances where undertaking competitor research can be very useful:

1. When you're the new kid on the block and entering an existing industry, it's advantageous to understand what to expect, and a competitive analysis provides an overall view of the marketplace, including gaps, opportunities, and outlook. A competitor analysis will provide a profile on what you need to know about each competitor, including how other competitors and customers view them.

   What are their offerings? Will they continue to support all of them, or will there be an opportunity as they wind down in a specific market? What is unique about each? What are their strengths and weaknesses? To whom do they sell, and what are their distribution channels? What is their reputation? Armed with this information, you can now specifically determine whether there *is* indeed a place for you in the industry, and, if so, you can work to differentiate your offering and identify why a customer would be interested in your product or service.

2. One of the most useful pieces of competitor information is learning that competitors are distracted by other events, such as possible mergers, acquisitions, or legal problems. When companies are busy with these other concerns, they don't pay as much attention to their customers, which provides you with an opportunity to woo them. Similar opportunities occur when there are key executive changes, product recalls, loss of a major customer, or a potential change in advertising agencies.

3. Competitor information is part of understanding the entire competitive environment in which you operate. You cannot ignore competitors any more than you would ignore any of the other elements—customers, distribution channels, materials, features, and so on. Specific competitor profiles will alert you to the differences or similarities between you and your competitors and provide an opportunity for you to consider how you can distinguish yourself. But—and this is a big but—it only makes sense to differentiate yourself in a way that your customers want, to be different in a way that matters to customers.

4. When you are preparing a business plan or a presentation to investors, it's expected that information will be included about the competitive landscape and competitors. Doing so demonstrates a deep understanding of the entire competitive environment, how your company is differentiated, and how you will attract customers.

5. When you are trying to determine why other companies are more successful than yours, you may need to focus on your competitors in general or on specific aspects (new feature, packaging, different customers, marketing, distribution, etc.). While this information is critical to know, it points out that you are unaware of what's happening in your industry or with your customers and their wants/needs. A corollary is to seek input on weaknesses in your product or service line via competitor successes and analysis.

6. When you want to determine why "your" customers are buying from an unknown company when they could and should be buying from you, go one step further and buy your competitors' products or services to understand what it's like to be their customer.

Back to the Main Question: Who *Are* Your Competitors?

Let's face it: Every business has competition. The last and only movie theater in a town still faces competition from television, bowling alleys, DVDs, PlayStations, arcades—any place customers spend their money in lieu of the theater. And with the increased use of the Internet to buy goods and services or to download content, that theater is no longer competing with just the immediately neighboring venues.

As evident from the preceding example, competitors are any businesses offering a similar or substitute product or service that makes your own offering redundant. If your customers spend money for those products or services instead of with you, then those providers are your competitors. You need to be constantly on the lookout—not only for them, but also for possible new competition that is ready to snare your customers. Think broadly and wildly for who they are.

We have heard far too many companies proclaim that these other providers aren't their competitors. That's viewing it from an internal perspective, not the customer's. This assertion indicates a lack of objective information and an inability to recognize the reality of the marketplace.

Competitors fall into one of three categories (also briefly covered in Chapter 3):

1. ***Direct competitors:*** Companies offering the same or similar products or services to the same or similar customers.
2. ***Indirect competitors:*** Companies in *related* industries or with related capabilities (primary or secondary) who are selling the same or similar products and services to the same or similar customers.
3. ***Substitute competitors:*** Companies in *different* industries offering the same or similar products and services to the same or similar customers.

There may be some discussion or disagreement over which industry fits into which bucket (refer to Table 4.1), but the primary point is that companies have significant competitors that they don't view as competitors. However, if companies are attracting your customers or prospects, they *are* your competitors, and you are losing that business.

Table 4.1

The Competitor Landscape

Type of Competitor	Financial Planning	Meals	Video Rental
Direct	Certified financial planners	Restaurants	Blockbuster or local video store
Indirect	CPAs and accountants Insurance companies Brokerage houses Banks American Express	Restaurant take-out (with or without sit-down space) Restaurant delivery Supermarkets Personal chef	Netflix Amazon Internet DirecTV TV on demand Libraries Supermarkets and drug stores
Substitute	Software Internet Books Attorneys	Coffeehouses Cafés Home shopping (QVC) Mail order Internet Movie theaters Department stores	Dining out Movie theater Bowling Hanging out

Direct Competitors

Competitors come in all shapes and sizes and from many more directions than ever before. It's all about competition for the customer's dollars, depending on whom you target as your primary customer. A direct competitor for your company is the competitor that fills the same buyer need that you fill, in the same way you fill it. Direct competitors are the companies readily identified by your customers, named by your trade association, or mentioned in the press in articles about your industry. They exhibit at conferences and are listed in the same directories. Even if these companies perform other services, they are viewed as direct competition for specific offerings. Companies and industries easily deny or dismiss new or different competition that they don't view as direct competition. Broadcast TV stations dismissed CNN and other cable stations, and we all know what happened there.

Indirect Competitors

Indirect competitors are a bit more difficult to classify and identify. The accepted market definition of an *indirect competitive product or service* is one that is a reasonable and accepted alternative. Chapter 3 describes a financial services client who had entered the campus card market. The client's indirect competition included phone companies, hospitality companies, card manufacturers, and even security companies whose cards were performing the very same functions for the very same customers.

Classification of competition as *direct*, *indirect*, or *substitute* may change, depending on the industry. Tire retreads are a direct competitor to the truck tire industry because truck tires are expensive. For car owners, however, new tires aren't very expensive relative to retreads, so this is not as viable a market.

Compounding this confusion is the fact that customers can also be competitors. They may be customers of yours for select products, but competing against you in other situations.

Substitute Competitors

Substitute competitors are the most difficult for companies to acknowledge, let alone pay attention to. For example, Swiss and Japanese watches compete with cell phones, and Coke competes with bottled water. In short, substitute competition is *any other business* that can fulfill your customers' needs or solve their problems using a product that isn't yours. This means that you have to *look at your customers* and how they behave to truly determine who your competition is.

Are you being blindsided by unexpected competition? Apple Computer started in the computer business and then moved very successfully into the music arena with its iPod and the highly successful iTunes online store. Now it has moved, once again successfully, into the telephone arena with its highly successful iPhone and the growing business of apps (applications).

New Competitors

It's frustrating that new competitors don't announce their arrival in advance. All of a sudden, they're there, and your reaction to their entrance will determine whether you continue to dismiss them or use this as an opportunity to reach out to your customers. New competitors cannot gain customers—existing or new—unless they are offering something that you and your direct competitors are not. This is how you get blindsided. To what extent this happens depends a lot on when you notice them and whether or not you choose to ignore, dismiss, or underestimate them. It's difficult to accept that new upstart as competition; remember that your company probably also started off small.

The American automotive industry failed to respond when the original Volkswagen Beetle came on the scene, and again when the Japanese automotive industry started offering products to the American market in the early 1970s. Even after Japan had established a foothold on the American highway, Detroit again dismissed Japanese carmakers when they began offering lines of luxury cars. The question Detroit failed to ask, the one that every producer *must* ask when confronted with unexpected competition, is this: "Why do they think they can attract our customers or prospects?" What are they offering that we do not? Did Apple ask that very question when Google entered the telephone arena?

Cars are fairly big-ticket items, but what about the more mundane, such as coffee? That is evident in the battle between Starbucks and McDonald's. No one could possibly conceive of these two giants as competing in the same space, and they didn't until 2008. In 2007, Starbucks announced a decline in stock value, and McDonald's revealed that it was hiring baristas and buying sleek, expensive coffee machines to make fresh, high-quality coffee drinks to compete directly with Starbucks. Was that a good strategy? Time will tell, of course, but McDonald's coffee is rated quite high and offers a lower-priced alternative. At this writing, Starbucks has announced a 97 percent drop in profits, while McDonald's has improved its own bottom line. Enough said.

While competitor intelligence is important, it must be done within the confines of the greater competitive landscape. Limiting yourself to your own industry and your direct competitors will make you miss important changes in consumer behavior and expectations and will put you at risk of disappointing or even annoying those consumers.

The famous Chinese general and military strategist Sun Tzu (400 BC), frequently cited in the competitive intelligence community to defend a company's focus on the competition, offers this quote: "It is said that if you know your enemies and know yourself, you will not be imperiled in a hundred battles. If you do not know your enemies but do know yourself, you will win one and lose one. If you do not know your enemies nor yourself, you will be imperiled in every single battle."

This would be more applicable to business if, in fact, business had clearly or discretely defined "enemies" or competitors, or if this was not a reference to war.

He also proclaimed that "It is best to keep one's own state intact; to crush the enemy's state is only second best." As it relates to business, a company's primary goal is to have a profitable, viable, and growing business. Competitors that are diminished because of your good decisions and cleverness are necessarily a consequence.

Knockoffs and Innovation: More Competition?

There is a lot that can be said for and about "me too" products. While the new ones might be better than those that already exist, a lot of these "me too" products will not offer much differentiation. However, if you are obsessed with what your direct competition is doing, you will likely end up copying the competitor's new concept or product. A number of companies have been quite successful with that strategy, although most garner very little market share; witness the iPod and its poor cousins. Even if you do succeed being second in the marketplace, you are at best a smart follower.

We conducted many investigations for Rubbermaid in the early 1990s when it was one of the most highly regarded companies across a wide spectrum of categories. We noticed that whenever Rubbermaid came out with an improved product, there were specific companies who produced knockoffs of its products. Their strategy was to let Rubbermaid figure out the details of the improvements and then offer a similar product for approximately 30 percent lower cost. This is a viable strategy that relies on the good decisions of the company you're pursuing, but may not fit your vision of your company. And while this approach may work for some, and for a limited amount of time, the original innovator is continuing to forge ahead and is likely already working on a newer and better widget that will be its next big product. The question is, will your customers stay with you or move to back to the original innovator or to another knockoff company?

An alternative strategy is to strive for differentiation through innovation. Most of the products or services that companies claim to be innovative are really just improvements. There are very few true innovations—that is, completely new products, services, features, strategies, or marketing approaches. The purpose of innovation is to provide something of value for the customer, not simply to create something totally new for its own sake. Customer value is far more likely to result in new customers and additional sales, because you're giving customers what they want. Something totally new but without the benefit of an in-depth investigation often results in a product or service that the company is enamored with, but the buying public isn't, as our clients have discovered. This is a huge disappointment, and a costly finding, but the good news is that the competitive intelligence investigation saved all the costs associated with proceeding.

Peter Drucker has a more expansive view. Innovation "endows existing resources with enhanced potential for creating wealth" ("The Discipline of Innovation," *Harvard Business Review*). In this article, Drucker outlines seven sources of innovation, all of which are revealed with good competitive intelligence: industry and market changes; unexpected occurrences; incongruities; process needs; demographic changes; changes in perception; and new knowledge. Drucker continues to affirm that "the easiest source of innovation opportunity [is] the unexpected." And that's what a changing marketplace continues to offer.

Detect Opportunities From Change, Not From Competitors

The past several decades have been ones of constant *surprise* and unpredictability during which what actually occurs is unexpected. This is one area in which competitive intelligence really proves its advantage for those executives who are open to hearing, considering, analyzing, and understanding these changes and surprises. As a best-practice strategy, executives should be listening for, observing, or looking for the unexpected—day in and day out, month in and month out.

Surprising information is usually ignored, dismissed, or under-estimated because it doesn't make sense in the context of what is currently known. All it takes to understand this type of information, and why it makes sense today and may be a huge competitive advantage, is to know the back story. That is, more explanation is needed to see how the new information evolved logically from the old familiar information. Connect the dots.

The downside to being an innovator and a leader is that once competitors start copying your successful ideas, you fall into a similar complacent situation. You must differentiate your offering and continue creating that unique competitive advantage. Retailer Target created a strategy that was unthinkable—selling lower-priced goods from high-end and fashion-forward designers, including Isaac Mizrachi and architect Michael Graves. Once other retailers became aware of the increased revenue (Mizrachi accounted for 3 percent of Target's apparel and accessories business) and enviable reputation of Target's strategy, many copied it (J.C. Penney, Kohl's). Target's uniqueness has been reduced to the unique offerings of its designers rather than the unique marketing idea.

Executives often prefer innovation to incremental improvements as a way to differentiate themselves from their competitors (and to score a big hit). Innovation is sexy and attracts buzz, while improvements and small changes are viewed as unexciting, easy to copy, and not particularly worthy. But relatively few companies have gained success with *truly* innovative products or services.

The good news about incremental changes is that they are an acknowledgment of their customer's constant desire for better, faster, easier, or cheaper. This includes more features, more usable space in the same exterior space (refrigerators), or faster speed (computer bandwidth). Toyota is known for its incremental changes, the Japanese philosophy of Kaizen, earning a reputation of being in touch with its customers.

There has been considerable research documenting the fact that first-mover advantage leading to market dominance is not accurate. Companies that are credited with innovative products, processes, or services may not have been the innovators of them, but rather those who were better at marketing. Amazon did not create online bookselling. Two other companies preceded Amazon by several years. Two Chicago brokerage firms launched the first Internet-based stock trading services before Charles Schwab or E*Trade. Xerox developed many innovative products, but did not have the requisite marketing savvy.

The Anti-Competitor Strategy: Red Ocean–Blue Ocean

Blue Ocean Strategy by W. Chan Kim and Renée Mauborgne details companies that recognized a gap in their industry and took a road different than their competitors. These businesses carved out new space that expanded their industry rather than taking away sales from competitors:

1. Cirque du Soleil created a new definition of the circus.
2. Curves developed a different gym model, 30-minute *circuit training,* focusing only on women.
3. California Pizza Kitchen transformed the everyday pizza into a specialty, gourmet option.
4. Pinkberry offers a totally different taste for a familiar product— yogurt.

"Red ocean" companies operate within the confines of their existing industry, where they are trying to steal customers from rivals. As more and more entities enter this same market space, profits and growth are reduced. Products attain commodity status, and the resulting cutthroat competition "turns the ocean bloody red."

In contrast, Blue Ocean Strategy is the anti-competitor message. The primary theory of this very popular book, which spawned an Institute at INSEAD (the world-famous graduate business school based in Fontainebleau, near Paris), is to uncover opportunities that are not currently served by your competitors. Blue oceans denote the industries that may not yet exist. This is part of the goal of what competitive intelligence will uncover. Successful blue ocean companies have certainly created a differentiated company.

In blue oceans, the demand is created rather than fought over. Businesses create a new niche within an existing industry from within the red ocean, as Curves did in the fitness arena. Cirque du Soleil is a circus, but it does not compete with other traditional circuses.

Operating in a blue ocean provides much greater opportunity for profit and growth, because you can set the rules for this market space. In order to do so, you have to study the customers to see what appeals to them and to determine what the competitors in the red ocean are *not* providing. Armed with this new perspective, you can create new competitive space in the same industry. After all, why go up against direct competitors when you can have a piece of that market all for yourself?

Last Word on Competitor Intelligence

While CI shines a light on competitors, competitive intelligence truly focuses on more than your competitors. This due diligence allows you to consider and analyze *all* the elements in the competitive landscape, including the industry, the distribution channels, the economy, the legal and regulatory arena, demographics, culture, technology, and, above all, the customer. All of these affect a firm's ability to compete and offer a better, clearer pathway to success.

The goal in business is to make a profit. This profit can be increased significantly by minimizing risks, and that's just one of the many benefits that competit*ive* intelligence brings to the table.

5

Three Critical Distinctions

What's in a name? That which we call a rose, by any other name would smell as sweet.
　　　　　—William Shakespeare, *Romeo and Juliet*

Shakespeare may well have been right that "a rose by any other name would smell as sweet." However, that aphorism does not apply to competitive intelligence. The terms *data, information,* and *intelligence*, while often used interchangeably by many businesspeople, do not carry the same meaning. It is not a matter of semantics; the differences between these terms are fundamental; they underscore the quality of the input for decisions and strategy.

Strategy is not built on data, nor is it built on information. Strategy is built on intelligence—insightful, current, relevant, accurate, and sufficient intelligence. Insights are bigger than data or information. They make you think differently about what you know and help you understand it in a new way.

Using the wrong name creates confusion and may be misleading because of the limitations of each term. For instance, data is but one element of information. And when all those elements are given context, they *then* constitute information. After appropriate *analysis* of the information, the results become intelligence, with the ultimate goal of using that intelligence to develop or improve a company's strategy and its decisions.

The purpose of this chapter is not merely to clarify the differences between these terms, but also to explain why these differences matter— *really* matter. Discarding any one of these three elements leaves you open to being blindsided.

Focus on the Goal

The goal of gathering data and information must never be simply having the information itself, unless of course, you are seeking "just the facts." Rather, the goal is analysis of information that is sufficiently useful to yield *actionable intelligence.* This is important enough to *repeat: The purpose of intelligence is action.*

Successful companies build their firms on smart business decisions centered on what is happening with the customer and the marketplace, not on data such as price points or units sold.

Pricing, although important, is among the least successful strategic element. Survey after survey has shown that, even in recessionary times, pricing is not at, or even near the top of, the list of what's most important to customers. Most often, it is customer service. Dozens and dozens of our competitive intelligence projects have demonstrated similar results. Clients often believe that price is most important to their current or potential customers and that knowing their competitors' pricing will be a major factor in greater success. Yet our findings prove consistently that other issues are much more significant. These include the ease with which clients can do business with a company, reliability of delivery dates, minimal returns, proper packaging, relationships, product quality, and—oh, yes—also price.

Of course, many companies and salespeople have a tendency to point to pricing as the reason they didn't make the sale. The reality is usually that customers have not perceived sufficient value from your offering, value they consider to be commensurate with the price that exists, and hence they cannot differentiate your product or service from others. So the product becomes a mere commodity to the buyer. Pricing offers an advantage for the moment—until another vendor lowers its price—and it is a short-term advantage. Competitive intelligence moves the conversation away from pricing and toward issues that uncover relevant and long-term advantages.

Components of Data, Information, and Intelligence

There is overlap among these three groups to some extent. For example, news can fit into any of the three categories, depending on the degree and level of detail. Furthermore, what is considered by one person to be intelligence may be mere information to another.

In the introduction to his book *The Information Resources Policy Handbook*, the founder of Harvard University's Program on Information Resources Policy, Anthony G. Oettinger, says, "What a vice president for marketing, production, or finance thinks he knows is just data to the chief executive officer's staff. What a scientist thinks he knows about the merits of a flu vaccine or the safety of a nuclear reactor is just data for presidential policy and politics."

In other words, data is noisy; intelligence is quiet. Data gets lots of attention, and it's easy for people to talk about it; it's something that we understand quickly and easily. Intelligence, on the other hand, requires context and thoughtful analysis, contemplation for what it really means. And it may require a far more expository presentation. Intelligence is much quieter, and it doesn't garner the same attention. But it has a much higher probability of being useful and creating noise in the near future.

In the quest for faster answers, it's easy to be enticed by the seeming validity of data rather than accepting the necessary time to develop intelligence.

Data: What Exactly *Is* Data?

Data generally refers to facts, statistics, or even a single number. When you truly look at data within its context, you begin to realize that data really presents some form of a given. It's something that has occurred in the past: We sold so many widgets; we sold them for this price; it cost this much to produce them; we spent this much on marketing; we have this number of customers or outlets or SKUs.

Data is extremely important and highly valued. It's easy to understand, to compare, and to discuss. Executives include lots of numbers in conversations to convey their point, especially to the financial community. Data is the basis for many business decisions and often appears to be the foundation of MBA discussions. However, data by itself can be misleading, seriously misleading, as the following examples show.

1. Breast cancer statistics are frequently cited something like this: "One in eight women will get breast cancer." The reality is that this statistic is true *only* for women who reach 85 years of age. A woman's risk of developing breast cancer is one out of 2,525 by age 30, increasing to one out of 50 by age 50, one in 14 by age 70, and one in 10 by age 80. (Source: National Cancer Institute Surveillance Program.)

2. Sources of similar data may have different and unstated bases. Online brokerage houses have included different firms and different data to state their earnings. Some may not include "noncore" items; some may exclude pretax charges or gains. Investors may even receive reports with different earnings numbers for the same company, according to the *Wall Street Journal*. Another article in the *Journal* notes that "Manufacturers and auto industry data analysts each rely on different figures

for measuring used-car demand." Bottom line: Comparisons between firms or product lines may actually be apples to oranges; you simply don't know it.

3. Rising household income is less about higher income per se and more a reflection of the increase in multiple earners per household and more people working full-time. While the actual data is true, the underlying story may be quite different; the data tells only part of the story. Further, the 2006 median household income, which increased from the previous year, is actually down from the peak in 1999. Two very different perspectives.

4. It seems as though everyone quotes a particular statistic about the divorce rate, that "50 percent of all marriages fail." In fact, the divorce rate per 1,000 people peaked in 1981 and is closer to its lowest rate since 1970. There are good reasons for this: The number of unmarried couples who live together has increased; Americans are getting married at an older age; and people are open to seeking solutions to problems. Yet the statistic, "one in two marriages will end in divorce," continues to be repeated by news and other sources.

5. Similar to this is the oft-stated assumption about the percentage of high school students who are having sex. The fact is that this number decreased 54 percent between 1991 and 2005, and, in 65 years of recorded data, the teen birth rate reached an all-time low in 2005. While it has increased slightly in recent years, a commonly held belief is that the percentages continue to increase and that *every* teen is having sex.

6. When we provided research for an author, we learned that unemployment statistics are measured three different ways, but that only one metric is reported, thereby skewing the real understanding of what's occurring. The unemployment percentages that are stated do not include those who have given up looking, and they don't reflect information about those who want to work full-time but are forced to settle for part-time work.

7. Car sales do not reflect rates of satisfaction. No more explanation required here!

Barack Obama resigned his Senate seat in December 2008. This is data. Imagine that we know nothing else, that we are without any contextual information about this "news." What are we to make of it?

Why did he resign? What does this mean? Is he sick? Is he or was he involved in a potential scandal? Was he convicted of a crime? Was he just plain tired of the job? As we can see, facts alone have limitations and can lead to *lots* of speculation.

Author and futurist John Naisbitt, in his book *Megatrends*, said, "We are drowning in data, but starved for knowledge." In other words, there are plenty of *facts and statistics*, but a paucity of information that is analyzed for meaning. Intelligence is often drowned out by data.

Businesspeople appear far more comfortable with quantitative information than they are with non-quantitative. It's harder to dispute statistics, and it's easier to defend numbers than intelligence. Data is likely to be accepted, while intelligence is more apt to be debated and argued. The business world regards data as far more significant than it is and often puts a higher premium on hard information than may be warranted. Data and information are considered real, solid, and irrefutable; the more precise the data, the more easily it is accepted.

Mathematical models and statistical analyses are revered and rarely questioned. The big *however* is that they ignore non-quantitative and noneconomic realities. They rarely factor in social, political, and cultural behaviors and beliefs, which can totally shift the meaning of the data.

Data can be misleading, and when it isn't clear-cut, CEOs often take on the role of referees rather than strategists. They have access to all the data, but can never be quite sure of its relevance or accuracy without validation of the input along with analysis. As has been said many times, volumes of data alone often mask the truth. Without context and sufficient supporting information, data may well be misleading. Yet business presentations, meetings, and conversations are replete with data, charts, graphs, and statistics. To what end?

The Toyota Camry was the number one best-selling car in the United States in 1997, and sales were increasing. While this data was widely reported, readers rarely learned that the Toyota brand ranked number 30 in customer satisfaction. The sales data was great, of course, but not so the *other* information—important information, at that. As a car buyer, wouldn't you consider this *other* information relevant? Would you reconsider your decision?

The way data is presented can consciously or unconsciously give the wrong impression. The major advantage of using graphs and charts

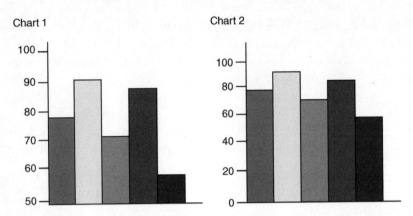

FIGURE 5.1   Percentage of pupils earning grades A to C in five academic subjects

http://hospitality.hud.ac.uk/studyskills/usingData/InterpretingData/misleadingData.htm.

to represent data is that they give an instant visual picture of the relationship between the variables, but this picture can easily be altered by using different scales and different ways of presentation.

In the example shown in Figure 5.1, which presents the percentage of students who achieved grades from A to C in different classes, the *same data* on exam results is presented differently. The graph on the left uses a scale of 50 to 100 percent, while the graph on the right uses a scale of 0 to 100 percent.

The performance of the pupils suggests two different stories. Chart 1 gives the impression that results for the subjects represented by the fifth and third bars, respectively, are quite low, the result of using different scales in Charts 1 and 2. Though the differences in scale are easily seen in this example, this is not always the case, as usually only one of these graphs is presented. Therefore, when comparing graphs, it is important to pay close attention to the *scale* that's used. Many similar charts, especially in newspapers, do not use a 0 to 100 percent scale; it's more likely to be a subset to support the story and present a different or dramatic slant.

It's worth repeating, *data is and can be very useful.* Data provides the numbers and the basic necessary information for the next step, building toward intelligence. Data is powerful; but it can also be powerfully misleading. It represents the past, while to see the present (and future) you need additional factors.

Metrics: Are You Data Rich and Information Poor?

For at least the past decade or longer, management appears to have adopted the mantra, "If you can't measure it, you can't manage it." Rubbish! Certainly, there is merit to measuring and comparing what is appropriate and useful, but to believe that it should be applied across the board is absurd.

Not everything that is important can be measured or, for that matter, needs to be measured. My mathematics degrees provided a deep, visceral understanding that *just because you can measure it doesn't mean it provides value* or that it should be measured. Conversely, just because you *can't* measure it doesn't mean that it doesn't have value.

Intelligence is not data-based. While data may be part of it, intelligence is light-years from pure data. Intelligence includes insight, analysis, understanding, perspective, and other higher-level reflection and reasoning that cannot be measured but offer considerable value.

Metrics, also referred to as *key performance indicators*, is one of the buzzwords of today's management thinking. While there is considerable emphasis in business today on metrics, this concept needs a reality check. The business of sports is heavily metric-centered. Yet, how often does the last place team beat the top ranking team? How often do sports announcers state that "This has never happened before"?

Although metrics have the appearance of certainty, it's noteworthy that vital data may not be included. Consider this: Information Resources, Inc. (IRI), the primary and widely used source of data on supermarket sales, does not include Wal-Mart's sales, yet Wal-Mart accounts for more than half the sales of many packaged-goods categories in food, drug, and mass-merchandise retailers. An unknowing purchaser or reader of a report with the IRI data may not be aware of this significant omission. (Wal-Mart has banned its sales data from syndicators since 2001.)

Metrics are familiar, easy, comfortable, and have the appearance of objectivity. Metrics are simple, but business today is increasingly more complex, and decisions require the addition of more subjective information that is revealing and insightful.

Respected business sources have, for several decades reported that 75 to 85 percent of all mergers and acquisitions are unsuccessful. How can this be so, when companies pour over every number and statistic?

It's simply because they focus on financial, operational, or manufacturing data, while softer information is ignored or deemed far less important. This includes understanding the corporate culture and the likelihood of employees fitting together, demographics of the two workforces, values, work styles, and so forth. While the companies have reams of data to analyze, the purchasing companies are obviously not looking at all the *right* information or their mergers would not be so likely to fail.

This is where we make a strong case for competitive intelligence. In speaking with many private equity firms, investment bankers, and others involved in the M&A community, we are repeatedly amazed at how little market due diligence is undertaken. They engage in financial and legal due diligence, and study the operations, but either don't conduct market due diligence or rely on the company to educate them about the marketplace. Metrics aren't enough, and even more so when they exclude significant decision components.

Metrics must be directly comparable to be meaningful. They must measure identical parameters; otherwise it's an apples-to-oranges situation. Highly regarded nonprofit TV station PBS usually does not get into the ratings game of its broadcast siblings. But they made an exception for Ken Burns's series, *The War* (about World War II). PBS boasted that its airing attracted an "estimated gross audience" of 18.7 million viewers, a number that indicates a ratings success. It turns out that PBS was deliberately using a different standard than other broadcast networks use. When applying the same standard, the PBS audience was a much lower 7.3 million. The importance of TV ratings cannot be underestimated, as it's the source of future advertising revenues.

Similarly, during the height of dot-com investing, "some of the largest Internet brokers . . . presented investors with two different sets of earnings numbers . . . one that includes items such as the amortization of goodwill and one that doesn't," according to the *Wall Street Journal*.

And then there's the not uncommon issue of incomplete or nonstandard data. The *Wall Street Journal* reported in December 2007 that "at least five search companies, including Google and Yahoo, announced their top searches of the year, based on the first 11 months." Since when does the word *year* comprise only 11 months?

That wasn't the only problem. Raw numbers for most popular searches usually exclude adult terms, such as "porn," which ranked number three on AOL's preliminary list of the top searches from mobile devices. The final news release excluded porn, without a statement that it was being excluded. There are numerous similar examples depending on the site and the filters (e.g., using most popular versus fastest-growing in order to mix it up and not have similar lists perennially).

Metrics must reveal *all* relevant information. As mentioned earlier in this chapter, a woman has a one-in-eight risk of developing breast cancer, but only when she reaches her eighties. Somehow, that last part is often omitted, especially when the figure is used for fund-raising and to gain press attention. One more point: The statistics are more positive when only those who don't have cancer at the beginning of the age interval are measured, according to the National Cancer Institute. I'll bet none of us knows *that* statistic.

How do we know what information is missing when statistics are presented to us? The frequently quoted and highly respected Fortune 500 lists did not include retailers (e.g., Wal-Mart) until 1996. Until then, it was a list of industrial companies. How could this be a list of the "Fortune 500" when an entire category was excluded?

The media widely reported, in early 2009, that 1,900 manufacturing jobs would be lost from Dell Inc. in Ireland. While that fact is accurate, it's grossly misleading, as it suggests a shrinking Dell workforce. The true picture is that Dell is moving its Irish manufacturing operations to Poland in early 2010, and the 1,900 figure represents one-half of Dell's current workforce in Ireland. The company is keeping 1,300 jobs in Dublin and 1,000 in Limerick. Knowing the accuracy of number of employees is a *critical* metric, and it has more meaning than just a data point.

As if this weren't enough, what about information that cannot be reconciled? For more than a decade, the U.S. Bureau of the Census has reported that there are 1 million more married women than married men. This was true even before same-sex marriages. How do we deal with this disparity? I started following this in 1994, when there were 57.0 million married men compared to 58.1 million women (both over the age of 18). The gap is decreasing, as the statistics reported 63.6 million married males and 64.0 million married females in 2006. Okay, perhaps more men are admitting that they are married (www.census. gov/prod/2007pubs/08abstract/pop.pdf).

This disparity is not a problem if you don't need exact data, which is most of the time. But if preciseness is required, then more investigation is necessary to ferret out what data is *not* included and why. That might be the more important part of the story. It's not acceptable to merely state that the data cannot be reconciled. It means you don't have the complete picture, and that could lead to bad decisions, even if exact data is not crucial.

When companies really buy into metrics, it can obscure all reason and other judgments. For instance, it has been said that nothing in Oregon goes unquantified, thanks to the Oregon Benchmarking Experience, the state's "results-oriented measures" for the purpose of creating a "high-performance organization." This includes everything from child immunization rates, vehicles driven, and cleanliness of parks to the quality of life. The state measures (statistically) how clean a park is and how residents rank quality of life.

Many believe that this official state policy has gotten out of hand, measuring everything (or so it seems) even if it's impractical, immeasurable, or totally frivolous. This is a good example of data collection gone wild and being confused with intelligence. The emphasis appears to be on developing and reporting data rather than on engaging in insight, understanding, and analysis, which would provide better decisions for the citizens of Oregon.

Sometimes the basic measure or accepted norm upon which a statistic is based may change and fail to be noted when the data is discussed or compared. For many years, cholesterol levels above 220 were considered in the high range. Then it changed to 200, and now 180 (and lower) is considered the standard. This causes two potential problems. First, discussions may not include the previous norm or desired number. Second, because the number has been lowered, there are now many more people who fall into the high-cholesterol range who didn't before. Does this higher number reflect more health problems, or is it due to the changed metric?

Schools, at all levels, focus on metrics that range from report cards to standardized tests to SATs. But would you consider hiring someone *solely* for his or her metrics? What about the importance of problem-solving skills, creativity, work ethic, passion, street smarts, and ability to communicate? No doubt you've come across, as we all have at some point, interviewees or colleagues who have graduated summa cum laude, yet they can't make the kinds of decisions your business needs. Academic intelligence does have limitations if you cannot translate that into the real world.

Finally, the way that data is presented can often mislead. The year 2008 appeared to be the champion for selective data, particularly when it came to reporting on the number or percentage of homes in foreclosure or missing mortgage payments. The constant barrage of bad news about foreclosures made it appear that almost everyone was in danger of losing their home. What most of these reports failed to include was context.

The statement that "One in 10 American households with mortgages is overdue on payments or in foreclosure" means that 9 out of 10 mortgage holders are okay. Do you recall any news program stating that 90 percent of homeowners pay their mortgages monthly? And that 90 percent statistic doesn't even include those who have paid off their mortgages (about 30 percent), which would increase that number to 90-plus percent. Presenting the negative number, even when it's small, creates a subliminal message of poor performance that at best feeds into people's fears and at worst becomes a self-fulfilling prophecy. While more homes are in foreclosure than ever before, these "facts" simply do not portray a true picture of how many homeowners are actually doing fine.

The secondary message here is find out exactly what the number refers to. Is it U.S. or global, retail or wholesale, gross or net, under 18 years of age or everyone, and on and on.

Intuition, Gut, and Experience: The Immeasurable

Intuition and experience certainly cannot be dismissed or underestimated as valuable input for business decisions. The problem is that many executives rely too much on what they "know" and don't temper this with facts and solid information. Those executives frequently state that it was their "good judgment" or "experience" that got them to their current lofty positions; therefore, why wouldn't they continue to rely on this successful approach?

The major problem with intuition, gut, and experience is that all these are based on the past. And while they *are* critical to success, they must be tempered with the reality of the present. In a constantly changing business environment, the same thinking and decisions cannot be applied even to what appears to be similar events. Today's problems and issues are not like yesterday's problems; they differ in both seemingly trivial and highly significant ways.

The bar for all products and services is constantly being raised, even when we are unaware of it. That's what competitive intelligence uncovers. If your salespeople and executives cannot specifically identify those changes, then you are creating opportunities for another company to fill the voids that are being created. Take the challenge and detail the changes that have occurred in your industry and in your business over the last five years. The last year. The last month.

Experience has shown us and our clients that reliance on data or information combined with an overexuberant belief in intuition, experience, and assumptions, does *not* equal intelligence. It's more likely, in fact, to result in poor and costly decisions.

It's important to reiterate that data is backward-looking and cannot be used as a forward-looking tool. Hard data is important for context and foundation; so is experience. But it's less reliable for moving forward with surety. And the more often that decisions are based on data alone, the greater the likelihood that these will infer yesterday's decisions and increase risk.

The Intelligence Pyramid

Where does data fit into the context of information and intelligence? Figure 5.2 illustrates the general flow from data to intelligence.

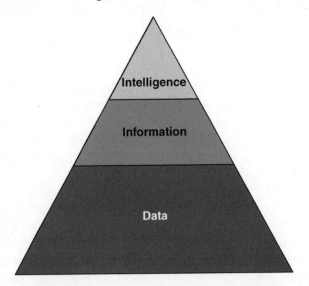

FIGURE 5.2 The Intelligence Pyramid

Data is the most available of the three segments, and it's the largest segment. Data is the easiest to gather, requires the least skill of the three, and more people can get it.

Information, however, provides more value than data. Moving up the pyramid, information is more difficult to uncover and fewer people have the skills to provide it.

Intelligence really is the tip and the top of the pyramid, and this visual is a true reflection. There is far less intelligence than data; very few people understand what it is; and even fewer appear to have the skills to provide it. (See Chapter 3 for our discussion of the components of competitive intelligence.)

The pyramid goes in only one direction. You can't get to intelligence without data, but you can have data without intelligence. And data may be sufficient; not every situation requires intelligence. (See Chapter 11, "Demystifying Competitive Intelligence," that discusses the myths about CI.)

For example, the Los Angeles traffic signal system is the envy of planners worldwide. According to the *Los Angeles Times*, "Sensors and computers collect massive amounts of data about traffic patterns and congestions." But they don't "help engineers plan for the city's growing transportation need or determine how development is affecting traffic," because the city doesn't save the data. They use it for real-time traffic movement, such as how quickly lights change.

City planners do not appear to understand that the same data can be extremely useful in developing strategy. This is a good example of great data that is used—and equally, an example of not moving data to intelligence.

The goal in competitive intelligence is to gather accurate and current data, then use that data to move to information and from there to intelligence. Bottom line: Move to the top of the pyramid.

What Is Information—and How Do We Get There from Here?

There can be little doubt that the word *information* has exploded to the point of near absurdity: We are in the information age; we are an information society; we live in an information economy; we suffer from information overload; we travel the information superhighway; we are engaged in information warfare (cyberwar); and on and on. But does information move us to intelligence?

Companies often delude themselves into thinking that information and intelligence are one and the same. Those who believe that information equals intelligence have a less sophisticated and more limited approach to what's valuable to their company. We do business today in sophisticated and complex times, so the input must be equally sophisticated. Using simple or common information is a distinct disadvantage.

Information is important, and certainly a big step up from data. It will result in a better decision than one might make having *no* information, because at least you have some of the pieces, even if not all. Smart decisions are dependent on sufficient amounts of the *right* information. (See Chapter 10 under the heading *"Enough Information?"*)

At first blush, the definition of *information* is clear and unproblematic; we all believe that we know what it is. But upon closer inspection, it is all too evident that we can't specify the exact meaning of the term and that it's often used interchangeably with *data* and *intelligence*. How does one differentiate between the three?

Information is both qualitative (data-driven) and quantitative (adding context or more meaning). In that sense, information is the interim point between data and intelligence. It's a level up from data, and it is useful and important for what it is: a portal to intelligence.

It's a step toward getting to intelligence, but it is *not* intelligence. So, information is a contextual construct. Table 5.1 characterizes each of the terms.

Consider the example of Hospital A in Table 5.2, which has a reported death rate of 2 percent. That's data. What does it mean? As a single data point, it has no meaning. It's impossible to determine whether this rate is good or bad.

Let's next add Hospital B to the mix, with its reported death rate of 3 percent. Now that we have additional data, one could easily conclude that Hospital A is a much more desirable hospital in which to be a patient. While this conclusion is based on extremely limited information and the most basic analysis, judgments are often based on comparably limited information. It's not unusual for companies with comparable amounts of data to arrive at a conclusion with similar limited information. Further, it's not unusual to hear a news report that presents a single data point that does not reflect the news story.

Table 5.1

Characteristics of Data, Information, and Intelligence

Data	Raw material: number, statistic, fact, image
	Single, isolated item
	Discrete
	No context
	Static
	Component of information
Information	Grouping or collection of data
	Puts data in context
	Good for comparison
	Reveals more than data
	May or may not be sufficient
	Subset of intelligence
Intelligence	Sufficient and right information that has been evaluated and analyzed
	Dynamic
	Reveals patterns; connects the dots
	Leads to insights and implications
	Results in decision or action
	Highest level

Now add just a few more pieces of information. Hospital B performs many more difficult surgeries than Hospital A. Hospital B attracts better doctors to deal with these situations. Hospital A refuses the sickest patients that Hospital B admits. Would that change your decision about which hospital to visit? Do you consider this important information? Do you want it included before you make a decision?

Yes, this example is *very* basic and simple. It points out the significance of how your thinking would change if you had more information, especially if that information was more important. It's

Table 5.2

Evaluating a Company: Moving From Data to Intelligence

Data	Raw material: sales, profits, number of beds, branch location, number of employees, image Isolated piece information (fact or statistic), discrete No context Static Component of information	Hospital A Death rate 2%
Information (Rudimentary Analysis)	Grouping of data Puts data in context Good for comparison Reveals more than data May or may not be sufficient	Hospital B Death rate 3%
Conclusion	Go to hospital A: lower death rate and higher likelihood of survival	
More Information	Hospital B has a much higher percentage of difficult surgeries Hospital B attracts better trained and highly respected doctors Hospital B takes patients that Hospital A won't admit/sicker patients Direct comparisons of procedures between two institutions – B has better outcomes	
Intelligence (Analysis of Relevant Information to Get to the Desired End Result)	Need right info Have sufficient info Analyzed information Dynamic Reveals patterns Leads to insights and implications Results in best decisions	
New Conclusion	Hospital B: more experience and better outcomes	

not a big leap to understand the value of doing one's research and having the necessary input, especially for all but the least important decisions.

A scenario similar to that displayed by the hospitals in Table 5.2 is often found in articles describing companies, in that information brought to management is equally wanting and misleading. It is just another example of limited and basic information, and proves what Sherlock Holmes observed, "How dangerous it is to reason from insufficient data."

Consider the business case shown in Table 5.3, in which Hot Company revenues decreased from $300 million in 2008 to $100 million in 2009. The company's competitors are quite excited by this news, because it suggests that Hot is not doing well, which creates an opportunity for them to acquire some additional business or customers. They care little about what happened or why and are primarily interested in Hot's revenue decline.

Just a little more digging uncovers considerably more specific information, which reveals that Hot Company is in a stronger position in its market than it previously was, despite the significant drop in revenues. Accordingly, Hot's competitors really don't have much to be excited about and shouldn't be so quick to dismiss the company.

Obviously, it is easy to be taken in by what you want to hear and not probe further to discover all that should be known. Again, this is a very simple example, but not different from the limited information many companies have. Think about how much and what type of information is included in your decisions or assumptions.

Information is a commodity that is available to all, including competitors. However—and this is a big however—*very* few companies actively seek information, have the right information, have sufficient information, or know how to turn it into intelligence. Accordingly, and done in even the most modest of terms, CI has the potential to be a commodity that provides advantage, because it uncovers insights—and insights drive differentiation.

As with the preceding examples, there are legitimate situations in which modest amounts of information are sufficient, instances where you don't need analysis or a deep understanding. This might be when you are first exploring a new endeavor and a handful of articles on the company or topic is adequate.

Mark Twain said that "Figures lie and liars figure," and that oft-repeated quote seems to apply to many situations. While it may well be an amusing bit of exaggeration because figures really don't lie, there is no question that data can be manipulated, and it can certainly be misinterpreted. But it's usually a case of not having the correct information or of having insufficient information. In these circumstances, it's not too difficult to come to a wrong conclusion.

Table 5.3

Example: Moving From Data to Intelligence

Data	Raw material: sales, profits, # branches, image Isolated piece information (fact or statistic), discrete No context Static Component of information	Hot Company 2008 Revenues $300 million
Information (Basis for Rudimentary Analysis)	Grouping of data Puts data in context Good for comparison Reveals more than data May or may not be sufficient	Hot Company 2009 Revenues $100 million
Conclusion	Company not doing well; significant decline in revenues; less of a competitive threat; possibly going out of business	
More Information	Outsourcing some functions Using more technology More highly skilled staff/reduced staff Divested part of the company Selling higher margin products Instituted more effective operations More effective marketing; selling online, selling ads on website Profits up 50%	
Intelligence (Analysis of Relevant and Sufficient Information to Get to the Accurate Assessment)	Company is retrenching in order to put them in a more saleable position - or Company is shifting core and downsizing existing business – or Company is focusing on most profitable segments (products or customers) – or Company is putting themselves in stronger position to expand - or Company is buying new business; wants to keep company at manageable size	
New Conclusion	Company in far better shape than data or preliminary information indicates	

Table 5.4

Example: Moving From Data to Intelligence

Data	Despite the gloomy economy in 2008, the Census Bureau reported in 2009 that median household income in 2007 had grown 1% over the past year, after adjusting for inflation, from $49,586 to $50,233.
Conclusion	Economy must be better than reported or believed.
More Information	When you segment income by age groupings, only one segment increased, householders ages 55 to 64. The number of working men and women in this age group increased 2.3 and 6.4 percentage points, respectively. Both the number of householders working and their incomes increased. They are in their peak earning years *and* postponing retirement.
Intelligence	What looks like good news (increasing household income) is misleading. All household groups except those over 55 are losing ground.
New Conclusion	Market only to those households in the 55–64 age range. Or market differently to those under 55.

Source: *American Consumers Newsletter*, August 26, 2008.

Take the example shown in Table 5.4. The first part (data) sounds like a typical TV news report, and the pieces in the information box are rarely included.

Obviously, we move from data to information by providing both the right information and the proper context. The next step is to analyze what we have learned and glean the true meaning of our findings, which will elevate the information to that next level: intelligence. The most advantageous path is to move from data to information to intelligence. The prize for this obvious move is enormous and extremely advantageous. It will allow you to achieve truly effective decision making, minimize risks, and avoid surprises—all desirable outcomes.

The Big Cheese: Intelligence

Now we come to intelligence. One view of competitive intelligence is that it is *data mining* (i.e., gathering significant amounts of data) purely for calculations, measuring, monitoring, and especially for detecting patterns. Perhaps that's why data mining, sometimes referred to as *business intelligence*, has grown so much in recent years. Companies are beginning to recognize that they have useful data that they're not analyzing.

How often have you seen evidence in your own company of reams and reams of data, but nothing useful is done with it? There's no question that there is value in data mining. But that is not intelligence, because it does not include nonquantifiable information, which we believe is more valuable. Data mining produces data and information about the past. A good start.

Intelligence, on the other hand, means using the right data that's been appropriately analyzed and put into proper context, where unimportant data and information have been filtered out. CI attempts to develop key insights, draw better conclusions, make smarter recommendations, understand players and events, define problems, and then generate appropriate actions—actions and decisions that will not require a do-over. How often has your company had to go back to the drawing board because the initial decision did not produce the desired results? It likely was because the data was wrong or insufficient and even more likely that the company didn't have all the right information, both quantitative and qualitative, internal and external.

Strategy and Intelligence

Intelligence drives strategy and smart decisions, and reduces risk. The idea is for the business to better understand its customers, identify their needs and wants, determine what potential services may be in demand, and especially to learn what they don't know. It helps executives understand actual market conditions, and sets forth today's reality with a view toward the near future.

Intelligence provides advantages that are not available with data or information alone. It paints a more complete and, therefore, a more accurate picture. Intelligence elevates thinking by providing the tools, foundation, and components to reason, process information, see patterns, and become aware of the broader macroview.

The benefit of intelligence is that it moves us from focusing on information that supports what we believe, to additional, higher and improved levels of information that reflect changes that we don't know or have not yet recognized. This is where the *real* value lies, in having our assumptions and information challenged by an unknown reality.

A recent McKinsey Global Survey, "Flaws in Strategic Decision Making," included evidence that "satisfactory outcomes are associated with less bias . . . an objective assessment of facts . . . " They seek "contrary evidence . . . ensuring that decision makers had all the critical information . . . . And this applies regardless of what type of decision a company was making or what the outcome was." One of the conclusions was that "collective intelligence tools . . . can nullify many pervasive biases."

That's just one of the benefits of competitive intelligence: to reveal biases. This is closely related to assumptions that companies have made about their own industries. It's not uncommon for these notions to no longer be true and, in some instances, to have never been true in the first place. They are urban myths that are perpetuated in certain industries. Every industry has them, so be on the lookout for those in your business.

Assumptions

Assumptions take on a life of their own; they are not easily eradicated. It takes smart companies to continually seek the most current intelligence even when they think they already have it. A client of ours, a successful manufacturer of garden tools, was looking for growth opportunities. The company decided internally that combining the features of two separate tools into a single, dual-purpose tool would appeal to a segment of customers and expand its market. We conducted a market analysis of the two separate products, which served as a foundation for validating our client's decision and continuing to the next step.

The client was encouraged by the results and proceeded to develop this "two-headed" product. It took two years to achieve the quality and cost structure the company was seeking. At the end of the two years, the client requested follow-up research to verify that the market was the same as presented in the first report and to have solid information to present at a trade show, where they would be introducing this new product. Much to the surprise of everyone in the firm, the market had changed significantly:

- More than 50 percent of the products were now made from plastic, a reverse of the dominance of metal.
- The primary distribution channel had shifted to home centers from mass merchandisers.
- The pricing had decreased significantly, almost 50 percent.
- The market leaders had lost their dominance to second-tier players.

As a result of these new findings, the client quickly modified its pricing, marketing materials, and strategy to fit in with the changed market and had a very successful introduction at the trade show.

It's quite clear that the more data and information you include in your presentation, the more closely your presentation focuses on a historical perspective. It's backward-looking, which is really not enough.

During the height of the pirate attacks off the Somalia coast in late 2008, EU Operations Commander Rear Admiral Phillip Jones stated, "The goalposts are moving all the time. The pirates are very agile. They learn quickly. They're adapting new tactics all the time for how to try to defeat what we're doing to deter and disrupt them. So, we have got to be very agile, too." This reasoning applies equally to businesses. Can you say the same about your company?

Information and intelligence are dynamic; the only way to be successful against the "pirates" out there is to constantly update information to develop better tactics.

Companies often downplay intelligence, believing that competitors have access to the same data and even the same information. Well, everyone also has access to a wide array of fruits and vegetables, yet many don't eat them or eat very few. Access does not translate into intelligence or action. Your competitive advantage includes executing good analysis of the right information and then figuring out what all of this means for your company.

Moving from intelligence into action is extremely difficult, since implementation is challenging and rarely done well. Those who seize the opportunity and develop an effective plan that can reasonably be accomplished have a significant competitive advantage. Understanding these differences is crucial, as very few companies make decisions on data or information, and they don't get the value that intelligence provides. They're stuck at the analysis, the report.

Execution is very difficult. It's easier with good intelligence, but still difficult. Intelligence is not the same as execution or competitive advantage. Rather, it's the step that enables you to *develop* and create a plan or strategy and therefore have a good shot at competitive advantage with a successful execution.

The real purpose of competitive intelligence is to learn and to act. It is not to gather data and it is not to develop information. Most companies collect a large amount of data from their operations. Some even analyze that data so that they have the right information upon which to act. Even fewer companies seek external, objective information, which is critical to intelligence.

Competitive intelligence is a product (findings) and a process. The analysis provides an overall broad understanding of where the market has been, where it is now, and where it will be going in the near future, along with opportunities and potential threats. It provides more than numbers; it allows management to interpret the meaning and significance of the information, to act on their knowledge, and to make smarter business decisions.

Data and information are often used to present a company in the best possible light or to convey a particular viewpoint. It's not unusual for a company to state that sales growth during good economic times is due to its product management or strategy, while the truth is that the economic recovery improved the entire category. The reasons why a product or company succeeds are complex and layered and cannot be explained in simplistic terms. True learning results from an assessment of numerous gauges and insights—from intelligence, not from data.

Competitive intelligence is created when data is collected *and only* when that information is analyzed, refined, and distilled into something that has very clear implications for decision making. Higher on the food chain are important decisions and actions, particularly those with big upsides and downsides. That's where and when competitive intelligence can significantly reduce risk.

6

All Information is Not Equal

All truths are easy to understand once they are discovered.
The point is to discover them.

—Galileo Galilei

f information is the core of intelligence, and all information is not equal, then what is the *right* information?

Information is a term that can be sliced, diced, parsed, and prepared in any number of ways. There is fact and there is opinion. There is objective and subjective information. There is primary and secondary information. There is noise and there is constructive information. And there are other aspects of information, as discussed in Chapter 5, "Three Critical Distinctions," which distinguishes the differences between data, information, and intelligence. Knowing these differences will work to your advantage and keep you from being blindsided.

Suffice it to say that all information is not created equal, and the wrong information always has consequences, especially when businesses use any that is outdated, irrelevant, misleading, or flawed in some critical way. We find that when companies seek data that does not answer their specific problem they are laden with disappointment. They end up with information that is more in the nice-to-know category, when what is required is *need-to-know* information. This occurs most frequently when information is developed from Internet sources, when the competitive intelligence practitioner does not have the necessary skills, or when the client (internal or external) does not have a sophisticated understanding of the purpose.

The challenge is not to be duped by information that has the appearance of being important, but is, in reality, limited in its value or scope. On one hand, we easily accept very limited information and don't realize that, while it's accurate, it's also misleading. The Hot Company example in Chapter 5 explicitly shows how we draw conclusions from very little information. Conversely, clients may request massive amounts of data that don't translate to meaningful insights or good decisions.

A client asked us to investigate pricing in preparation for designing a market research survey. The company originally requested 20 data points for 50 products across half a dozen brands. The end result would have been to create a matrix of more than 5,000 data points, at a prohibitive cost and with relatively little value.

By further probing for the purpose of the request, we realized we could scale down the project and deliver input that would be much more useful, and that made all the difference. The client initially was looking at its competitors and what they were doing. We suggested a different approach that looked at the customers and the distribution channels, which was much more relevant to the client's goal. Pricing is all too often identified as the brass ring when the real issue is elsewhere.

Need-to-Know Information

In general, business information can be divided into what you know and what you don't know (Figure 6.1).

The segments in Figure 6.1 are fairly evenly divided at 50 percent. We're not suggesting this division is absolute; it's merely a representation. However, when you ask most successful executives to draw that same circle, they depict their "know" segment as very big and their "don't know" as very small. In today's volatile environment, does that hold up? And why is this important?

Imagine a stage where every single one of your decisions is based upon good-quality, up-to-date information that supports it. The return on investment for this scenario is easy to calculate. Possessing information gives your business a competitive advantage; it improves your decision making and strategy; it saves time and money; it garners all the customers you want and need; it captures the share of market you aim for; it provides the foundation for new product and service ideas; and so on.

With this basis for classifying information, the steps that follow show you how to put it into use for your business.

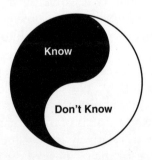

FIGURE 6.1 Sphere of Information 1

Step 1. Start with What You Don't Know— but Ask the Right Questions

First, there must be acknowledgment that you don't have all the relevant information. Unless you've done a decent investigation, and very recently, changing times presuppose new information that you probably don't know.

All too often, business executives underestimate the importance of what they don't know. They tend to be dismissive of their ignorance and can't imagine that they may be unaware of any information that is really important to know. Consequently, executives believe that they know—they *really* know—what they need to know and that this includes all the necessary information to make smart decisions. In too many instances, however, that falls short of the mark.

This may be due to the lack of an integrated information collection and sharing process, or to lack of investment in keeping up-to-date, or to not encouraging employees to share all information, especially with what's changing or different. Whatever the cause, this very information that is not known by a company often opens an opportunity for a new competitor to enter the market, one who recognizes the value of what the industry and its leaders don't know.

What makes this identification so important is that it recognizes a knowledge gap, which then sets into motion the steps required to fill that gap. Once filled, the decisions that result will be that much stronger.

In the example used earlier in this chapter, our client originally requested pricing for some 50 products, which would not have addressed the real issue. After conducting hundreds of CI studies and asking thousands of questions, one fact is clear: While there may be no bad questions, there are certainly a lot of irrelevant ones.

So, how do you get to the right questions, the more useful ones? To ask the valuable questions, you need to start with the basics, to identify what you are trying to accomplish. Then you might want to add another set of questions, such as "Why do I want to know *this* information?" "Will this information address the issue?" "What are the industry and consumer dynamics affecting this issue?"

The idea here is that the information must, in some fashion, meet your business goals. If it does not, then this rightfully remains in the realm of information you don't know. If the due diligence you seek *will* meet your business goals, then you are asking the right question.

Step 2. Identify What You Know: Is It Current and Relevant?

Begin the process by detailing what you know and, more important, by verifying that the information remains current and is still relevant. It's important for the material to meet those criteria, because while what you know might still be current and accurate, it may no longer have the same significance. In that case, you have the opportunity to replace it with information that's more relevant. Like so many perishables, information has a shelf life; at some point it will be outdated or wrong, and, consequently, so will the decisions based on it.

No matter how fabulous yesterday's information was, or how enticing predictions and forecasts are, nothing trumps information that is current and matches reality. It still has to be verified to make certain it's accurate and that it also makes sense for your company.

Our garden tools client, discussed in Chapter 5, rechecked the relevance of findings from an investigation two years prior to its new product launch. The big surprise was learning that several critical pieces of information had changed, enabling the company to react before the launch. This is similar to our financial services client who, because it understood the credit card business, believed that it could penetrate the college campus card market. After our client's unsuccessful foray into this arena, we found that its knowledge of credit cards was not as relevant as many other factors at play in this market. As a result, this company pulled out of the market.

Identify What You Know: Is It True?

The information you know is segmented into what's true and what's no longer true. (Figure 6.2).

Business regularly hangs on to outdated information, unaware or perhaps denying that it is no longer true. It's very easy for information to be repeated so often within the company or industry that it becomes part of conventional wisdom and is rarely challenged. That's often how urban myths, which everyone believes to be true, gain currency. Further, it's an annoyance to constantly learn new stuff, and, conversely, it's not always easy to unlearn what's no longer true. We prefer to leap over this step, whenever possible.

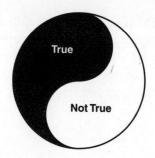

FIGURE 6.2 Sphere of Information 2

Conventional wisdom today is just not as reliable as it once was, and it is even less so in today's tumultuous business climate. The financial crises of 2008 and 2009 unearthed multiple unknowns—and even more "unknown unknowns." As a consequence, many companies and individuals acted impetuously, without sufficient information and intelligence, and/or resorted to the familiar—actions they had taken in the past and that they *assumed* would bring desired results. We still have not recovered from that strategy.

The lesson here: Review what you know and verify that the information remains current, accurate, and just as relevant for your business. Be very open to the idea that a good portion will have changed. If you haven't identified new information (covering important aspects of your business), then how do you reconcile the lack of new information in your company with a changing world?

Step 3. Identify What You Know That's No Longer So

Competitive intelligence analysis will reveal what is true and not true, and it is especially obvious when information of the conventional wisdom type no longer applies.

By the mid-1980s, the overwhelming majority of cars were purchased or influenced by women. Conventional wisdom continued to proclaim that men were the primary car buyers. Managers at car dealerships and their salespeople directed their comments to the man (when present) or, even more absurdly, asked the woman to come back after she had discussed it with "her man." This continued well into the

1990s, at which time the percentage of female buyers and influencers reached over 80 percent. Dealerships resisted hiring female sales personnel and continued a dismissive, disrespectful attitude toward women. This was one of the reasons why Saturn attracted a disproportionately high percentage of women, especially in its early days. Saturn did not play the conventional game; it actually had a policy of hiring female salespeople. Saturn was mocked for its strategy—its successful strategy.

Automotive examples abound. The Chrysler minivan, introduced in 1983, sported a visor mirror only on the passenger side. When I purchased my minivan in 1984 and asked why no mirror existed on the driver side, the response was that *men don't need it.* The manufacturers either didn't know or chose to ignore the fact that minivans were purchased by families and driven largely by women. Imagine such inadequate information and insight for a (then) 35-cent item.

Sometimes there just isn't enough data to make wise decisions. Consequently, important decisions are based on little or no information, with commensurate consequences. These situations are inexcusable when there is sufficient time to get the information, although companies routinely proclaim after the fact that they didn't have the time. Funny how there seems to be time to redo a poor decision.

But the bigger problem arises when a decision is made on information that is no longer true. The consequences here might be catastrophic, since a company would act with a level of costly commitment from which it might be unable to reverse course. Even if not catastrophic, the cost of being informed is rarely close to the costs of a bad decision, which doesn't even include the impact on morale, the time wasted, and the potential loss of timely opportunity.

Step 4. Identify What You Think Is True (but May Not Be)

In a world that is in constant upheaval and changing in wildly unexpected ways, companies have to continuously search for information about what they don't know and verify what they believe is true. You can't rely on assumptions, and that necessitates getting current, valid information on a regular basis.

That's where competitive intelligence will be of enormous assistance, by including new information. Because the information is not known, it needs sufficient detail to connect the dots between what is known and unknown. For this, we highly recommend independent verification. Failure to investigate this box leads to blind spots, missed opportunities, threats, and other undesirable outcomes.

Another financial services client approached us with the task of identifying how the Hispanic population invests differently than the population at large, which our client believed to be the case. It is an absolute waste to search for information just to confirm an idea, unless the client is open to the entire range of findings. The client was in fact wrong about the specific investment items it identified. Nonetheless, the firm chose to follow its beliefs, and, consequently, it never did capture much of the Hispanic investment dollar. As difficult as it is to let go of strongly held beliefs, think of how difficult it is to lose money associated with that erroneous decision.

Customer Loyalty versus Company Disloyalty

Put on your disruptive hat. One of my favorite concepts is the issue of customer loyalty. What most executives believe about this just ain't so! There is a pervasive belief in the business world (B2C as well as B2B) that customers are generally disloyal and will easily shift from one vendor to another. This is explained and rationalized by proclaiming that price is the dominant reason. Neither position is true. The reality is that customers are not disloyal; it's the reverse. Companies are disloyal and they have, in fact, abandoned their customers.

Customers truly *are* loyal; they prefer to stick with their existing vendors or brands, retail or commercial. They know what to expect; they've established a relationship (real or not); and it's easy and comfortable to remain with that vendor. Customers don't want to change unless it's in their best interests—that is, to get what they want. They will usually stay with a company or brand for a considerable period of time, even after they begin to be dissatisfied, just to make it easier for themselves.

Conversely, customers expect "their" product or service to keep up with changing needs or new offerings. When their company no longer does and another company, new or unknown, fills in the gap, the customers eventually will buy from the new company. This is not disloyalty; customers buy from the company that offers what is desired. A loyal customer is a satisfied customer.

When the brand no longer satisfies the customer, or when another brand satisfies the customer more, the customer status and loyalty shifts from one vendor to another. The truth is that *the company is no longer loyal to its customers*. It's the company making the moves here, not the customer. Therefore, the questions to be asked regularly are: "What else do my customers want?" "Is there a better way to satisfy them?"

If that's not enough to deal with, think about this: How often have companies exacerbated the situation by offering rebates or discounts to *new* customers while offering *nothing* to existing, loyal customers? Does this make sense? Does it engender loyalty from existing customers when you treat newbies better than those who have been with you for months or years?

Think of how often companies offer specials to new customers, and the only way current customers can get the same benefits is by canceling their existing membership or subscription and joining as a new member. Again, this is not customer disloyalty. This is companies treating prospects better than current customers and failing to reward those who have been supporting their product or service for a significant amount of time.

Change your perspective on customer loyalty. You'll keep your customers and convert them into positively raving word-of-mouth customers who tell their friends, share their experience on product sites, and declare their satisfaction on Facebook, Twitter, or other social networks. News of dissatisfaction travels very quickly today.

Executives Defending Their "Knowledge" of What Their Customers Want

It's simply fascinating to me how customers get blamed for a company's failures. Too many executives claim to know what customers want better than the customers themselves. The executives are so embedded in their industry that there is little doubt about their knowledge. And when it turns out they are wrong about their view of the customer, the customer is viewed as the problem.

Detroit automakers have taken this position for the past 40 years, even as their market share has declined. When their new products, services, or features didn't garner the sales expected, the companies were stymied and blamed the customer for not knowing what's in their best interests. The poor quality of the materials, blind spots, undistinguishable styling, or unacceptable comfort is not part of their understanding and ranks far lower for the company than the buyer.

Smart companies recognize that customers are in the best position to know what improvements they want. It doesn't matter whether the company agrees; the only reality is the customer's reality. Customers are the best communicators of changing needs. They know better than the company or the experts what they are willing to buy. But since they can't always articulate those needs in a way that is directly related to a product, it's up to companies to figure out how to translate these needs into products that will solve the customers' problems. As Henry Ford said, "If I had asked people what they wanted, they would have said a faster horse." Ford figured out how to give customers a faster horse—in a slightly different package.

Businesses must constantly question what they know or believe and view these dissenting bits of information as an opportunity to *unlearn* what's no longer true. This certainly applies to the perspective on customer loyalty. Fortunately for the consumer, there are many examples of companies doing it right!

- Amazon founder Jeff Bezos is famous for his focus on customers: Figure out what they want, and figure out a way to do it. This has been his mantra from the beginning and apparently still is, as Amazon continues to outpace potential competitors by staying ahead of them and satisfying customers. Amazon's Adam Selipsky explains: "Amazon's goal is to be the most customer-centric company in the world." This company actually walks the talk.

- Irene Rosenfield, chair and CEO of Kraft Foods North America, stated that her mission was "to move Kraft from a manufacturing-focused entity toward one that creates products based on consumer needs." "We're talking to consumers more than we ever have and we're trying to bring more products that fit with what consumers want," states Bob Becker, senior vice president for New Products, in a *Brandweek* interview. Even though Kraft's business model has been one of making meals easy, its customers have told Kraft that they want the products to be even easier. Kraft didn't respond by citing its already easy-to-prepare products. The company went back to the drawing board and, in response to consumer demand, is changing packaging or products. This includes new packaging design for Cool Whip in an aerosol can that's refrigerated, pudding mix in powder packets that can be prepared almost instantaneously, and single-portion products that are just right for one person.

- Boomers increasingly want and need hearing aids, but they have largely resisted buying them because hearing aids haven't been designed to look they way they want. Swiss-based Phonak Group is offering its new "Audeo" hearing device, which resembles a sleek earphone rather than the traditional hearing aid, in 15 fashionable colors. Boomers don't want to look like their grandparents, so a hearing aid needs to be a hip, high-tech product that improves the quality of their lives. Further, the company reinforces its understanding of this market by advertising its product as "a personal communication assistant."

- Jackie Mason is a comedian who has been performing for more than 50 years. His secret? "The best way to stay relevant is to simply listen to your audience."

- Restaurants (regardless of price) immediately know whether what they're offering matches what the customer wants. Fast-food companies constantly respond to customers' changing desires, stated or not, and to exploring new growth opportunities. McDonald's and Burger King find out very quickly how customers are responding to new offerings. No arguing, no defending.

Customers resonate with products and services that meet *their* needs. It's the difference between buying and being sold. Successful salespeople listen first to what customers say they're looking for and then suggest products/services that will meet those needs, along with possible suggestions for additional features or services.

Companies that don't train their salespeople—or that train them to do what is best for the company—generally don't get high marks; by doing so, they create an opening for customers to shop elsewhere. Think of the stereotypical computer salesperson who boldly proclaims all the features and then goes on and on with too much technical detail. Or retail clothing stores that do not include mirrors in their dressing rooms because they want their salespeople to comment on and influence the selection rather than letting the customer decide.

Step 5. Does the Information Reflect Today or Tomorrow?

Today is the current business environment in which you operate. Tomorrow is unknown, unpredictable, and likely to be unexpected. Tomorrow is the "Undiscovered Country" (with all due respect to *Star Trek*). (See Figure 6.3.)

Tomorrow is literally tomorrow, or it may be next month. Regardless of how you define the time frame, that's when you sell your wares. Therefore, getting an insight into tomorrow is crucial. There is no reasonable expectation that today's information will be useful for tomorrow. Consequently, it's imperative to stay updated on the information used in making decisions.

And that includes observations. Any number of clues and indications are available if you are open to them.

Semco Group has been a very successful manufacturer in São Paulo, Brazil, since 1952, selling cooling towers for large commercial buildings. When the company heard constant complaints about companies that maintained its towers, Semco turned it into an opportunity to offer additional satisfaction to its customers. It developed its own maintenance business, which turned into a $30 million organization in just five years. Semco listened and created an unexpected revenue stream. It never planned to be in the maintenance business, but the business found Semco, which was open to hearing the signals . . . and growing its business. What are you doing to listen?

How great would it be if you knew of business opportunities before they existed, or if you could predict when your "loyal" customers would abandon your ship? It would give you a big head start on

FIGURE 6.3 Sphere of Information 3

planning how you might tap that opportunity and have things ready well before either scenario even comes up. This is what can be accomplished with competitive intelligence; it goes beyond looking at trend lines that are based on, to a degree, what happened yesterday. Noticing problems or opportunities is one way to let today crash into tomorrow—in the most advantageous manner.

Step 6. Get It Right:
The Correct Information

The right information is more than just accurate or current. It also has to be the most appropriate, pertinent, and fit the context to provide value.

Syndicated conservative radio talk show host Michael Medved noted, after Obama's election, that talk shows that "cultivated a niche audience rather than the Republican mainstream" needed to reassess their strategy. "A radio show that draws just 5 percent of the available audience can achieve notable success in ratings and revenue, but a conservatism that connects with only a disgruntled, paranoid 5 percent of the public will wither and die."

Leverage the Right Information to Develop
Growth Opportunities

The right information is available, but understanding what it is and getting to it are not easy. The right information is an underutilized portal to information on growth opportunities, threats, market changes, and tomorrow. Clues and signals to opportunities are in our face daily, in anecdotal observations, in random comments on the street or television, and in newspapers and trade publications. They're hidden if you don't know what to look for—that is, if you even look.

According to a survey conducted by CareerBuilder.com, one in five veterans returning from active duty in Iraq or Afghanistan said they were having difficulty finding a job. Their biggest obstacle was "employers' inability to understand how military skills can fulfill qualifications for civilian positions." This quote should be an immediate heads-up opportunity for a small training firm. Using this survey, a company could approach veterans' organizations and propose a class on teaching veterans how to sell their military skills, how they transfer to and provide exceptional value for the civilian community.

Every complaint or unfilled need is a possible opportunity to explore. It may not be realistic, but that's where intelligence can be of assistance. Ferreting out what the intelligence means and how to use it will make sense to some company. And that company could be yours!

Every company has areas in which it excels. In addition to selling a product or service, companies should consider their expertise and evaluate whether this is a potential additional revenue stream.

Training has been a growth segment across a wide spectrum over the past few decades. Personnel training includes issues of sexual harassment, negotiating, communicating, working together, and leadership. Education classes range from learning new software to new marketing approaches to new physical labor skills. The latter is especially true for women, who were previously shut out but who are moving into formerly male-only careers, such as climbing electrical posts, doing carpentry, and providing odd-job skills to homeowners. One of the heartening observations during the last economic recession was the number of workers who recognized that their jobs may no longer be relevant or return. Many have sought out and paid for training in fields they have determined will increase, such as Detroit workers studying nursing.

Consider your company's expertise and whether it makes sense to offer classes to others, even competitors:

- BMW teaches motor safety and maximizing exhilaration from your car (even if it's not a BMW) at the BMW Performance Driving School in South Carolina.
- Sephora University, targeted primarily at employees, also offers master makeup classes to the public.
- Ritz-Carlton Leadership Center teaches the Ritz-Carlton Way, capitalizing on its stellar reputation for customer service and superior standards (noted in Chapter 7).
- Toyota may well be the leader in leveraging its highly regarded reputation to create growth opportunities. According to *Business-Week*, Toyota's sideline businesses would have ranked it number 192 on the S&P 500 in 2006. Other Toyota businesses include

sports (golf course operator, pro soccer team), housing (prefab houses), aerospace (helicopter operator, airport management), gardening (rooftop greenery, ornamental plants), consulting (Toyota Amenity), advertising (Delphys), as well as resort developer and financial services.

The takeaway from this chapter is to proactively and aggressively conduct due diligence; look for information that both reflects the present reality and is also forward-thinking, to see where the market is headed. In short, look for, see, and get the right information and turn it into intelligence. The right information is found in multiple spheres, including customers, distributors, internal and external industry experts, a wide array of publications (e.g., newsletters, trade journals), competitors, and other collaborative sources. The goal is to focus on what demand will likely be and what action is required on your part to move your company from "what is" to "what will be."

7

Knowing When and Why to Power Up the CI Engine

"You can't expect your knowledge of yesterday to carry you through tomorrow."

—James Champy

8

Next Steps for You and Your Company

Perhaps you are reading this book because you are interested in competitive intelligence as a subject. Perhaps you have been shocked into learning about it because of some dramatic adverse change that has taken place in your business or industry and you don't want that to happen again. Perhaps you've read about companies in other industries being blindsided and you don't want to find your company in that position. Regardless of the reasons, the mere fact that you are even considering the subject marks the reshaping of how you look at your business. The challenge is to turn that curiosity and that new beginning into some concrete action that will result in taking a new direction.

What are the next steps?

After digesting what you have read so far, and with an understanding of the role that CI can play in minimizing risks, the following lists, actions, and insights guide you in creating the setup that will be most useful. We break this down into what *you* as an individual can do and what *your company* can do as next-step actions. We end this chapter with a questionnaire to start the conversation within your company about what's important and what advantage you can gain by just asking these questions.

Your Next Steps

There are a number of steps that you can take, even if you do not create a formal CI department. The most important quality that an executive needs is a mind open to new, different, or contrary findings. Here are some of the factors needed for success, along with your next steps.

Get Up to Speed Very, Very Quickly

A very effective way to get a broad and yet specific view of an industry in just a few hours is to subscribe to trade publications or the relevant business publications for your industry. Get a sample copy from three or four of these journals and determine which one(s) appear to provide the level of information you're seeking.

After you identify the ones that appear valuable, buy a year's worth of back issues and scan those for the most useful articles. In just hours, you will learn about what's happening, and about the concerns and issues facing that industry, and who the industry leaders are. The same advice can be applied to industry newsletters. You will likely really be astonished at what has happened in your industry during the last year that you didn't know about. That alone should compel you to engage in competitive intelligence.

There are likely to be 30-300 trade publications related to your industry. If you don't know which ones to request, check *The Standard Periodical Directory*, *SRDS Business Publications*, and one of the newsletter directories. (Sources are discussed in Chapter 9).

Listen to Your Own Staff

Your employees are on the front lines of your business. They are not just the arms and legs that run the company; they are also its eyes and ears. Whether you realize it or not, their feedback and opinions can play a vital role in the success of your company. They have a lot of input about the product and the company because of their constant exposure to customers or via third parties. Even those who don't deal directly with customers may hear about issues from those who do delivery or repair.

Employees help identify the needs for future product improvements. They can help resolve some of the inevitable inefficiencies that creep in when a company has been in business for years, since they have to work with the systems and processes in place. It's easy to become complacent and rank their comments as not important.

Employ tried-and-true suggestions for soliciting employee input. Come out of your office; visit with your employees; start a company suggestion box; and establish a monetary "president's award" for the best "change" idea that has helped the bottom line. Your sales employees can also provide information for competitive analyses. They are familiar with the market and often have wide-ranging contacts throughout their respective territories, which may provide some inside information. Use that to your company's advantage.

New employees who are unfamiliar with your industry will provide an external perspective that may be similar to new customers. Yes, they may ask dumb questions, but they will likely point out copy that isn't clear, or functions that aren't convenient, and so forth. Encourage them to speak up.

Get Your Staff's New Ideas: Explore Them and Reward Them

Do you know where the next big thing for your product or service will come from? Some businesses have a strategy of buying ideas or other companies whose products they believe will be the next big thing. Although that may have some merit for companies with deep pockets, it is not a universally available approach.

On the other hand, the Japanese style of adding small improvements to existing products, known as *kaizen*, is a proven way to add value to a company's bottom line. Where do these small improvements, some of which turn into new products, come from? From a company's own employees.

Establish a reward system for ideas, which will ensure new proposals from staff members. They know your company, your product, and your customers better than anyone, and they want the company to grow and succeed. They can be a great source for new ideas if given the proper outlet and encouragement. Monetary rewards are welcome, but employees usually prefer widespread acknowledgement of their contribution (and a few bucks wouldn't hurt). Think broadly about who has valuable information to share. It's not just salespeople and customer service. Tap into people who repair and deliver, as well as those who answer the phones. Due diligence resources surround you, once you start looking. Anyone who "touches" your customer has input.

Value the Importance of Dissenting Voices

Creative dissent can actually enhance business. Consider the cost to your business when dissent is not permitted to surface. For decades, Detroit carmakers have been fighting the notion that a large segment of their consumers might prefer automobiles that are safer and more fuel-efficient than the gas guzzlers they have been producing. Coca-Cola ignored evidence that New Coke would fizzle and launched it anyway. And eToys, that once-dominant force in online shopping, ignored advice to align itself with the brick-and-mortar giant, Toys "R" Us, only to fade into the dustbin of history with the crash of the dot-com era. NASA is said to have refused to listen to input about the danger of foam tank insulation, with the resulting loss of the seven astronauts on the ill-fated *Columbia* shuttle.

This propensity to maintain silence is widespread and prevalent in both the private and public sectors. Part of this reluctance can be attributed to fears that management will not like the idea or will ridicule and shame the dissenter into silence. Challenges to the conventional wisdom are often suppressed or discouraged. While contrarians can be annoying, they often speak the truth. Upon hearing a panel of CEOs discussing this issue, one seasoned veteran leaned over and whispered to a newly minted CEO: "This is the last time you will hear the truth."

Who is responsible for silencing dissenting voices? Executives. They don't listen; they refuse to hear; they cut people off because of their "certainty" of the direction they are taking. Executives set the tone for how much disagreement will be tolerated. If they acknowledge and encourage it, managers also will be more likely to accept it. If you are after good decisions, contention and challenges are essential; they can point to the flaws or potential pitfalls of taking a certain direction that may not have been considered. Decisions are seldom better because the dissenting voice has been silenced.

Host Mandatory Meetings to Feed the Company's Collective Mind-Set

The last two subsections clearly indicate our view that your sales and front-office employees know a lot about your business, competition, and customers. But that doesn't mean they necessarily share what they know. You need to take the time to gather this information by listening to your employees and customers, both of whom present an opportunity to improve the overall company performance.

A collective meeting with both internal and external employees will also allow for recollection and/or corroboration of information that may not have been shared in other venues. The mandatory strategic meetings could be conducted over a catered lunch, which will not interfere with the day's work. And, the nicer the lunch, the higher the attendance and the increased willingness to share.

Use the Supreme Court Approach: Write Dissenting Papers

We are big believers in the value of dissension; that's why it is used by the Supreme Court, and even by the Roman Catholic Church when considering a proposed beatification. The church appoints a devil's advocate to critically examine the facts and then to vigorously put forth the argument against approval. This represents an essential way to avoid regrettable errors.

Competitive intelligence can be employed in a similar manner for an opposing viewpoint in the corporate environment. If that dissenting opinion is valid, it will help avoid mistakes; if it proves wrong, then you move forward with greater confidence and with even greater support from your staff. At the very least, it alerts you to possible problem areas.

Clever Solutions from the Unexpected

A number of years ago, a tall truck got stuck on New York City's FDR Drive when it drove under an overpass. New York City engineers and the company's owners huddled, trying to decide on how best to remove the truck with the least possible damage to the structure. A young kid on his way to school stopped to watch. As he listened, he saw the problem as it really was and suggested, "Why don'tcha let the air outa the tires?" The adults were thinking traditionally and wore blinders to the obvious, easy solution.

There are at least a few people in every organization who spot the obvious weaknesses. Give them the opportunity to share—and reward them. Those entry-level employees are just as likely to occasionally notice or hear about areas of improvement.

Use Technology

There are several flavors of CI technology, including knowledge management and data mining. This is where tracking and analysis of data already in a company's possession is used to ferret out useful information, but that is not what we are advocating here. Instead, we are talking about the use of technology to create a database of information. This can take the form of an electronic whiteboard, an internal company blog, and/or a wiki on which everyone who has any information about a product or competitor can post and add to the knowledge base.

Use the free Google Alerts for blogs and news monitoring. There are also new mind-mapping software tools that can be used in CI discussions.

Reevaluate What You "Know" Every Year

If you are the typical executive, you revisit your marketing strategy on a regular basis. Perhaps once a year, perhaps more often. In much the same way, you need to reevaluate, at least once a year, what you know about your market and customers and the competitive environment.

Can you really believe that there haven't been any significant changes in the last year? At the very least, you will want to know whether the competitive landscape is still the same. Have new competitors entered the market? What are their strengths and weaknesses? What new features or products have they introduced? Can you identify what makes them unique? Do you know which end of your market they are targeting? Have some existing competitors fallen out, and what are the implications for you?

Then do some basic checks on your market. Has it changed, and, if so, how? Have your customers changed, and, if so, how? Do your customers still buy from your distribution channels? What about your distribution channels? Are they unchanged? Are there some that are emerging?

Finally, examine your products and determine their relevancy in the marketplace. Have you taken any product actions in the prior year to alter where your product stands? One company we know appointed a new president, and his first act was to increase sales right away. He did so by pushing more of the product into the marketplace. The result: His retailers believed the company was "dumping" the product prior to its "killing" the product line, and that became the end of a very successful product. Consider whether any actions devalue your products. How are your customers and distributors reacting?

Once you've taken that critical, albeit cursory review of these elements—the competition, the market, the customer, and the product—you will have the strategic foundation to either continue what you were doing or take the necessary corrective steps.

Monitor the Market for Any Shifts—and Don't Dismiss Anomalies without Checking Them Out

Market shifts are your opportunity to keep up with your customers. The bar is constantly being raised—whether that refers to changes to features, ease of use, or any other area. We just want "it" to be better for us. While examining the customer and the marketplace, note any disturbances in the water. Don't be too hasty to dismiss those aberrations that don't fit preconceived notions of what the answer should be. The economic world right now is littered with the remnants of missed warning signs and the consequences of having dismissed what are now recognized as early warning signs of things to come.

The same forces appear in every field, and changes, for better or worse, are always clues to shifts. As someone once observed, "customers are sneaky people." They change their buying habits, and they change their opinion of your products. If you don't pay attention to what your customers are doing, your business can disappear, because without customers, you have no business. So, if you note a change, check it out. It may save your very existence. This doesn't mean you have to take immediate action. This is an opportunity to monitor the change and decide if it's right for your company.

In the early 1990s, it was a sure bet that e-mail was the next big thing, and in the intervening years, that became a reality. In the 1980s, it was a sure bet that we were moving to a paperless world. We are still moving in that direction today, but there is a shift taking place in the digital world, and people are beginning to move away from e-mail. What are they shifting to? Texting, blogging, or social networks like Twitter and Facebook? Only time will tell, but good CI can help move this analysis along.

I recently visited a Los Angeles restaurant. The food was very good, but even better was the enthusiastic young chef who visited every table. We had quite a spirited conversation about restaurants, food, and cities we each had visited. Before leaving, he asked for my e-mail address, and within a day I received an invitation to be his Facebook friend. Is this a new trend? Will this do away with the traditional e-mail? I don't know. But this would be an area to check out.

Read Beyond Your Usual Horizon: You're Not Alone; Others Are Also Interested in Your Market

When a client asked us to get him information on a big, privately held candy manufacturer, we found the information he wanted, but not in the usual candy industry publications. Instead, it appeared in a technology magazine, where the competitor provided considerable insight into its operations. The focus of the article was on the company's technology.

This is not unusual as every business deals with issues that go beyond the finished product or service. This wasn't a resource that our clients would tap into, and yet we urge that you take that very broad look. Why? In an increasingly tumultuous marketplace, you have to keep seeking and learning. Because the more you learn, the more likely you are to stay ahead of change and to implement changes when and where necessary. If you don't want to or don't have the time to read technology publications, assign this task to someone in your group or team and ask them to report back.

This does not mean it's necessary to analyze every piece of data or hunt down every mention. But it is advantageous to have a voracious appetite for knowledge from anywhere and everywhere that ultimately leads you to improve the depth of your knowledge. In other words, expand your horizons. Get your information from as many channels as you can, and have your staff members broaden their reach. Subscribe to a broad array of trade and business publications and encourage all employees to scan them and suggest ideas.

Do all of this in pursuit of different ideas, concepts, and changes affecting your product, your market, and your customers. Explore the larger world to identify tomorrow's opportunities for your business *and* so that you are not blindsided.

Consult the Blogosphere about Your Company and about Your Competition

Find out what others say about your business, as it often contains some truth. And if it's not true and potentially harmful, this alerts you to action. Because a lot of people are putting content on the Web, someone is likely commenting about your company or your products. If you follow what is happening online, you quickly realize that consumers trust each other more than they trust business. The question is, how do you tap into this, and how do you turn it to your advantage?

Put someone or something in place to monitor conversations about your brand, such as Google Alerts. This tool will scan web sites for your company's name (and that of your competition) and send you a daily e-mail with these mentions. You can also use a search engine to monitor blogs. Then, if someone pans your business, you can address the issue and fix the problem before it snowballs out of control.

It's tempting to dismiss comments as mere opinions, as that viewpoint is irrelevant. Opinions are precisely what people hear and pass on. They don't know if it's true or disinformation. They deserve some attention, even if they merely indicate that the public isn't interpreting your company's message in the same way that you are. It's the company's responsibility to stay in charge of their message.

Go Beyond Mere Data Collection

Even after decades of digging up insightful and useful information and analyzing it for intelligence, I'm still amazed at how many companies turn to collecting massive amounts of data. When we are asked for data, we probe the company to determine the purpose and use for the data. It's often clear that they don't need data; rather, they need information and intelligence. Remember, data only reveals the past.

Unless you are looking for the details of an industry or product and how it has evolved or how or where it's selling, data may not yield useful results. Companies request data because that's what business does. It's relatively easy to obtain (compared to intelligence) and it lends itself to pretty charts and graphs. Although data tells the backstory, it never tells the *whole* story, and certainly not what's changing and emerging.

As a responsible executive, it is equally important for you to not only get the data, but to develop a full understanding of *what* that data means. If you're planning to be in business tomorrow, data is only the first step.

Do Your Homework

Being in business requires constant learning. Expand your industry thinking and find general business trends, as well as industry trends. Subscribe to at least three or four trade magazines and newsletters to determine what is new in your industry and what is changing overall in business. They're not unrelated and by not being aware of the larger business community, you're missing what's new, different, passé.

Scan the table of contents from two publications, one from an industry that is indirectly related to your industry and one that isn't. Get trade publications from colleagues and friends who are in totally different industries, or read publications when you're in the doctor's office. Read those articles, regardless of the industry, that discuss trends or changes or that may be general in nature, as they likely contain some insights useful for your industry. You will be surprised at what you can apply to your business by reading about successes in other industries.

Alternate the industries over the course of a year to become exposed to a wider range of businesses. When possible, include newsletters or blogs (by highly regarded businesspeople, such as Tom Peters's electronic newsletter, *Tom Peters Times!* www.tompeters.com).

Establish Excellent Communication Lines

It is a given in both good times and bad that businesses must be more customer-centric than ever before, and good communications is an important element in that focus.

Companies seldom listen to their company's voice-mail message or perform post-sale satisfaction surveys with customers or distributors. All too often, even when a company fields a customer service desk, it is more likely done to resolve the immediate issue rather than to learn or to leverage the opportunity that this service desk creates.

BusinessWeek magazine reported in late 2008 that Toyota had overtaken GM as the world's biggest carmaker. Big news. Yet, Toyota dealerships "continue to score poorly in customer satisfaction surveys that rate the overall car-buying experience" (the Prius brand notwithstanding). Good communication with customers, dealers, and the company's own in-house staff can work to alleviate the negative attitude.

Customers, suppliers, and distributors expect companies to communicate and to be easy to reach. The lack of clear and open communication channels is rarely discussed, but it creates an undercurrent of annoyance and a decreased desire to do business.

Your *Company's* Next Steps

The company itself has a number of steps that can be taken:

- Create a competitive intelligence culture.
- Establish a CI department or group.
- Listen to your customers; use complaints as an opportunity.
- Deploy an innovation challenge.

Create a Competitive Intelligence Culture

How do you create a CI culture? Start by recognizing that everyone in the organization knows something about the company, the competitors, the customers, the marketplace, and the broader industry in which your company operates. In a sense, you can view these as independent competitive intelligence agents, who generally operate in a silo and who are never asked to share. One way to overcome this issue is to create a forum where each of these CI agents can meet on a regular basis to discuss emerging issues, share experiences and knowledge, jointly solve problems, and generally interact. Another opportunity for a company-paid pizza lunch.

Forums of this type tend to eliminate silo mentalities and allow every one of these CI agents to be involved in the creation and implementation of possible solutions. When they become part of the process, the end result has a higher likelihood of success because of general buy-in and acceptance. As participation is recognized and rewarded, a competitive intelligence culture becomes embedded in the social fabric of the organization.

- Put together teams of disparate functions to identify wish lists, no matter how improbable, for the company to accomplish. Publish results and distribute them to all in the company. Do this every three months, and revisit previous results with different groups.
- Create "What's In? What's Out?" lists at the beginning of every year. Discuss the implication for the company.
- Make regular presentations to schoolchildren (second- and seventh-graders) about what your company does. These audiences will ask questions or suggest ideas that will have some nuggets of good thought. And their feedback will simplify your message.
- Do the same with someone in a totally different business. A total stranger to your business will make assumptions or ask questions that will trigger some good thoughts.
- Be skeptical of conventional wisdom. After all, if the business world is changing, how can conventional wisdom continue to hold true? Are there new opportunities out there? Are there customers who don't fit the standard profile? In the early 1990s, plastic surgery moved from very wealthy patients to those in the middle class when doctors began offering patients extended-payment options, similar to payment coupons used by car financing firms.

- Understand that new does not always *replace* old. It may reduce the volume, but is often unlikely to replace it. Radio did not replace newspapers; TV did not replace radio; VCRs, DVDs, and on-demand movies to be viewed at home did not stop people from going to movies. In fact, movie theater revenues are at their highest. As author Douglas Adams, of *The Hitchhiker's Guide to the Galaxy*, said, "No technology really ever dies."

Creating an open CI culture and getting people to openly share takes time to develop and nurture. But it's hard to argue with the success that will result from being prepared and making smarter decisions.

Establish a Competitive Intelligence Unit

The goal of competitive intelligence is to produce actionable intelligence for decision makers; and to do so, you need to have that intelligence. What better way to gather that intelligence than by creating your own CI unit?

How do you go about this, and how do you determine what will work for your company?

There is no single approach to starting an effective CI function. Done correctly, competitive intelligence involves collection, analysis, interpretation and deduction, dissemination, and, finally, decision making. If any one of these elements is not made part of the whole, then the intelligence process cannot succeed. Key considerations include the number of people you need and what each will do.

The unit does not have to start big. At the very least, you will need to staff three functions. First is an information researcher for electronic databases, as well as for printed research not available electronically. Then you will need a direct contact researcher who is skilled in telephone and trade show elicitation. Finally, you will need a highly skilled analyst who can analyze, interpret, deduce what the findings mean, and write the report in an engaging and useful manner.

The *database researcher* does not have to be an in-house staffer. This is a function that can be outsourced, provided that the person you choose can access all the commercial databases and knows how to do research on the Web. That same person should know how to deeply dive into the more arcane levels that most of us never get to see, including non-electronic sources. As discussed in Chapter 9, limited business information is available electronically, so the researcher must know and be comfortable accessing other sources.

The *direct contact researcher* makes phone calls to speak with those who have the information or know where it will be found. This is a more difficult position to outsource. Individuals who can fill this role have to have the skills and dogged personality of a reporter. They should be friendly and personable, articulate, detail-oriented, with good listening and interviewing skills, and not easily riled, because they may have to think quickly on their feet. As for doggedness, they need to be on a constant hunt for something interesting and worthwhile in their search. They also can be tasked to attend trade shows to collect the requisite intelligence.

The *analyst* has a greater role to play and should have a managerial-level position so that the organization appreciates the value of the CI unit's input. This person will supervise and direct the collection of data and then perform the requisite analysis of that strategic intelligence. But most of all, the analyst needs to be a creative thinker who can understand the implications to the company of what the CI unit has uncovered and have the ability to present the findings so that they will be heard and understood. The analyst needs a deep understanding of the company's business and what is or could be important.

The direct contact researcher and the analyst can be the same person if he or she truly has both skills. If so, and if the database researcher is outsourced, the company can start with a single staffer.

As we have indicated several times in this book, moving from data and information to intelligence is done by the interpretation of that data and information. It requires a skill to put the information into a contextual setting. It means going way beyond reporting the facts and moves the context to an understanding of what it means. Finally, it requires that the individual understand business and how it operates, along with what's important to successful businesses.

Is a move by the competition indicative of a new direction, a broadening of its product line? Does the passage of a new law offer new opportunities or greater challenges? Is an increase in customers' defection rate from your products a sign of dissatisfaction with your offerings, or is there a new competitor in the landscape?

The analyst puts the information into a context that may or may not be accurate. While facts can be validated quickly with other sources, the perspective brought out by the analysis will take more time to bear out. Still, it is a very necessary function, because this analysis will help identify potential risks and allow a company to prepare a substantive response.

Without good communication skills, the findings may not be read, understood, highly regarded, or utilized. Vary the way the findings are communicated—from internal alerts, to single page overview, to newsletter format. Make the format fit the findings; not the reverse.

Whether the CI unit is large or small, every company should have this function operating as part of its core business. But since this may not be realistic, plan B is to create an atmosphere within the company where all will share and be heard.

Listen to Your Customers; Use Complaints as an Opportunity

At a conference we attended, one session was titled "Your customers are your livelihood, so why can't you let them have their say?"

There's little doubt that customers are more demanding than ever. As products and services have improved, so have customer expectations, largely due to company-approved marketing and advertising statements, as well as executive pronouncements that promise more than they deliver. And when the expectations don't match customer experiences, customers are ready to skewer the companies.

The airline industry certainly felt the needle by consumers demanding action from Congress, and the blogosphere is full of complaint content that might make the proverbial sailor blush. When customers feel soured by their experience with a company or its products, they are not willing to keep their anger to themselves. As statistics have shown, a satisfied customer may tell as few as three people about his or her positive experience, while a disgruntled one will talk to as many as twenty. And that was *before* the advent of online communications.

In a sense, the online world has provided an opportunity where everyone—customers and companies—can engage in conversations about what is good, what is bad, what can be improved, and what needs to be done. This is also an opportunity for companies to become more transparent and more honest, a quality customers highly value. This could be your differentiator.

You can ignore complaints at your company's peril, or you can engage this medium and use it as an opportunity to fix what ails your product, to keep in touch with your customers and solidify a positive feeling. Most recently, Virgin Air's Richard Branson elected to respond personally to a customer letter, and that letter and response made headlines around the world. It did not hurt Virgin's image one bit.

How do you listen to your customers? Start a suggestion box on your company web site; deploy a customer service toll-free number; send a customer satisfaction survey; occasionally do a personalized follow-up phone call; talk to your distributors; go into stores and speak to your purchasers directly. In short, work with your customers to improve your company, your products, and your lines of communication.

Deploy an Innovation Challenge Program

Are you seeking growth opportunities? If yes, part of your company's strategy has to include innovation as a key factor. Can you have innovation outside the lab or engineering functions? Yes, you can!

When I worked in advertising, one of our clients developed a new product. The company gave each agency employee a sample of the product and a specification sheet. We were asked to submit our ideas for what might be done with this product. The response was over-whelming. The ideas generated actually helped improve the product and also gave the client several new potential markets to explore. This idea can be applied to most businesses.

In select situations, it may not be the invention itself that creates a market revolution; it may be how the invention is applied. That is where establishing an "innovation challenge program" can yield great benefits. You start by capturing the collective ideas of your own employees to help solve crucial strategic challenges. Take a product (one of yours or one of your competitors) and ask the necessary questions as a challenge. How can we use this product in other ways? How can we improve the product? How can we better explain and promote the features? Then have individual employees or teams of employees write a concept plan to address the challenges posed by the questions. The next step is to conduct competitive intelligence to determine whether this is a sound idea and if there are buyers.

Questionnaire

The goal of competitive intelligence is to produce actionable intelligence for decision makers, and to do so you need to ask the right questions. But what are these "right" questions? We have developed a series of pertinent questions, organized by category, of some things you always want to know. Start by selecting the questions that you and your executives *can* answer. Randomly, at meetings or during coffee breaks, ask other questions of employees. The responses will alert you to what's unknown and to responses that vary from your own.

Change

1. Do you have a system (formal or informal) for spotting or tracking changes?
2. How do you figure out how to apply these changes?
3. What are the best resources for keeping up with changes in your industry?
4. Can you specifically identify how customers are changing—in your industry, in other industries that indirectly deal with yours, and in other geographic regions (southwest, United States, or globally)?
5. What changes from outside your industry could affect your business?
6. If so, how and what are you doing about it?
7. How vulnerable are you to changes in the market?
8. Do you know what's new and changing?
9. Do you know what's no longer true?
10. If you don't, could you be missing an opportunity?
11. Do you have a "canary in the coal mine" alert system?

Information/Intelligence

1. Do you have the right intelligence to drive your strategy and grow your business? Or do you have information only?
2. If you don't have a CI system in place, what do you do to stay up-to-date?
3. How important is due diligence to the decision—nice to have, or need to know?
4. Do you know enough about your market? What's happening with your brokers, distributors, suppliers, or reps? How often do you speak to them and probe for potential problems or opportunities?

5. What trade and business publications do you read regularly? Do you share new information with your staff?

6. How paranoid are you about unexpected competition? Does your staff regularly inform you about possible competition, especially from unexpected companies and/or industries?

Questions a Company Should Be Asking Regularly

1. What would you do differently if you found out that current assumptions are wrong?

2. What do you do to find out? What don't you know?

3. How certain are you about your knowledge of your industry, customers, competitors, external factors or threats, and alternative uses?

4. What have you heard that you dismissed—from a salesperson, company maverick, customer, or supplier?

5. What has surprised you?

6. How often are you surprised by competitors introducing a product or service or feature you never considered but now seems obvious?

7. How often do you learn something new, and what do you do with it?

8. How do you respond to bad news?

9. Do you and your customers agree on what customers want? How do you respond to customers' challenges or complaints?

10. Do your customers describe your company or products/services the same way you do?

11. What's in your peripheral vision?

12. How do you handle multiple pieces of disparate information? Do you have a designated person responsible for putting the pieces together?

13. Do you know and can you describe customers who don't fit your target profile or usual demographics?

14. Are you framing the questions too narrowly

15. Are all the "right" people in the room (which may relate to their position, their experience, or their ability to think differently)? Do you have a contrarian in your organization, and how do you view that person and his or her comments?

16. Do you assess initiatives, bad decisions, or poor investments that didn't go well?
17. When discussing technology, for example, are you also including areas such as financial or social or marketing?

Create a Checklist That Stakeholders Answer Annually

1. What has changed in your industry in the past year?
2. What new or different complaints are you hearing from your customers, or via your salespeople, customer service reps, and delivery people?
3. Have your customers been asking about a feature or service you are not currently offering?
4. What new customers are now buying your product? Describe why they are new and how they are different from your traditional target profile.
5. What alternative uses have you heard about for your product or service? Does it warrant a closer look for possible extension or a new offering?

The goal here is to start thinking about what's important for your business and what information and intelligence will propel your firm to the next level. Preparation, insights, and unlearning are key to success, more rapid success, and a far easier journey. Are you ready to take the next steps?

9

Understanding and Evaluating Information Sources

There is a deep-seated belief that whatever we need to know we can find on the Web. If so much information is publicly available, then why do we fail to find the specific business information we need? We give up after 30 or 60 minutes, frustrated by how little useful information we found.

There is no question that the amount of information available today is almost breathtaking and continues to increase daily. But when the focus is narrowed to business information, the reality is quite different. Yes, there is extensive business information, and, yes, some can be accessed electronically. But that information is limited in terms of *what* specifically is available, the validity of the sources, and how current it is. The reality, you may have realized, is that not much solid, insightful business information is available on the Web. Three reasons for this are the "hidden" Web; less business information available electronically; and extremely limited strategic information.

The hidden Web (also referred to as the deep Web or invisible Web) refers to information that is not accessible via metasearch engines (Google, Ask, Bing, Yahoo!) but may be located in databases down a level or two—either from the source itself or from a third-party provider. That means you have to go directly to the *New York Times*, *BusinessWeek*, or a trade association's web site (e.g., www.adhesives-mag.com for the adhesives and sealants industry).

The second reason is that most useful business information is not available electronically. Finally, there is little strategic information within business articles or websites. There is some, but it's very limited. Occasionally you will find what you're seeking, but expectations are best kept at a low level.

There's a lot of business information on the Web, but it's probably not what you're seeking, unless you're looking for background, history, overall sales, etc. With all the hype about there being so much information out there and that no human being can cope with all of it anyway, my purpose for this chapter is to provide a general understanding of the types of business information available. It's also to underscore, as firmly as possible, that there is an incredible array of openly available information unknown by most.

This chapter is not focused on how to *find* information. Rather, the goal is to provide insight into an expansive view of the sources of and for competitive intelligence. It includes what to expect from published sources and human intelligence (*humint*) information, sources of information that are less familiar, suggestions for underused but rich sources, and a different perspective on the specifics of sources of information. The goal is to select the most robust method for the specific inquiry rather than relying on just a few sources or approaches.

Because of the prevalence of "ginormous" amounts of information and the considerable hype behind it, most people believe that they can probably find everything they are looking for. They often rely on their Web-based college skills to find the information. Think back to all the times you looked for specific business information and just couldn't find it. Think about the times when you read an article just the day before. You obviously knew the name of the publication and yet you still couldn't manage to locate it. We have all experienced that scenario far too many times, yet we continue to believe that given just a few more minutes, we would find it. "Just another minute, please, Mom?"

Unfortunately, even if you spent another week searching, you still might not find it. Searching is simply neither as easy nor intuitive as we think. While information found on the Web may be enough to satisfy the most basic or limited search, it's not likely to uncover the depth necessary to satisfy a business question; and in many instances, it may not even be enough to offer executive summary information. Finding the information you seek requires more than mere search skills and tenacity. See Chapter 10 for the characteristics of a good searcher.

For a contrary point of view, it is interesting to note that some claim that the type of information that we are likely to find on the Web may even have a *negative impact*. Paul Boutin says in a *Wall Street Journal* review of Neal Stephenson's novel *Anathem* that "Intellectuals fret that the Internet's instant-answer machine may be making us dumber, as we learn to solve problems without applying long-term mental effort." That is, the opportunity to uncover substantive and useful information and turn it into intelligence has to be more than a simple exercise in Internet searching.

The inability to find what you expect to find results in frustration with the spare results. Searchers then attribute their failure to the fact that the information probably just doesn't exist. This is just not so.

When executives hire graduate students to do their research, they are even more certain that if the information could not be found, it didn't exist. They believe that students would *definitely* know how to find the information, and the bonus is that they'll save the company money. The results? We hear the same refrain from our clients who have gone down this path: Students produce a nice research report, but it usually does not reveal anything new—no insights, no implications, no satisfaction. Worse, students give them commonly available information. At best, it's a step up from research papers done for university courses.

Would you hire an accounting student to do your taxes? Do you believe he or she could find most of the deductions your experienced accountant could? Grad students have limited skills that are sufficient for university projects, but not for serious business decisions. It's just not as insightful or as deep as business requires.

And it's just not easy. To get the specific and strategic business information that you're likely to need requires skill and expertise, and cannot be limited to database researches. While some information will be available via the Web, there are far better sources, even when your search is limited to printed and published documents. These include associations, fringe publications, private newsletters, conference proceedings, and other traditional venues, such as popular trade and business magazines. Many of the sources mentioned require either membership or payment to access the data, and there is surprisingly good information available for free. But what is free today may not be tomorrow, and vice versa, especially as publishers seek to gain revenue.

Published Information

Information from published sources is also called *secondary* or *open source*. The term *open source* was originally a government term, but is being used increasingly in business. Occasionally, information is referred to as *printed source*, meaning documents available from a source (an association or a university) that hasn't formally published the document. It usually does not show up on a search engine. On many occasions, we have received survey results, a white paper, or market data that the source makes available for its own or members' use and is willing to share, when asked (nicely).

Broadly speaking, *published*, *secondary*, and *open source* are synonyms referring to publicly available information that is not proprietary or confidential. Availability is not consistent. Some sources are widely accessible, and others are obtainable on only a limited basis or at the discretion of the institution. Documents subject to the Freedom of

Information Act are now much easier to obtain than during the previous administration.

Published information is frequently viewed as the stepchild to humint information, *hu*man *int*elligence sourced directly from people, discussed later in this chapter.

The best information is the one that provides what you need *and* is current and accurate. As with most things, there is no absolute or right source for good, substantial information. Each method has its advantages and disadvantages. Living in New York City is not better than living in Kansas City, and chocolate mousse is not better than apple pie. (Actually, mousse *is* better, but please don't send an e-mail.)

What's more important is *appropriateness*: Which choice is better for the specific task in question? Using each search method to its advantage is the best way to get the most from each. When starting an investigation, we consider all sources, and judging the type is less important. Getting the information you are seeking should be the goal. A great meal is a great meal, whether it's complex or basic. A dish with 27 ingredients that takes three hours to prepare can be just as delicious and satisfying as your favorite bread, cheese, and wine. This concept is important, because people and firms dedicated to one or the other may consider the other inferior, and this includes firms that use only software solutions.

Many investigations are best served by starting with a search of secondary sources. Each article from a reliable source can be a miniature investigation that provides a decent understanding of the industry, product, or company.

The earlier point, the common belief that everything you could ever want to know is on the Web, is both true and untrue. Generally, if you know where to look, you will find some information that is current, comprehensive, and accurate. It may take a long time to find it, but the more important thing is to understand and believe that it *does* exist. Published information covers a wide spectrum of sources, but rarely includes strategy, future plans, or pricing information. Even if it does, it probably will be very limited and not sufficient and need to be supplemented with humint input.

Sources

Numerous sites serve as portals to other worthwhile business sources. For instance, *The Standard Periodical Directory* lists more than 60,000

U.S. and Canadian periodicals (magazines, journals, newsletters, newspapers, directories, and yearbooks). Most industries are covered by dozens of trade publications, far more than the 3 or 4 which are generally known. There are 78 listings for the newspaper industry, and this does not include the specific 6,000 newspapers for each locale. There are 663 for automotive and 150 for trucking, 159 listings for metals and metalworking, and 72 for the grocery industry, not including 340 for food and food preparation.

There are almost 13,000 journals (business, professional, technical, and scientific) and 15,000 newsletters. Of the 60,000 listings in *The Standard Periodical Directory*, only 29 percent (17,000) are available electronically. Surprised? And, among those that *are* available electronically, a specific issue usually does not include all the articles from the print version. Even if it does, you're not as likely to find it as you are when scanning a paper version.

Then there are additional complications. It may be far more difficult than you can imagine to find the article you want in that issue; titles of articles are changed; small articles or mentions are often excluded, as are sidebars and graphs or tables. Finally, searching an individual issue electronically does not yield all the information that's found when manually flipping pages.

Where else can you go? There are more sources for business information than any one person can possibly deal with. The first step is to narrow the universe to recognized business sources, including:

1. Trade sources. Associations, industry publications, studies, surveys, newsletters, directories
2. Academic institutions
3. Government sites
4. Industry experts. Names that are often found in articles about the industry or company
5. Speaking presentations, including CEO investment presentations (often on the company web site), and speeches
6. Conferences, some of which sell downloads of presentations
7. Security analysts' reports
8. SEC filings

The following sources represent just a small amount of what's publicly available, and many are available at little or no cost:

1. Management articles from MIT Sloan, Emory University, Knowledge@Wharton. These cover a very wide range of general business issues and politics that impacts business. They often write about specific company case studies, current topics (e.g., global impact of the economic meltdown, the rise and fall of the Russian economic machine), and studies on how to deal with change. This is a very desirable source of current thinking, especially as it relates to changing business events.

2. Catalogs and reports of aggregated studies from other institutions. These include the Conference Board, Marketing Science Institute (MSI), *Research Alert*.

3. Research reports from educational or business institutions. Among these are the Center for Retailing Studies, Food Marketing Institute (retailers and wholesalers), *The Lempert Report* (supermarkets), Harvard Business School Publishing. Some (e.g., Hoover's) offer both free information and a fee-based option for more extensive information.

4. Industry or company research reports offered by firms who sell off-the-shelf reports. The primary advantage is immediate availability of electronic copies upon payment. The downside is that the report may contain only some of the specific information required, the research may not be current, and the quality varies considerably. Some reports are available by page or section. Commercial firms offering these include www.MarketResearch.com, http://reports.mintel.com, www.gartner.com, www.datamonitor.com, www.freedoniagroup.com, www.ibisworld.com, and www.packagedfacts.com.

5. Management/financial reports. These include Risk Management Association's *Annual Statement Studies*, brokerage house investment reports and analysis, Bain's Top Management Tools.

6. Demographic focus. These offer more depth on narrowly defined groups, *Marketing to Women*, *Minority Market Report*, *Hispanic Business*.

7. Special issues. More than 3,500 magazines have special editorial content focusing on industries or companies (see www.special-issues.com).

8. Trends. *TrendWatching* (www.trendwatching.com) and *Springwise* (www.springwise.com) are sister online newsletters that

report on new products and services globally, insights, and new business ideas. PSFK is a daily-trends news site (www.psfk .com). There are no specific sites for trend information, which is usually included or buried in trade or general business articles about the industry.

There are thousands of reliable and current published sources, and many are free, although free doesn't mean readily available. It takes time to learn what they are, but if they provide the information you are seeking, then it's important to learn about them. To begin to understand the scope of what's available, check Gale Directory Library (www.gale.cengage.com/DirectoryLibrary/available.htm).

Many of the web sites mentioned in this chapter do not provide free access to the contents of these directories; however, some are available in local libraries, where access is free. Business sources and directories are more likely to be located in the business section of a library or in academic (college and university) libraries (especially those with business schools). Check the general reference sections in the library, as they may be housed there.

Your local library provides free access to numerous and very expensive reference books, such as those discussed—*The Encyclopedia of Associations, The Standard Periodical Directory*, and *Directory of Newsletters*. If you are primarily interested in just one or two industries, make an incidental copy of the specific industry pages (likely permitted under the fair use doctrine) so that you can easily refer to them in your office.

One of the best secrets is that many libraries make their collections available online to cardholders, enabling 24/7 access from your home or desk. This includes searches for magazine articles from large databases such as EBSCO and searches of major newspapers from ProQuest. We recommend you obtain library cards for your local community library as well as for any larger nearby city or county systems, as each may use different portals, which will enlarge your range of available sources.

Find Articles is a general online database for free and fee-based articles and is good for business articles (http://findarticles.com). HighBeam Research (www.highbeam.com) is a fee-based database of magazine, newspaper and journals. The Securities and Exchange Commission (SEC) enables online searching of U.S. public company filings, including annual reports, prospectus, and quarterly updates (www.sec.gov/answers/publicdocs.htm).

Associations

Almost every industry, profession, and nonprofit has at least one association, and many have several associations. The lesser known ones may have a very narrow focus that provides more specific information than the better-known associations. The *Encyclopedia of Associations* includes descriptions of more than 25,000 associations, and it has an international edition (www.gale.com). The *National Trade and Professional Associations Directory* includes information on 7,800 associations, professional societies, and labor unions and their 20,000-plus executives (www.columbiabooks.com).

Both directories include information on the trade periodicals published, as well as conferences and special reports. We have found that a phone call to these associations is very helpful when we can't find what we want. There's a lot of information that is not listed but is available when speaking to the right people.

Trade Magazines

Contrary to conventional wisdom about where the publishing industry is headed, thousands of new titles are published annually, often for more narrowly defined niches. While many who work in a given industry can name the two or three that are considered the bibles of the industry, there are usually dozens more printed trade publications for each market segment. Solid, current information is available from numerous sources, often as many as a dozen for a specific industry. And it's not unusual to find as many as 30 to 100 trade magazines that cover an industry.

The Standard Periodical Directory (SPD) lists more than 50,000 trade and consumer magazines. Although it is less detailed than the SRDS, the SPD includes many smaller business and trade periodicals as well as newsletters. Don't dismiss the ones you've never heard about. All these publications need decent editorial content to attract advertisers and subscribers; hence they make good sources to check out (www.oxbridge.com).

Standard Rate & Data Service (SRDS) Publications offer several discrete issues (for businesses, consumers, newspapers, etc.). SRDS Business includes the top 5,000 trade magazines for the purpose of detailing advertising specs. It's useful for locating the top trade publications, while SPD lists many more for each industry. SRDS includes a brief description of the publication (helpful in determining whether it has the focus you're seeking), circulation numbers, and availability of special issues (www.srds.com). It also has a dedicated book for health, listing 3,000 health-focused periodicals.

Ulrich's lists international magazines and newspapers (www .ulrichsweb.com).

Newsletters

Newsletters can be incredibly valuable. They are the most current type of periodical and require the shortest lead time to publication. And, like many trade periodicals, they can be very narrowly defined. *Newsletters in Print* includes publications such as *Retailing Issues Letter* (from the Center for Retailing Studies at Texas A&M University), business management newsletters, *McKinsey Quarterly*, as well as newsletters for highly specialized topics such as *Safety Compliance Alert, Wire Industry News, Computer Architecture News, National Fundraiser, State Recycling Laws Update, Inside DOT & Transportation Week*, and *No Salt Week Newsletter* (www.gale.com).

Newspapers

SRDS Newspaper issue lists more than 3,000 newspapers, segmented by state and city (www.srds.com).

These next two sources are outstanding for current news about a specific city and keeping up with the companies located there, as well as overall issues facing the local business community. There are more than 40 business journals focused on business news for a city or area, such as *Dallas Business Journal* (www.bizjournals.com). Crain Communications (www.crain.com) covers newspapers not covered in www.bizjournals .com, such as *Crain's New York Business*.

The *American Journalism Review* (www.ajr.org) has information on more than 25,000 daily, specialty, alternative, campus, and other newspapers.

General Business Publications

There are hundreds of solid, well-documented business publications that have a general rather than a specific industry focus and cover a very wide range of industries and companies. *BusinessWeek, Fortune*, and *The*

Economist are particularly useful for their analysis and information. They do not publish articles that don't contain new insights; therefore, if companies want press coverage in such prestigious publications, they will need to provide information and some good nuggets not revealed elsewhere. Accordingly, these sources may contain a treasure or two about new products or new strategic initiatives.

Some of the smaller publications may provide in-depth information on a company that is not covered by the trade magazine for that specific industry. For example, some years back, *Inc.* magazine wrote about Larry's Shoes, the largest men's shoe store in the United States. This 4,000-word article detailed this *privately held*, independent chain store's story—including strategy, missteps, successes, and its advertising budget. The article also described its turnaround, as well as a comparison (shoe industry versus Larry's Shoes) of sales, inventory, store size, and so forth. When the chain ran into trouble, the *Wall Street Journal* explained what happened; again, the article was loaded with specific statistical information.

You may not find comparable depth of information on a specific company you're investigating, but you might be surprised at how much you can find if you venture beyond—way beyond—the Internet and the company's web site.

Specialty Libraries

There are numerous libraries across the United States that focus on a particular industry or activity. Many universities also have several specialty libraries, including those dedicated to business, art, and medicine. The *Directory of Special Libraries and Information Centers* (www.gale.cengage.com) lists more than 30,000 international libraries that specialize in architecture, nonprofits, chemistry, environmental design, psychology, and hundreds of others topics. And most are open to the public.

Three specialty libraries we used locally in Los Angeles had far deeper collections than any database or online source. We were able to utilize their databases and to make copies from the thousands of specialty print publications, both magazines and books. The Paul Ziffren Sports Resource Center covers every conceivable sport, along with the periodicals and databases serving those sports (www.la84 foundation.org). The Margaret Herrick Library at the Academy of Motion Picture Arts and Sciences is the place to go for information on cinema (www.oscars.org/library), and the Center for Nonprofit Management contains a deep collection of resources on nonprofit funding and management (www.cnmsocal.org).

Your trade association will be helpful in identifying specialty libraries and other unknown sources.

Unexpected or Unknown Sources

Local Publications

When you can't find the right or sufficient information about a company, an excellent source is the newspaper in its headquarter city and/or cities or towns where the company has branches.

The primary Japanese car manufacturers have their U.S. headquarters in Torrance, California, a suburb of Los Angeles. The *Los Angeles Times* covers Honda, Lexus, and Toyota when there is news to report. But the local newspaper that serves Torrance, the *Daily Breeze*, provides far greater coverage of these companies than does the *L.A. Times*. The Japanese automobile companies are far more important to the local community than to the greater Los Angeles area. Accordingly, the *Daily Breeze* is a better source and one that complements the coverage from a big city paper.

One of our clients was looking for information about its competitor in a small Pennsylvania town. We contacted that town's local newspaper which occasionally wrote about the company, and gained a lot of good information for our client—information that had appeared nowhere else. Another company under investigation was a small manufacturing firm in upstate New York. A search performed via the LexisNexis database found very little, and even that contained little of substance. A call to the local newspaper, however, revealed an article chock-full of information that highlighted the firm's growth—including details on the number of new hires, new strategic directions, planned equipment purchases, additional square footage, and so on. This newspaper was not available electronically, but the staff was perfectly willing to fax the article to us.

City or country magazines occasionally feature a local business, even though the publication may be oriented toward consumers. While this is a less likely source for solid business information, few businesses turn down the opportunity to be featured, and they usually provide more company information than they realize.

It's difficult to praise your own firm without revealing specific information, and the interviewees are more open with a non-business publication. Check out publications that focus on local business executives, such as *Dallas CEO* and *Washington SmartCEO*, listed in *The Standard Periodical Directory*.

Hoover's, which is known for its brief company overviews, includes the top three competitors, which may offer a surprise or two. It's not unusual for one of the top three to not be on your company's radar. Unless you are in the soft drink, beer or automotive industry, market share may not be readily available and companies often have no idea of industry rankings.

Associations that Cover Indirectly Related Industries

Think about other sources that have an interest in your product or service. There is very little public data on market size for medical imaging equipment. One unexpected source that we uncovered when researching a specific type of imaging equipment was the National Electrical Manufacturer's Association, which has a Medical Imaging and Technology Alliance division that targeted our exact area of interest.

Always ask yourself, "Who else is interested in this subject?" For example, you can be sure that the plastics industry is quite interested in and may publish articles on both the petroleum industry and crops that could provide another source of materials for plastics. Trade publications are looking for news, including copy that is tangentially related to the industry. These articles about *other* industries are interesting and may be useful in indicating an opportunity.

Legal Filings and Lawsuits

This is a hidden source that may include some company or market information that is not generally known and that a company does not want known. Check to see whether major players in the industry have been involved in lawsuits.

A company's *prospectus* (a legal document used to describe security offerings) provides a wealth of information on the company—financial mostly, but also legal information, including litigation, bios of top executives and board members, and the marketplace. The prospectus is particularly useful for its section on risks or market outlook. For example, the prospectus for a bond mutual fund we recently looked at included 15 separate risks, which are the principal risks that can affect the value of the fund's investments. Among these were interest rate risk, credit risk, market risk, emerging markets risks, leveraging risk, and management risk—each accompanied by a paragraph or more on the specifics of the risk.

Every business will have different risks. The prospectus for a water company included competition (identified by name), regulations, customer usage, natural hazards, costs and expenditures, market disruptions, reliance on third-party suppliers, eminent domain, and other factors. The value here is that it may include areas not considered by the company.

Company Information and Web Sites

Now we get to what most businesspeople think is a great source of information about a company—its web site. Perhaps that's true, but then again, probably not. In general, what companies put on their web site is information that has been carefully designed to tell the story *they* want to tell; and it's not necessarily the one you want to read. Unfortunately, for a company outsider, there is no way to determine the degree to which the company web site may be a fair and objective portrayal of the company and what might have been omitted or underplayed. The same is true for annual reports, even if not to the same degree.

Companies' web sites are most useful for finding out their:

1. *Positioning.* Their web site broadcasts how companies want to be perceived, what's important to them, and how transparent they are.
2. *Company focus.* Companies that are customer-centered include lots of product information on the site and make it easy to find and access customer service and technical assistance.
3. *Job postings.* Reveals new capabilities or expansion of existing ones.
4. *Change in direction.* This may be indicated by links to partners, alliances, other domain names, and so forth.
5. *Leadership.* There may be a company directory, organizational chart, or bios of top executives.

6. *Product line.* Text or photos and varying degrees of specifications.

7. *Product guarantees/warranties.*

8. *Articles about them.* These are likely to be selected for their positive coverage, but will also contain more balanced commentary, including weaknesses and comments from competitors and other outsiders. Some may include nuggets on strategy, new product initiatives, successes, and so on. These articles note the publications that cover them, which may contain other articles and be a good source of information on the industry. And they will include press releases which cover new products, executive appointments, new facilities, etc.

Keep in mind that companies may prepare parallel internal- and external-facing web sites—that is, one they want the public to see and one for clients or internal use. The company's web site is one-sided, the face the company wants you to see. It may bear limited resemblance to what the company is doing, as they will carefully select what's included.

Don't overlook chat rooms and angry-customer web sites (e.g., untied.com, about United Airlines, and walmartwatch.com), where company products and services, as well as the firms themselves, are "reviewed." These sources contain both great and flawed information, which must be verified, and may contain hints of problems that could be turned into opportunities for your firm and may be useful to your sales force. You have to be more vigilant than ever about the reliability of the information, especially if it's from a personal web site (not always obvious) or from a blog. Posted information may be from a disgruntled former employee or disinformation (from an employee in a competitor firm.)

Doing Your Own Searching

It's clear that executives are doing more and more of their own searching and will continue to do so. The next few pages will provide some tools and perspectives on expectations for those who are not experts in this field but want to improve their results.

According to a study from Forbes.com and Yahoo published in July 2009, the Internet continues to be the most influential and important source of business information for C-level executives, in companies with

$1 billion-plus in sales in the United States, at 74 percent. But do they find the information they're seeking? As with any profession, it's the experts who have studied and learned the requisite search skills who can uncover what you want. After all, while you *can* cut your own hair, lay your own tile, sew your own clothes, design your own landscaping plan, and make your own cheese, you usually don't do these tasks, because your efforts will likely not produce the quality you want and need.

It's much the same for information and intelligence. If the information is important to you or your company, then let the experts do it. They will find the information you can't; it will be current, reliable (usually corroborated by several sources), and on target—as opposed to information that's "kinda related" to what you want, but is not quite specific enough.

Competitive intelligence professionals are not librarians (no disparagement is meant) and do not simply rely on the Web for answers. Instead, CI professionals are skilled in a number of different areas and have the expertise to partner with you and determine what information is best suited to your purpose. They will ferret out the information from areas you might not even consider, analyze it for meaning, and present it in a manner that will convey it best. In this way, you increase the chances of acquiring the answers or intelligence you need.

That said, however, we recognize that many of you will continue to do your own searching, so this chapter will provide some guidance to specific areas for useful business sources—and point out the pitfalls of others.

Commercial databases such as LexisNexis, Factiva, and others are the best and fastest sources for uncovering business information from a wide range of publications. These sources are not easy to use, and they can be accessed only for a fee. If you want specific information that is organized and properly analyzed in answer to a specific question or problem, you will have to pay a professional to get it for you. As with choosing a surgeon or any other professional, make certain that the person performs this type of search on that database regularly and is familiar with its quirks.

Google and Wikipedia are both terrific and extremely popular first sites for searching, as both have extensive filings and might provide some of the information you're seeking—but just *some*, as they don't specialize in business information. According to comScore, a leader in measuring search rankings among the major search engines, Google accounts for almost 60 percent of all searches, followed by Yahoo! with 21 percent, Microsoft with 9 percent, and AOL with 5 percent. Google's share is significantly greater in Europe, at 79 percent.

Search Google News rather than Google, as the former contains more business news than does the latter. Google News aggregates 4,500 English-language news sources globally, including most of the major newspapers (*New York Times*, *Washington Post*, *Al-Jazeera*), business publications (*Forbes* and *Fortune*), media outlets (Bloomberg News, Associated Press, BBC News, CNN, bizjournals.com), many of which will not be found on *regular* Google.

These tips will improve your Google search:

1. Use explicit phrases in your search. If you are looking for information on garden tools, use quotes to make the term a phrase: "garden tools."
2. Remove the quotes from the same phrase to broaden the search if you're not getting sufficient results (quality or number).
3. Reverse the order of the word(s), even if it sounds absurd.
4. Specify the type of document you are looking for. If you think the area of inquiry was used in a PowerPoint presentation, type in "garden tools" .ppt.
5. Use the Google advanced search feature. If you can't remember the operators used in your search string, use Google's Advanced Search (the link is right next to the Search button).
6. In the search box, try both limited words and phrases (e.g., business blogs) and descriptive phrases or questions (e.g., What are the best blogs for business information?)
7. Use synonyms: cars, autos, vehicles—or place the tilde sign (~) immediately in front of your search term, ~cars.
8. Scan a minimum of 10 pages before changing your approach. Better and/or more current sites may show up on page 10 or 15. The first few pages are not necessarily better.

We recommend that you access at least 3 or 4 different meta search engines, each of which enables access to multiple databases. Two other meta search engines that cover business include: www.nlsearch.com (Northern Light Search) and www.bing.com, Microsoft's answer to Google. Wikipedia has an extensive list of search engines on their site.

Advantages and Disadvantages of the Internet and Google

The Internet/Web makes information far more accessible from a greater variety of sources than from any other single source. The Web also makes that information easier to disseminate, so it spreads the word(s) ever more quickly than at any time in history. But there *are* limitations. As you have no doubt figured out, the Internet does not contain every piece of information ever written. Millions of books and articles have been published over time, and only a fraction of them can be found on the Internet. After all, someone has to put it on the Internet for you to have the possibility of finding it, and we are far from that being accomplished. There is a lot out there in cyberspace, but not necessarily what you are seeking.

It's just not true that everything you seek is available on the Web. The Internet is infinite, unfiltered, and unverified.

Business Information Review (http://bir.sagepub.com/) noted that "Answering broad business information questions by using Internet search engines can provide results which are at any point on the continuum between spectacularly useful and incredibly irrelevant." Then, too, there is a question about the credibility of what you get. Since no one "controls" the Internet, anyone can post information on it, and no doubt some of what you find will be garbage. Keep in mind that just because the information appears out there does not make it factual, credible, or even reliable.

Many of the sources will be unknown and may be just opinion. Before you accept the information on the page you linked to, check the source *and* the date. Information changes too quickly to rely on outdated comments or articles. Before we open a link on Google, we check the source, which can prevent time-consuming viewing of an unknown and unreliable blog.

Having said all this, the Internet remains a good place to start, and it's where we often begin our research. However, it's *only* the first step.

The first place most people turn to find specific information is one of the large, broad-based electronic search engines, such as Google or LexisNexis. Google, Bing, Ask, Yahoo!, and others are free, whereas LexisNexis and Factiva are subscription-based and require greater research skills and experience. In essence, you get what you pay for.

Google and the other search engines can be fabulous sources for general information, but they are not very good for business information. Very few, if any, of the major newspapers or trade publications or specialized newsletters appear in your Google and other search engine results, although a fugitive business article may occasionally appear. Major newspapers may offer free access from their own sites, but their articles rarely appear in Google or other search engine results.

The next time you're conducting a search on Google, note the URLs for the first 20 entries and see how many include known, serious, or highly regarded sources. Do this for the next five searches to prove to yourself that it's not an anomaly for a single subject area. Second, for the few that may appear useful, when you link to the full article, can you find the date (should be current) and the source, or is it identified only by an individual or an unknown entity?

Some experts even claim that typical search engines like Yahoo! and Google pick up only about 1 percent of the information available on the Internet. In fact, one expert compared searching the Internet to "sifting the sand of the Sahara to find a specific grain." While you are likely to catch a lot of sand in your bucket even by skimming just the surface of the vast desert, you are going to leave even more behind, because most of the information is hidden in the deep or invisible Web. Whether that 1 percent figure is accurate or not, it certainly applies even more to business information. The message here is that general search engines should not be relied upon as a business source. Not venturing beyond the first step can blindside you to believing the information is not available to you or your competitors.

To be clear, I am not suggesting that searching Google or Yahoo! is a waste of time. On the contrary, they are both perfectly good starting points, and they certainly deserve 20 to 30 minutes of your time. Occasionally, they will link to a source that you might not otherwise find, or identify a source worth pursuing. These metasearch engines can include press releases (the company's story) or articles from the Associated Press, the latter of which includes reportorial business information that frequently appears in respected sources.

Although you may find very narrowly defined, basic business information that you're searching for on the Web, be aware of the following:

1. A limited number of articles from highly regarded business publications (*Business Week*, *The Economist*, *Forbes*, *Harvard*

Business Review, strategy+business) or trade periodicals (*Adhesives Age, Supermarket News, Mortuary Management, Multifamily Executive*) will come up in your search.

2. Article citations from highly regarded resources such as the Conference Board or *McKinsey Quarterly* will not appear, although an occasional search may include a random article from the *Wall St. Journal*. Every once in a while, one of these sources will appear, but a 1 or 5 percent hit rate is just not sufficient.

3. Few studies or surveys published by trade publications, associations, and companies who specialize in the field appear in the results.

4. The more specific and strategic the information that you're seeking, the less likely it will be found electronically or in a library, unless it's from a directory, which is usually not available for free online. Conversely, the Web will occasionally unearth information you would not easily find if searching the usual sources or even the hidden Web. In a project where our client targeted its product for universities, we actually found a 100-plus-page document detailing a specific university's experience with this particular product.

If you find a specific article requiring a subscription, you may be able to obtain it by searching Google with the title in quotation marks. This is particularly effective for articles that appear in multiple sources.

According to Bonnie Hohhoff of the Society of Competitive Intelligence Professionals (SCIP):

- There is little overlap in results from each of the search engines.
- The same site can rank high in one engine and low in another.
- Search engines change their relevancy algorithm constantly.

Finding information online, whether general or specific, may be more challenging than anticipated. I have both print and online subscriptions to the *Wall Street Journal*; yet quite often, when seeking an article from the online *WSJ* published just a day earlier, I can't find it! Even using the exact headline almost never yields the specific article I want. The print and online editions use different headlines. You would expect that the article would be listed, as the subject is the same, but my search results say, "No content matches your search criteria." This has happened repeatedly, and it is not due to misspelled or omitted words. (I do recheck my typing.)

But don't dismay: There is a solution. Now when I look for an article on the venerable *WSJ* site, I search by the reporter's name. This approach has been successful every time, and it may work for other journals and publications.

Invisible Web

Also called the *hidden* or *deep Web*, the invisible Web is the part of the Internet that is not available via the commonly used search engines. It's the difference between *surface* and *deep* information. The surface Web is the most familiar, available from search engines like Yahoo! and Google. The deep Web can include subscription-only web sites, restricted sites, obscure databases, or those that are not linked to other sites and must be found independently. Professional associations often have research centers, trade newsletters, or magazines that aren't accessible via Google. Going directly to their sites may uncover a windfall of industry findings—articles, studies, experts, conference proceedings, and directories.

The invisible Web, which is estimated to be several hundred times larger than the traditional Web, requires considerable time commitment to search. Each URL/source must be researched individually, unlike Google, which aggregates many sources. But it's time well spent to go directly to the source. It's similar to hiring a real estate agent. While you can drive up and down and up and down endless streets, and you may find a house you like that's for sale (which is comparable to searching Google), only an agent (comparable to the hidden Web) will know which houses are for sale that have the features you want and which ones will be coming on the market.

Competitive Intelligence Software

Robert Steele, CEO of OSS, Inc., and producer of more than a dozen open source conferences, said it well in *Open Source Intelligence: Executive Overview*: "Over the past couple of months, we have run across many people who believe that a software solution is all that is required for a business intelligence system to be in place in their organization. Sadly, this will not deliver the intelligence directors and senior managers value. . . . At this point in time, the human mind is still the only computer available to put together all the pieces of the jigsaw and devise a competitive strategy."

Chapter 11 describes CI myths and presents a detailed discussion of CI software.

Human Intelligence (Humint)

*Humint, hum*an *int*elligence, is information gathered from direct contact with people. It gets less attention than the Web or published information, but can prove more valuable. Humint provides a unique perspective because it is developed from human sources who are subject matter experts (SMEs) and those in the know. They have the experience and are involved in industry issues on a regular basis. Their comments are comparable to "expert witness testimony" for corporate development initiatives, according to Dan Himelfarb, who writes extensively on humint in SCIP's *Competitive Intelligence* magazine (www.scip.org). Numerous books and articles detail exactly how to do this most effectively.

The practice of human intelligence is not merely picking up the phone, finding the right people, and asking questions. You also need strong *listening* skills and a dogged but creative mind to uncover information an ordinary person might not even think to inquire about. This is generally what good reporters who are knowledgeable in interviewing and elicitation do.

Great intelligence evolves from knowing *how* to elicit information in concert with understanding *what* information is useful for business in general and for that specific business in particular. It's developed by asking clarifying questions (e.g., "What do you mean by that?" "Could you explain that in greater detail?") or allowing some dead time between the end of the response and before another statement or question is put out to the contact. People deplore a vacuum, so the person who is most uncomfortable is most likely to fill that space. This is an opportunity to hear additional information that would not have arisen during the conversations.

It's during such times that maintaining a focus on the purpose enables the CI professional to hear ancillary comments, such as random remarks about competitors (emerging and existing), customer comments and complaints, or rumors about competitive features or initiatives. This is how we capture information about reputation and positioning of competitors.

No one can doubt that we have made great technological strides in data collection, and with these huge technology advances in the past decade, we have been able to slice, dice, chop, and puree data to an incredible degree. Those advances notwithstanding, some of the best information gathered is still the result of two people talking directly to each other, and that is what human intelligence and elicitation is all about. This is not spying; this is not Dumpster diving. It can and must be done ethically. (See Chapter 13 for CI ethics.)

While some claim that humint is better than published information, the quality for both is directly related to the source. And each is better at providing specific kinds of information. Data-type information (market size and share, major competitors, sales by distribution channel) is usually more reliable from published sources, since a valid survey or investigation has been conducted, often corroborated by numerous sources. Humint is better for more sophisticated inquiries, those related to strategy, emerging issues, opportunities, threats, barriers to entry into a new market, the future, or pricing.

Humint results from information that is provided voluntarily and ethically. You contact and engage those who are most likely to know and can provide the best information, people directly or indirectly affiliated with the industry under investigation, including:

- Competitors
- Company employees, from the receptionist to the president (as high up as possible or relevant)
- Distributors, suppliers, and retailers
- Industry experts
- Academicians who study the industry, along with their assistants, who do the actual research
- Associations
- Reporters and bloggers who cover the industry
- Industry consultants
- Retired executives
- Financial sector individuals who monitor that specific industry

It may be surprising to find that any of the preceding sources would share information. My business colleagues have repeatedly told me that they would "never talk to anyone" about their business. My response is that they are in a state of denial, and they do not recognize that they are just as vulnerable to a soft type of inquiry as everyone else. Not long ago, a potential client contacted us to undertake a CI investigation. In the process of our discussion covering what we do and how we do it, the president of this company gulped and admitted he just had such a conversation three weeks prior to calling us.

You might question why people, even executives, would speak with us. The primary reason is cultural. Americans are very generous and like to help, even when they're working 10-hour days. Second, when you are speaking to people about their expertise, they are flattered and even more willing to talk. Add to this the reality that few people are usually interested in the work the contacts do; therefore, when someone, even a stranger, is truly interested and engaged, they *really* want to share. This appears to be less so in Europe and Asia; but even that gap is closing, as those in other countries increasingly are willing to provide information (although not as much or as detailed).

The primary concern about the value of information derived from this type of direct contact is its accuracy. Information garnered in this way will be more anecdotal than statistically reliable (according to market research standards) and usually does not stand on its own. Therefore, it will have to be validated by others who have the expertise or judgment to verify and otherwise corroborate such feedback. The likelihood of accuracy is very high for our practice, because we always make an extra effort to verify the information. We don't accept as fact the word of any one or two individuals, even those most knowledgeable. We validate what we've been told by others—in other functions, at different levels—so it's generated from a spectrum. We verify what we hear from carefully selected individuals by speaking with others, clarifying specifics, and then hearing new information, which in turn must be verified.

This process is very time-consuming, but no other method will produce comparable results. We have to identify the right people, then get the information and corroboration we are seeking. This requires speaking to a large number of people. The benefit of contact with many respondents is that numerous bits of information come together to complete the puzzle and identify patterns, which is invaluable. While these contacts don't generally reveal their company's strategy, if you've heard enough information and enough of the right information, you have a decent chance of figuring out the strategy or direction or issues.

Our success in uncovering information from human contacts depends on conducting conversations and having discussions rather than interviews. We don't start with a script, and we don't develop a list of questions to ask every contact, especially since some contacts are merely conduits to those who are most knowledgeable. This is what separates competitive intelligence from market research. The goal in CI is to not obtain statistically reliable data and information; instead, we're seeking clarity, insights, new perspectives, implications, and emerging changes. This is what good CI accomplishes. We're not trying to uncover a competitor's secrets or proprietary information; that would be a violation of ethics and really not necessary. The most valuable competitive intelligence leads to smarter decisions to increase sales, rather than knowing the competitors. (For more details on this point, read Chapter 3.)

Industry experts are also an obvious source of humint because they specialize in an industry or function that is important to the company. They provide deep, industry-specific information and context (history, competitors, distribution channels, etc.), and they can do it immediately. But experts are often no better than industry executives in having an external perspective. They often suffer from the same blinders, since they've been in the industry for an extended period of time and spout the same conventional wisdom. Expert sources and information change. Consider changing how you use experts, and use them for the most appropriate situations rather than expecting them to solve all problems.

For all the preceding reasons, humint is not a type of research that can be undertaken by a novice. Good humint requires specific and practiced elicitation skills that keep the contact talking—and talking about useful areas.

Humint intelligence is not completed and useful until all the feedback is aggregated, assessed, and analyzed—moving from information to intelligence.

Trade Shows and Conferences

Trade shows, conventions, conferences, and seminars are a rich source for competitive intelligence, both about the industry and specific competitors. Since these provide face-to-face encounters, they are another forum for human intelligence. Trade shows offer a unique opportunity to learn, observe, make contacts, find partners, and explore new markets or ideas. This is also a good time to toss out a balloon to selected individuals—to test an idea and hear a variety of comments to support the idea, to suggest that more work is required, to raise questions that the company had not considered, and to get feedback.

Jonathan Calof, professor at the University of Ottawa, and coauthor with Bonnie Hohhoff of *Conference and Trade Show Intelligence* (available from the SCIP web site at www.scip.org), states that trade shows are an untapped environment to:

- Identify new markets
- Pursue market opportunities
- Obtain market insights
- Identify key threats
- Validate rumors
- Hear new rumblings to monitor or check out
- Find joint venture partners

Most, if not all, of your competitors, plus a good many of their distributors, will usually attend an industry trade show, and there is nothing unethical about asking the booth staff a few pointed questions. People attend these venues to talk, to learn, and to exchange information. The talk is focused on the industry or the company; and the people attending or working the booths are part of that industry, so conversations are easier and can be more specific. That creates a great opportunity to enhance your knowledge base.

In addition to collecting their promotional literature, which can reveal some unknown information, it doesn't take much to get people to speak about their company, as well as to share what they know about competitors, new products, products in development, new customer accounts, and so on. After all, people like to demonstrate their industry knowledge, especially among their peers, suppliers, and customers. They have fewer filters when attending trade shows and may employ less self-control about what is discussed. The answers you get can be illuminating and may provide the very intelligence you need.

Most businesspeople will tell you that they just do not or would not share company information; however, as mentioned earlier, that belies the reality. When they are in the moment and face an inquisitive potential customer or even an unidentified but interested party, they actually want to talk up their company and brag about what they're doing, and so they share.

An inventor friend of mine told me of an electronics trade show he attended where he "discovered" a new way to program his product, simply from a conversation he had with competitors. They did not reveal any company secrets; they simply indicated the direction they had taken, and, presto, he understood a new way to enhance his own product.

Obviously, you can't just walk up to people and start interrogating them. You need to learn how to casually, concisely, and specifically discuss issues and make inquiries. But if you cover some of the same information that customers want to know, you can ask about their most recent product/service introductions, product delivery schedules, company and branch locations, quality of competitive products, competitive service strengths and weaknesses, who they see as industry leaders, and the like.

Do not misrepresent yourself or your company. Although you might think that when the contact realizes you are from a competitor that you won't talk to them, the reverse may occur. They are just as interested in learning from you. Your challenge is to gain the skills to share information, but not proprietary information. This includes talking about non-proprietary information that is not well known. In this way, you will have the conversation you didn't think possible.

Because trade shows may provide a gold mine of information to the competition, company employees require serious instruction about what can be discussed and in how much detail. Similarly, employees need specific and detailed instruction about how to maximize their time at the shows. While the conversations appear casual, the preparation and strategy for "learning" is anything but. Detailed information for developing plans, examples of successes, and tips on how to work a trade show may be found in *Conference and Trade Show Intelligence*, as noted previously.

Trade shows can also offer three other unexpected bonuses. First, many shows are attended by the press reps—from trade publications to general business magazines to city newspapers. This is an opportunity to connect with them and perhaps use them later as a resource to bolster what you have learned, potentially even to be featured in an article.

Second, companies that exhibit at trade shows may provide a speaker. Speaking provides two advantages. Hearing a speaker, especially from a competitive firm, may reveal unexpected information, especially during the question-and-answer segment. As many speakers will attest, there is a "rush" that they experience, and that vulnerability often opens the path for sharing a bit more than they otherwise might. Grabbing a speaking slot showcases your company's ability to provide solutions for dealing with a downturn and positions your company as one to be associated with.

Third, during periods of downturns in your specific industry or in recessionary times that hit businesses in general, exhibiting at trade shows broadcasts to your industry and competitors that you are doing okay. This is a desirable psychological advantage, similar to companies that continue to maintain their advertising. Competitors may approach you to help clients that they can no longer service because of downsizing. And suppliers prefer working with successful companies and may be more open to renegotiating pricing or other areas.

In the trade show book cited earlier, Dr. Alison Bourey states that companies waste 30 to 50 percent of their trade show budget by not having a collection plan. How do you "attack" a trade show? How do you become trade show smart? Here are some suggested steps:

1. Know before you go. Get the exhibitor list and floor map before you go.
2. Find out who is going to be there, and create a list of companies you have to see.
3. Don't limit that list to competitors. Suppliers and vendors to those competitors are also useful resources.
4. Use your floor map to do a walkabout to visit any new or unfamiliar exhibitors.
5. Collect all the literature that is offered, including business cards. These may be among the very people you contact when you do direct-contact research.
6. Stay open to information that may arise unexpectedly as you walk the show floor.

Develop a plan for who will attend from your company, what you want to learn, and who will be responsible for that information. Meet with the team nightly to discuss what's been learned and to download what you captured that day. It must be done immediately, as it's easy to forget, and there will be comparable material learned the next day.

This same approach is equally effective for conventions, conferences, and seminars. These events can be a gold mine of information if the attendees have a coordinated plan and the humint skills to find the treasure.

Conventional Wisdom

Conventional wisdom is what everyone "knows" to be true. It's the basis for assumptions and does not factor in changes, because it reflects the past. The job of competitive intelligence is to move beyond conventional wisdom.

Conventional wisdom should logically change over time as the world changes. While some may still hold true, even in changing times, some may not. The gap between the time when conventional wisdom is true and when it's not is an opportunity, as during this gap there are unknown or underestimated changes in behavior, attitudes, or reality.

For example, companies believe that developing loyal customers is the key to more sales. They follow the old 80-20 marketing mantra that 80 percent of your product is purchased by 20 percent of customers. Dr. David Corkindale's article, "Mistakes Marketers Make," published in MIT's *Sloan Management Review*, noted that "Beer is a common drink among Australian men, and many claim they wouldn't drink any beer other than their favorite brand. However, data on actual behavior show that only 10 percent of these men are loyal to a single brand. This is typical of the many repertoire markets in the developed world. But that doesn't stop some companies . . . [from] focusing their marketing effort on them. Ignoring the other 90 percent of the market restricts their sales." Dr. Corkindale further states that a far more successful way to increase sales is to increase the customer base by selling to more customers in the existing market space or by entering a new market.

The popular book *Freakonomics*, by economist Steven Levitt and *New York Times* journalist Stephen J. Dubner, made the case for why conventional wisdom is actually wrong more often than not. It's been wrong about the economy; it's been wrong about investment strategies; it's been wrong about the past several elections. Every woman, minority or "older" demographic cohort can easily discuss the myths of conventional wisdom. There are even articles that ask, "What Went Wrong with Conventional Wisdom." This tells us that conventional wisdom is not a source upon which decisions can be made—at least not with any degree of reliability.

Social Media Sources

Social Networking

LinkedIn, Facebook, and similar social networking sites have become increasingly used and useful for connecting to someone you don't know but want to speak with. This is especially useful for developing humint competitive intelligence, since it's almost impossible to call a company and be put through to the director of purchasing or the sales manager if you don't know that person. LinkedIn or Plaxo can provide the first, second, or third level of contact to gain an entrée or warm introduction, or, at the very least, the name of a person at the company.

That old adage, "It's not what you know but who you know," has achieved even more importance in this online era. And who you know can be part of a much larger group when you make connections through these social networking sites.

Blogs

Data, opinions, and other commentary from social media sources, especially blogs, must be used with *extreme* caution. These are opinions, many of which are purely anecdotal, unmonitored, unfiltered, unverified, and not necessarily written by an expert in the field—or even by someone with a thoughtful or valid viewpoint. At this time, social media can be considered as an option, albeit one to be carefully weighed against others for veracity and usefulness.

This is not meant to dismiss the usefulness of blogs, but rather to advise against jumping on the bandwagon for the newest tool. Blogs may be valuable for early warning of customer dissatisfaction, to hear what's being said about your company and the competition, or to open the company's eyes to other points of view. Despite all the twitter about Twitter and blogging, information that is the basis for decision making must be reliable and sufficiently comprehensive, and these sources cannot be relied upon for that.

Blogs may provide a signpost for information to be further checked out, but they do not yet warrant greater standing. Although the fictional Sherlock Holmes came on the scene more than 100 years before blogs, his methodology and thinking is more reliable than using blogs. His old-fashioned approach of careful reasoning, combined with observation and common sense, continues to be a very sound way to arrive at reality or truth. Blogs and other technology can supplement Holmes's approach by providing access to a greater variety of sources.

Blogs rarely constitute a good source of competitive intelligence because, as I pointed out earlier, most are opinions that are unsubstantiated, biased, and not thoroughly examined. They are useful for finding out what others are saying about your company (products, marketing, people), and they may also be useful for raising issues and generating discussions.

At this time, only a few business blogs deserve your attention—those from established experts such as Guy Kawasaki, Tom Peters, Seth Godin, and those who are highly regarded in your industry, whose blogs are extensions of their already highly regarded books and perspectives.

August Jackson, a competitive intelligence practitioner with a CI blog, offers the following perspective on blogs (www.augustjackson .net). Like many other kinds of newly emerging technology, blogs have both their strengths and weaknesses.

Potential Advantages of Blogs

- If used and explained properly, they can be extremely useful for obtaining and sharing information from the sales force, who often don't want to take the time to complete more time-intensive company forms.
- Internal company blogs are:
  - A source of company information that is easily disseminated to select internal groups or to the entire organization, and can engage many diverse individuals within the company (feedback, challenge veracity, add/supplement).
  - More timely and current than other methods.
  - A way to share information about competitors, suppliers, and so forth, along with facts or rumors.
- Blogs are useful for sharing new or successful methods or practices or success stories among your professional colleagues.
- Blogs may be good way to find thought leaders for the industry or general approach or thinking.

- They may be more conversational than other forms, less edited, and more forgiving in terms of grammar. They may be more engaging and encourage current and prospective participants to access them more often and comment more frequently.
- Blogs from competitors or the industry may be useful as a source of information relating to public relations, marketing, first indication of change (industry regulations, technology, etc.).
- Blogs may be an early warning of problems (complaints, threats), especially when they're from employees whose blog may or may not be sanctioned by their company.

Some Disadvantages of Blogs
- They are not a reliable source of information; facts and comments are not edited or qualified; they must be verified with appropriate, knowledgeable sources.
- It can be very time-consuming to find and monitor blogs, which may not produce useful results.
- Companies should assign an internal person to monitor what is being said about them on other blogs.
- Blogs rank lower for useful information than competitor web sites, humint information, the Internet, or published sources.

Evaluating Blogs
Jackson recommends the following two methods for determining the value of specific blogs.

1. *Reliability.* Has the information been published elsewhere (by other bloggers independent from the original blogger or by print publications)?
2. *Credibility.* Has this specific blogger provided accurate information consistently in the past?

Crowd Sourcing and Groupthink

There certainly is value in hearing and considering a wide array of diverse thinking. That is what we have been promoting in comments related to competitive versus competitor intelligence. Two recent popular books that address the concept of diversity are *The Wisdom of Crowds* and *Wikinomics*.

While there may be merit in these approaches for select decisions, I am not convinced of their viability for many business decisions. The exception is their use as a first step for developing ideas and fleshing out details of specific concepts from a wide group of constituencies. Part of the popularity of these types of ideas is their purported cost savings, which means they are less expensive than the traditional structured and careful methods. As with all new ideas, they must be used appropriately to add value.

Publisher's Weekly summarizes James Surowiecki's popular book, *The Wisdom of Crowds*, as "a crowd's 'collective intelligence' that will produce better outcomes than a small group of experts. The diversity brings in different information; independence keeps people from being swayed by a single opinion leader; people's errors balance each other out; and including all opinions guarantees that the results are 'smarter' than if a single expert had been in charge." *Wikinomics: How Mass Collaboration Changes Everything*, by Don Tapscott and Anthony D. Williams, addresses a similar concept of online groupthink. Both books are based on input that has as its foundation *opinion*—not facts, not deep understanding of the marketplace, and not carefully considered insight on what's changing.

Groupthink is not a substitute for competitive intelligence, and at best, is only a very weak supplement. The major disadvantage is that without careful and deliberate investigation, results usually reflect what is familiar and what has happened. What's changing is usually unknown or dismissed, so it is not factored into these opinions. And group dynamics may skew input.

Bottom line: There are innumerable good sources for information, which is both good news and bad news. The good news is that you have a good chance of getting the information you're seeking—*if* you use the appropriate source and have the skills to get to the right information. The bad news is that there is so much information available that more time and effort is required to get to that needle in a haystack. The title of Chapter 6, "All Information is Not Equal," captures this concept: determine the most appropriate sources to be used for each investigation. Be open and be selective.

It's time to broaden your scope of resources. Marshall Goldsmith, highly respected consultant and author of numerous management books, captured the reason why in his 2007 book, "What Got You Here Won't Get You There." Use these additional resources in this chapter to "get you there."

Enjoy the journey!

10

Performing Like a CI Pro

Getting Started in Competitive Intelligence: What You Need to Consider

Let's face it, no company wants to be at the mercy of the vagaries of the marketplace. For our clients and for us, this means learning what they need to know about the what, where, and why so that they can gain advantage from, rather than becoming victims of the marketplace. The intelligence that results from this investigation is only part of the story that will provide value.

The information must be the *right information*, and the right information starts with careful design and planning. What material is important, and where do we find it? The results must be presented in a manner that fits the person, department, or company. Great competitive intelligence that remains unread or misunderstood undermines the efforts and the results.

This chapter presents an approach and a point of view that delineates the competitive intelligence process and maximizes the results while supplementing other CI books that teach more detailed specifics on *how* to do CI. Many companies collect information on an informal basis about the marketplace and their competitors, but that is often undertaken in a haphazard method. It's often assigned to someone who knows nothing about CI—what it is or how to do it. Would you ask your recent college graduate to represent you in Superior Court? And it's frequently conducted on an ad hoc basis as a result of some event, or in response to some move made by the competition, so a well-thought-out, organized approach usually isn't part of the conversation. This is not due diligence.

What's the First Question?

Purpose, Purpose, Purpose

The starting point for any competitive intelligence investigation is to define the problem or issue, and that means getting a full and deep understanding of the purpose for gathering the information. Without this, you're spinning your wheels, not using time wisely, setting up all parties for disappointment, and leaving yourself vulnerable to being blindsided.

What is the problem you are trying to solve? What are you asking for? Why are you asking for it? Will the results address the problem? Who will use the results? How will they be used? The purpose guides the content and scope of the project and keeps the project focused. The purpose, content, and scope will vary with every investigation: Marketing and strategy arenas may focus more on the marketplace and what's changing; product development and sales may seek information on competitors, their specific products, and likely users; business development might be looking for background information on potential partners or alliances.

Scope

In our experience, the scope of the client's (internal or external) original request often becomes quite different by the end of the discussion. This is because clients often either have an unfocused view of what they need to know, get caught up in obtaining lots of data, or lack an awareness of what can be delivered—mainly because they are unfamiliar with competitive intelligence.

For example, companies that are considering entering a new market often focus on the size (revenues) of that market. They do some basic research, learn that the size of the market is "big enough" (whatever that means), which easily excites them as they assume they would get their share. How often have you heard an executive say, "If we capture just 2 percent of the market . . ."? This, of course, is not the correct question, and it's an absurd assumption.

Even a market as large as $5 billion may not be attractive once all the elements are known and understood. It's far more valuable to know whether this is a growing market and how and where is it growing. What barriers might exist to breaking in to it? How interested are potential customers in your new offering? Do prospects recognize your differentiators or is their point of view at odds with yours? How open are distributors to carrying a new vendor? What would be desirable from a new competitor? What do existing suppliers do well? Decision makers, too, often see opportunities that may not exist, as their focus is misplaced (on market size) and they haven't investigated the market for what's important to buyers.

Similarly, the scope must be clear from the perspective of how much information the client wants. Former president of SCIP, Ava Youngblood, seared in my mind what happens when you don't spend the time necessary to understand the scope. A member of her CI staff who was asked for information about a competitor worked diligently to gather reams of information. When it was presented to the requestor, he was astonished and perplexed with the quantity of material. The requestor did not state exactly what he was looking for, and the researcher was too intimidated to inquire. Ava referred to this extensive volume as "boiling the ocean." Getting everything you can on a topic is hardly a practical or useful approach.

- The scope is determined by considering a number of elements. How important is this information to the decision? Do you need an overview or an in-depth study? Is the focus on the market, the products, or competitors? The project scope should be as robust as necessary to answer the specific questions—and not more.
- I prefer a variation of the Socratic method of constant questioning to flesh out more about the scope than the client originally states. It involves asking numerous questions, even when the answers may be obvious or known. Open-ended questions solicit additional information from the requester, including opinions, perspectives, and details, in an unstructured manner. Sometimes referred to as "drilling down," this process may require several rounds of conversations, but will provide the best results. The purpose is twofold: to uncover all their needs (stated and not) and to stimulate thinking about other, preferred intelligence that can be provided but that the requestor did not know about or consider.

A prospect of ours had a seemingly simple request: "We need net pricing information for automotive parts from distributors." We started asking questions. How many parts? Are they specific parts or categories of parts? What do you mean by pricing? How many distributors? After several conversations to ferret out exactly what information the client was seeking, we learned they wanted pricing information (actual, not list) on 40 to 60 aftermarket products, for five or six foreign models, and from 13 U.S. distributors. Pricing didn't refer to a single figure: It included incentives, promotions, and trade discounts.

We're always skeptical of the value from massive amounts of data, and we doubt that all those data points will be useful. More probing revealed that the client was planning to use all this data for a survey to develop market potential for highest-profit products and to understand distributors' pricing structure. As the purpose became clear, we suggested an investigation that would produce more insightful and meaningful results. Some of our suggestions included discussing the distributors' discount policy and their criteria for offering discounts, understanding how pricing varies depending on brand or product category, determining pricing variations for factory-certified versus other brands, asking about bundling and minimum quantities, and identifying types of distributors that would receive these considerations. And yes, and inquiring about highest-profit items.

- Our repeated pumping for specifics resulted in an investigation that produced the comprehension our client needed, even though executives hadn't originally known how to frame the request. Yes, we could have gathered thousands of data points they'd ask for and given them lots of data, but this would have netted little intelligence. This is the point of knowing the difference between data and intelligence and of spending the time to work with the client to develop a better approach and better results.
- Expect your CI professional to guide the process so you maximize resources and minimize costs (time or money).

Presentation

It may seem out of place to discuss this in the earliest stages, but the final presentation should actually be framed *before* the research begins so that you can determine how much time the entire engagement will require. Further, knowing this in advance will help structure and clarify the final product.

Every company, department, and individual has a preferred style for reviewing the results. The closer the style is to what is comfortable or desirable for the decision makers, the greater the likelihood that the presentation will be read and the greater the impact of all the research. Do they prefer PowerPoint or a written report, or both? Do they prefer lots of graphics, tables, and charts, or more explanatory text, or are they okay with leaving it up to the CI practitioner? Do they want an executive summary and recommendations? Determine whether they prefer an executive summary that is one page or five pages. Some people expect a summary to be one page *only*, and if it's longer, they won't read it.

Intelligence is information that has been analyzed for deep understanding, insight, and implication. Determine whether the recipient has a bias for formal analytical techniques (SWOT or Five Forces), which should be factored into the scope. For analytic techniques written in understandable terms, we recommend *Analysis Without Paralysis: 10 Tools to Make Better Strategic Decisions*, by Babette E. Bensoussan and Craig S. Fleisher.

Finally, while the findings are the goal of the investigation, we believe it's desirable for our clients to know as much as we have learned, within reason and without providing unnecessary details. Our approach is to include in the findings as much as possible of all the relevant information that we've gathered. We want them to have a visceral sense of the findings, not just a report, and this is conveyed by providing as much as possible of useful findings or background information. In addition to the findings, this may include lists of contacts (especially those who have expressed interest in the unnamed product or company), details on conversations, quotes from contacts (so they can "hear" what was said), reports and articles that contacts provided, product details, and so on. This can be included in an addendum or provided in a secondary report to keep the main report shorter.

Planning the Project

To get where you're going, you gotta have a plan, so be prepared to spend a disproportionate amount of time planning the project. A good plan rewards all participants (researchers and recipients) with the best results; saves time and money (by not having to redo all or part of the project); and, most important, incorporates better decisions that result in significant competitive advantage. Some of this may be done prior to writing the proposal and some will occur once the work has been started.

Once the decision to proceed has been made, you may well be encouraged, pushed, and goaded into getting the project started—immediately. This is hardly the most desirable approach. You need time, perhaps a considerable amount, to clearly understand what your customer (the person requesting the information) wants and for the customer to understand what CI can reasonably deliver.

Engaging in multiple conversations does not preclude getting started quickly or getting a fast turnaround. Since the initial request and agreed-upon scope will vary significantly, the CI practitioner should guide the discussions to focus on the scope and the other elements mentioned earlier and also to bring to the table other aspects the requestor may not have considered.

For example, we often hear that there aren't other competitors in a particular field, or that the competitors don't offer what the market wants, or that a specific new feature is just what potential customers are looking for. I am hard-pressed to remember the last time the client's such assessment was accurate.

This is a red flag that the company needs an objective analysis of the marketplace, including assessment of the competitors and their reputations. It's time for a reality check. Decision makers too often believe in their company's uniqueness or see an opportunity that may not exist because they are thinking about it from a very narrow scope.

Other considerations may include an understanding of accepted distribution channels, comparing them to the company's capabilities to match what's necessary in *this* industry. How open are customers (especially B2B) to a new vendor? Are select regions of the country saturated? Are there regional variations? If so, how will the company deal with that? What are the gaps in or complaints about current vendors? What are the strengths of the current suppliers? It's the job of the researcher to raise questions and present additional issues.

Remember, the goal is to get useful results, *regardless* of the initial questions. And your responsibility as lead for the CI project is to guide the inquirer regarding what can be done and the best way to do it. The plan should include the overall project scope, organization, and resources, along with a detailed blueprint of the steps required for successful execution. Implicit here are ideas about the basic format of the research: How are we going about this? The basics must include methodology and sources and a determination regarding whether we are seeking secondary information, humint, or both. You also must establish, up front, all ethical guidelines, if this might be an issue, such as requests for competitor customer lists or pricing.

Prepare a Statement of Work or a Contract

Regardless of the size of project, and regardless of whether it's performed by in-house staff or by an external CI professional, *always* commit the plan to writing. This can be a proposal, contract, or statement of work, drafted on one or multiple pages. Most important, it will refine, for both parties, the client's request. This is the time for the client to clarify, expand, or eliminate segments of the proposal.

The proposal is a guide for the client to prioritize the issues of greatest interest or importance, thereby enabling you to decide how to apportion time to get the desired results. It will also serve as a guide if the budget needs to be reduced, as the less important areas can be eliminated. It will prevent or reduce any misunderstanding of the purpose, scope, and specifics of the research. Once agreement is reached on all aspects of the engagement, the document should be signed and dated to authorize commencement of the project.

The contract should include budget and timing. Some companies set up their CI departments as a cost center so that the staff is not bothered with constant, unimportant requests. The budget should reflect the scope, difficultly, time frame, and presentation and should not require any adjustments unless the scope changes significantly. We prefer a budget that is as transparent as possible; our proposals include all expenses, excluding travel, and do not vary from the agreed-upon fees.

The time frame for completion is a combination of (1) realistic time to complete the research and presentation and (2) consideration for client deadlines, such as board meetings. A time frame that does not match the stated scope should generate new discussions about the scope to fit a deadline. This is where the previous discussions regarding priorities will be particularly useful. The scope for an assignment to be completed in two days will be very different from one with a time frame of a week or a month. An option for a too-short deadline is to conduct the investigation in stages, immediately providing as much as possible of the most important information, followed by additional information that will be delivered after the deadline.

Do not agree to a time frame that is shorter than can be reasonably accomplished, or the results will be disappointing, and you will be blamed or unfairly criticized. Be forceful about what you can do in a truncated time frame: that you'll likely only be able to dig deep enough to tell clients what they already know. Dispensing already-known surface information is the quickest way to annoy clients and cause them to believe that the research is a waste of time. Worse, with a short time period, you probably won't uncover what's emerging, different, or no longer true, nor will you unearth what we consider some of the most useful information—nuances and unexpected issues that may already be in play but not generally known.

With the plan, the scope, and the priorities defined, you can now start collecting the information—almost. We strongly recommend starting with a kickoff meeting that includes all involved parties.

Kickoff and Updates

This is pivotal to getting the research started from the best jumping-off point. All parties from both sides, both management and CI investigators, must be present. The researchers hear directly from the clients, not from a written statement or from a member of the team, and they can ask the necessary clarifying questions. The kickoff will not be the same discussion as previous communication regarding the project. It's not unusual for clients to make some changes, as they have had time to think about previous conversations. They get excited about what can be accomplished and think about what else would be valuable. As a result, they may ask for even more. This is the time to refer to the purpose, priorities, and budget.

The goal here is for all parties to have agreement and trust in the written outline and expectations. Be prepared to discuss each item in the proposal, as well as to hear new thoughts from the client, which may be addressed after the kickoff. A new statement of work may be necessary.

Determine the frequency and type of updates. Do your clients want a brief update weekly or biweekly? By phone or e-mail? The updates are the appropriate time to discuss initial findings, as well as for each side to ask questions of the other, for clarification and to determine other areas of inquiry. Too many updates or written reports of more than a few pages will prolong the research, as the recipients will often ask for more. This is good news; it means they are enthusiastic about the findings. But it's not practical, so researchers must manage the feedback, by referring back to the purpose and scope.

The quality and quantity of the questions will be a major factor in the process toward good end results. Where possible, continuing the process of questioning throughout the project will refine and reposition the investigation, as necessary.

Definitions

Definitions and concepts change. Review industry jargon and probe for the meaning of terms with your clients, even if the terminology seems obvious. We ask clients for synonyms and alternatives for the terms they're using. This helps with the research and also in speaking with those in the industry who are likely to use a variety of terms. Occasionally, we find that our clients are using terms internally and in conversations with us that are not used by those in the industry. They don't think about this jargon or that it's used only within their company, so it's important to clarify a variety of terms. Here are some examples:

- The term *black-collar workers* once referred to those who worked in the mines or oil fields. Today, it more often signifies creative types (artists, graphic designers, video producers), who mostly wear black attire.
- The 2000 U.S. census determined that there were 28 million foreign-born residents. Of these, two-thirds identified themselves as white, compared to one-half in 1990. According to the census analysis, this statistic has been driven by Latinos, half of whom ticked off the "white" box in the 2000 census.
- The term *family* once meant a father, a mother, and their children. Now it refers to any unit that chooses to identify itself as a family—married or not, with or without children, related or not.
- *Tweaking* usually refers to minor editing or small improvements. But it also refers to methamphetamine use or obsessive-compulsive behavior.
- The definition of *rich* has changed dramatically, due in part to the rapidly increasing and then decreasing prices of homes and stock market losses and gains. Not too long ago, anyone with an annual income of $1 million was considered rich. Today, rich is also defined by those who choose not to work—who have the means, time, or attitude for different options.
- The concept of *cooking* has changed from preparing food from scratch, to assembling a variety of prepared foods, to adding an egg or meat to a packaged product, to heating something in the oven.
- Furniture was often described as "traditional" or "contemporary." A new category, "new traditional" is being used to describe a "fresher, more contemporary" version, blending classic and traditional styles, that doesn't look like grandma's furniture.

- Is a sports utility vehicle (SUV) a passenger car or a souped-up pickup truck?
- Remember when soap was soap? Now it requires adjectives to reflect today's numerous permutations in a changing marketplace: bar soap, body wash, liquid hand soap.

Ask: What Do You Know?

Find out whether the type of research you will be doing has been conducted previously, and, if so, use that report as a guide to determine what works best for your clients. Was it an off-the-shelf report, or customized? What was useful? When was it completed? Are they looking to update or start anew? If it wasn't useful, why not? Based on previous experience, get specifics on what they didn't get, what worked for them and what didn't, and what the expectations are for this assignment. In short, determine what information the client already has so that you don't replicate those results.

How Do You Know When You Have *Enough* Information?

When is enough enough? There are a number of factors at play in deciding whether a project has enough information and when to stop. Obviously, the time frame for completion is one factor in the decision to stop looking for information, and purpose is the other. Part of the decision in stopping the search depends on the importance of the decision. You need far less information when you're meeting with a prospect than when you're planning the company's strategy.

If the goal of content or time has been successfully reached, that is the point at which to stop. The goal should never be to reach perfection; that is unrealistic. Instead, the information must, at the very least, be sufficient for you to make a decent decision. You don't want to become bogged down in the search and not get to the decision point in a timely manner. One way to approach this question is to know whether the time frame is open or must be finished by a set date (for a trade show, a board of directors meeting, etc.). A set date limits the final delivery date. In that case, work backward to determine when the research ends and the writing begins.

Sometimes, it's as simple as when you've used up your budget of time or money. You've gathered what you could; now it's time to analyze, assess, and present. If you haven't learned some significant new information or updated old, then you probably haven't done enough. Conversely, if you're uncovering more and more of the same, then you've likely obtained most of what is reasonable or you may need to expand your search to a different, broader array of sources.

Finally, this is mostly an issue of judgment and experience. If you've focused your search on ferreting out the most valuable information and have not been distracted by data or nice-to-know information, then you will have a sense of when you've reached real insight into the issues you're investigating and can move on to analysis and decision. You can always revisit a specific aspect that needs verification or more detail.

How much of the information is important versus simply nice to know? You have enough when much of the information is important, or has the possibility to be important, or when you have consensus (i.e., similarity of reasonable, thoughtful information from numerous respected sources), and when the information can be tied to a better decision.

Is there such a thing as too much information? Is it possible to have a quantity of information that may confuse a decision? The obvious answer is yes, most likely when you are uncovering more specifics than necessary or when the quantity of data outweighs the ability to analyze it and directly respond to the purpose.

In Arthur Conan Doyle's first novel, *A Study in Scarlet*, protagonist Sherlock Holmes stated that "A fool takes in all . . . he comes across, so that the knowledge which might be useful to him gets crowded out. . . . The skillful workman will have nothing but the tools which may help him. . . . It is of the highest importance, therefore, not to have useless facts elbowing out the useful ones." In other words, the person conducting the CI must be skilled enough to separate the proverbial wheat from the chaff.

Competitive Intelligence Components

A clear objective understanding of the market for your business is a good starting point. Here are some of the elements that can be used as a guide to include or not.

Market Entry Investigation

These goals could also be used when requesting an objective view of your current industry to ascertain what has changed or in preparation for a strategy review. The overall goals are to:

1. Detail the industry as it exists today
2. Define where the industry is headed
3. Indicate the dynamics affecting this area (especially those beyond direct competitors and the industry)
4. Explore opportunities as well as countervailing and potential threats
5. Uncover market shifts and discontinuities that may impact business
6. Raise questions or issues to be monitored
7. Create a baseline for future strategy

The following is a menu of areas for possible inclusion, based on appropriateness for the particular investigation. This list applies to consumer, industrial, commercial, institutional, or nonprofit entities, and it applies to whether the product or service is sold business-to-consumer (B2C) or business-to-business (B2B).

1. Market/industry assessment
   - Definition: Identify exactly what the product or service is (e.g., beverage versus soda, cola versus citrus, regular versus diet versus caffeine-free, 8-ounce versus liter)
   - Size/sales/revenues, in dollars and/or units (U.S. versus regional versus state versus global); past, current, and growth trends or forecast
   - Market drivers
   - Keys to success
   - Barriers to entry
   - Discontinuities (changes in use, societal shifts)
2. Major competitors
   - Sales/revenues, as previously described
   - Who's gaining or losing and why?
   - Market ranking (first, second, third; or a range, such as "considered to be one of the top five")

- Emerging competitors (and why, they fill, niche, target customer, value proposition)
- Substitute or alternative competitors
- Joint ventures, alliances, consolidations
- SWOT analysis
- Strategy, as related to targeted customers or industries
- Competitors views of the other competitors, as well as how they view/position themselves
- Organization structure or chart

3. Products or services
   - Segmented by industry or competitors
   - Best-selling products
   - Fastest-growing or -shrinking products
   - Patterns and discontinuities
   - Emerging or anticipated innovations
   - Alternative uses

4. Target customers (primary, secondary, under consideration to add or delete)

5. Distribution channels

6. Pricing

7. Packaging

8. Advertising

9. Other
   - Opportunities, problems, and potential threats
   - External factors affecting the industry (economic, social, demographic technology)
   - Additional information that appears relevant even though not specifically identified

These *other* issues will identify erroneous assumptions that exist in every industry and also raise issues not previously considered. One of the most prevalent assumptions is that pricing is the reason why companies aren't doing as well as they or stakeholders expect. The reality, even for commodity products, is that price usually ranks fourth or fifth as a competitive advantage. Competitive intelligence uncovers the truth, which stems from issues relating to quality, reliability, consistency, delivery, customer service, innovation, ease of doing business with a company, availability, and other factors.

Success and Getting Buy-In

The success of a competitive intelligence investigation depends in large measure on whether the user accepts and uses the intelligence. Part of getting buy-in is to have those who will be involved in the execution participate in the kickoff and understand the process, to believe that the findings are accurate and credible.

We recommend that your clients test the findings by conducting conversations with customers or distributors or companies that are indirectly related to your industry, to get feedback and a sense of their assessment. This does not require replicating the CI to come to the same conclusion. These conversations shouldn't be defensive but, rather, casual discussions for the purpose of educating themselves on changes and new information. In this way, they can determine whether the results are sustained by their separate inquiry.

Success is also based on who is receiving the findings and how high up the company ladder that person is. Results delivered lower down the chain are often diluted as they move to the upper strata, and specific elements are eliminated or whitewashed. Unconventional thinking and surprising or less-than-desirable news does not travel upstream (to the CEO) very often or very well. It gets filtered or deleted, especially if the messenger is discouraged from presenting information that is contrary to what the company (or executive) believes or wants to hear.

There is fear of reporting bad news, and CI can often be viewed as "bad news" in the sense that it almost certainly challenges some of the company's beliefs. Be aware that bad news, or information the company doesn't want to hear, looms larger than confirming information. Getting buy-in, or at least a fair hearing, will be enhanced when you explain that:

1. CI is the opposite of bad news. It's the best information you can have, whether or not it matches the company line, because it represents reality and, therefore, offers opportunities.
2. Good CI is unbiased and does not shift the findings or enhance information to make it more acceptable to the company or to support company beliefs.

Some elements of the findings will probably not support the company's view of itself. When we're conducting direct contact conversations, we capture casual comments that are made regarding the reputation of competitors. It's very common for a firm to state that it is the technology leader, or has the best customer service, or is the most innovative. But, this internal viewpoint is rarely supported by competitors or major customers. For the open-minded executive, it opens the door to a reality check.

The Competitive Intelligence Process

The process starts and ends with data (see Figure 10.1).

This last step—more data—is easy to ignore. After all, you've just completed the research, why do you/would you need more data? Warren Buffett's letter to Berkshire Hathaway shareholders in the economic downturn in 2009 told them that he made mistakes he regrets. "I made some errors of omission, sucking my thumb when new facts came in that should have caused me to reexamine my thinking and promptly take action."

Competitive intelligence often stops at the results/presentation stage. But, new data may be just as important as the initial findings. It's not necessary to do the research again, but you must have your antenna out, day and night, actively looking for and incorporating new data. It

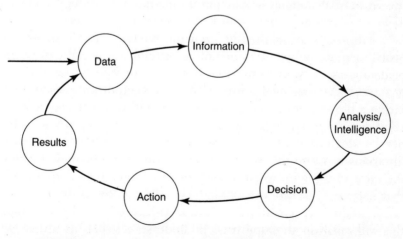

FIGURE 10.1 The CI Process: From Data to Results

may not be important, but you won't know that until you become aware of it and consider its import to your decision.

From the time that the findings (analyzed intelligence) have been presented, someone should be the point person for finding or being the recipient of new relevant information that will develop. Depending on the importance of the new input, it should be part of the process going forward from the decision stage. At any point, this new information may be relevant and must be made known to the decision makers, as it may change the decision or strategy. Decisions don't automatically lead to action. That requires a strategy and tactical plan for executing it.

Most Desirable CI Qualities, In-House or Outsourced

For many, when thinking about the best people to do competitive intelligence, librarians may come to mind, especially those with a master's degree in library science. After all, they have been trained and have expertise in information sources and how to find them. However, I disagree—strongly. In my experience, the best characteristics for a CI professional are different from those for librarians.

The best hire for competitive intelligence is an investigative journalist. If that is not possible, my second choice is a person who understands how business works, who knows what's important to business, and who sees how your specific company fits into the entire spectrum of challenges, opportunities, marketing, strategy, and so on. They can hire the people who know the specific sources.

Librarians are skilled at knowing sources of information and probably quite skilled in doing online searching, especially in a variety of databases. The missing piece is that their focus is on resources, not necessarily business sources. The more important reason for not hiring a librarian to do competitive intelligence is that they may have relatively little experience in business and what's important to business. A small caveat here: There is a shift in the skills that corporate librarians bring to the executive suite, as they increasingly recognize the value in using information to create intelligence and are providing that service. The librarian's view is changing to focus less on the information part and more on the intelligence part. Understanding this will result in an employee who understands that his or her job is not finding information; it's developing intelligence.

Outspoken CI voice Ben Gilad stated it all too well. "We are not information professionals . . . . We are not information service providers. We are not in the field of information at all! We do *use* information." In other words, information is our means to the end, to understanding, to analysis and insight and implications, and, finally, to good decisions for the company. Similarly, the doctor's skill and experience are more important than their tools.

Suffice it to say that the less experienced and sophisticated CI professionals are as they relate to the workings of business, the less useful will be their results. This means that you should not expect college students to produce competitive intelligence. They may be good at surfing the Web, but that is not the source of good business information, as detailed in Chapter 9. I have repeatedly heard from colleagues and clients that when they've hired students, even graduate students, they got a nice report but didn't learn anything new. Good competitive intelligence should include a fair amount of new and surprising information and intelligence.

Best Characteristics of a CI Practitioner

The ideal or preferred background for a competitive intelligence professional is a combination of several years' business experience *and* the characteristics of an investigative journalist:

1. Has a solid understanding of business, how it works, and what's important
   - Has business acumen; understands the industry as well as the company's big picture and strategic objectives
   - Possesses a macro-view of business and a specific view of the company's industry, along with an understanding that business is more important than the specific industry
2. Has plenty of intellectual curiosity, coupled with a need to know and understand
3. Possesses perseverance; doesn't easily give up, as it's not uncommon to run up against brick walls in trying to source information or contacts
4. Recognizes the potential value of anomalies; nonlinear thinker
5. Persistent and tenacious in probing a wide variety of sources; ability to consider nontraditional sources and approaches

6. Is insightful
   - Notices faint indications of opportunities to be monitored
   - Sees patterns and can connect the dots
   - Recognizes information that is buried or hidden or not fully explained but that may be useful
   - Is more concerned with meaning and implications than facts or statistics
7. Is comfortable with uncertainty and ambiguity and not necessarily certain that the findings are final; recognizes that some findings may be areas to monitor for usefulness and validity and that other findings are questionable (for source or validity)
8. Possesses good communication skills
   - Asks numerous questions of the requestor, more than expected, yet sufficient, so that time is well spent on the specifics of the request and not on a larger, unsought investigation
   - Has the ability to present the findings in the way best suited to the requestor, which may change
   - Is open to using a wide variety of deliverables, depending on the individual making the request, the purpose of the request, and the one that best reflects the findings
9. Is sufficiently skilled to discern important versus unimportant information
   - Has the ability to filter information quickly and to prioritize, to determine what's directly important and what might be worth monitoring
   - Can determine which part of the request is most important and which information is most useful
   - Understands that it's necessary to continually reevaluate priorities
10. Is organized
11. Is creative
12. Displays independent thinking and has a thick skin; must be strong enough to deliver news the company does *not* want to hear and have the personal skills to make the case for less than thrilling information; includes having a strong enough constitution to get the requestors to recognize new, different, and/or better information; should be prepared to present findings that don't match

clients' previous beliefs, old facts, and assumptions and to move them from old beliefs to new realities

13. Has the ability to present information in several ways, especially to persuade clients to see findings they are resisting

14. Is ethical

15. Can judge how long it will take to complete assignment and stay on course

16. Good interviewing skills to continually and delicately probe exactly what clients want and to offer other options, as appropriate, for that specific inquiry

17. Does not necessarily need to be a good searcher (electronic or otherwise), but knows what good information is, where it's likely to be found, and can direct someone who is a superb searcher

18. Ability to work within the organization, to build relationships that lead upward, both externally and internally (i.e., knowing what to share with others, what information would be useful to a wider range of staff)

One of the first things that an internal CI practitioner should do upon taking on this responsibility is to conduct an internal audit. This includes assessing both what information would be useful to decision makers and influencers and what information your company has and uses. Expect that most executives will not understand competitive intelligence and the scope of what can be accomplished.

Next, analyze the extent to which intelligence is valued and used. Start becoming visible to senior decision makers in your company and to influential people outside it. This can be accomplished by asking to sit in on select meetings, volunteering for in-house task forces, giving presentations within the company to educate various departments about what you can do *for* them. Ask key players to tell you what's on their mind. What will help them in making decisions? What would they love to know but are unaware that you can get?

Help the decision makers understand why you're one of their most valuable resources. Ask questions and present results so that they are seen as being central to the well-being of the company. Ask questions where the answers aren't obvious, questions that puzzle people and get them to think, "What should we do?" "Where should we be headed?" "Who should we be monitoring?" "What events might undermine us?" It's a great way to communicate trust and to understand what is on the minds of the people who matter in the company.

After the intelligence has been incorporated into the company's going-forward strategy, the same information must be circulated and communicated throughout the organization so that everyone works from the same playbook. Without this, some in the organization might revert to the old ways and to past mistakes. This can be an abbreviated document, i.e., one page with bullets.

If you're hiring an external CI firm, make certain it assigns its best people based on their skills in that subject area, as well as their ability to present the findings (written and verbal). They don't need to be subject matter experts (SMEs), but previous assignments in the general industry category may be useful.

Bottom line: Only an experienced businessperson can bring value to the firm. They possess an understanding of what's most useful to decisions and can convert the company to one that values competitive intelligence as much as marketing, sales, communications, and other areas.

Most Desirable Qualities for CI Content

We've discussed the issues to be addressed in a typical example of a competitive intelligence report, and we've talked about the characteristics of the person performing the CI function. But what of the end results? What are the most desirable qualities for CI content? The value of competitive intelligence is maximized when it leads to the best decisions. Decisions are based on a variety of inputs, including the right information.

The degree to which the following qualities are desirable will be dependent on the type and importance of the decision. However, it's hard to argue that accuracy or reliability or relevance is not important. Understanding the meaning of data and information helps executives interpret and use it properly. The intelligence has to be presented so that the decision maker appreciates its significance and so that the underlying information has been elevated to the level of intelligence. The information and intelligence must answer the question and be:

1. Accurate (i.e., from a trusted source)
2. Reliable (i.e., verified from a minimum of two good sources)
3. Relevant (i.e., relates to issue at hand)

4. Comprehensive/sufficient
   - Provides as much detail as necessary
   - Includes appropriate scope (global, local, wholesale, demographic cohort, units, profits, history, trends, etc.)
5. Timely/current
   - Usually not more than two years old
   - May be older if it relates to history of company, annual reports, executive profile, and so on
6. Broad-based (i.e., from a wide spectrum of diverse sources within and external to industry)
   - Trade associations
   - Trade publications
   - Special issues or reports
   - General business publications that are highly regarded (*Forbes, The Economist, Wall Street Journal, Marketing News, Across the Board*, etc.)
   - Experts
7. Cost-appropriate (i.e., related to purpose and importance, such as superficial versus in-depth, quick versus deep)

Clearly, good competitive intelligence requires far more than information. Spending the time to determine the purpose and scope, to understand exactly what the recipient expects and needs, to plan the investigation, to engage the right crew to do it, and, finally, to present the results in a useful manner is as important as the content. If the decision maker doesn't read it, or doesn't understand the crucial segments, or fails to take action (unless the action is to do nothing), then the value has not been realized. A great story with a lousy script, a lousy director, and poor actors will produce a film that no one wants to see.

The tools are all available. It's your job to put together the right team, and, with the proper guidance, you will have the basis for a winning decision.

11

Demystifying Competitive Intelligence, One Myth at a Time

Noted professor and lecturer Joseph John Campbell, best known for his work in the field of comparative mythology, believed that myths are an important element in human existence. He claimed that they've existed in nearly every culture that has ever roamed the world. Although Campbell focused on the spiritual and religious aspects of mythology, his work brings attention to the fact that we can also find myths in our everyday lives. They are essentially an organized collection of stories by which we explain what we *believe* to be true.

Reviewing stories in the proper light allows us to see that *every* business and every industry has its own mythology that it has consciously or unconsciously created. We all have our corporate heroes, such as Jack Welch of GE, Bill Gates of Microsoft, and Steve Jobs of Apple, whose mythic journeys we use to romanticize their various successes. Similar myths have grown up around businesses and products such as Coca Cola, a company that is, among other things, credited with creating the modern image of Santa Claus. We generally accept these cultural and business myths, to the extent that they tell stories repeated so often that they actually pass for truth, and thus become a shorthand narrative for what is accepted as truth. But are they true?

Not surprisingly, competitive intelligence has its own set of myths. This chapter addresses and challenges the most common ones:

1. Competitive intelligence is spying.
2. Everyone has access to competitive intelligence, so there is no advantage to doing it.
3. The most valuable information is already known within my company.
4. Our executives are very knowledgeable about our industry.
5. Information is free.
6. Intelligence costs too much.
7. There's no information about private companies.
8. Google is a great source for CI.
9. Every decision should include competitive intelligence.
10. CI software provides intelligence.
11. Data, information, and intelligence are the same.

12. Competitive intelligence is a waste of time.
13. Competitive intelligence is only for business-to-consumer (B2C) industries.

Myth #1: CI Is Spying

The media often drives our understanding or misunderstanding of competitive intelligence. Headlines certainly drive that idea, screaming: "The Corporate Spy Trade Is Booming," "Spying: Business as Usual," "The Case of the Corporate Spy," and "Corporate Spy Wars." They are provocative titles used to engage the reader, but they do not reflect reality.

First, "spying" implies doing something *illegal*. While spying in the corporate world *does* take place, it is rare, because companies don't want to find themselves in court. When Pepsi was offered the secret Coke formula, the company immediately alerted the authorities, and Coca-Cola took appropriate action against the secretary who was alleged to have made the offer. When a major employee problem arose between GM and Volkswagen, the matter also ended up in court. This was an area into which neither company wanted to venture; and their decisions to avoid it proved right.

The premier CI association, Society for Competitive Intelligence (SCIP), as well as those who speak or write about CI, strongly disavow any type of spying or unethical activities and in no way, implicitly or explicitly, endorse this thinking or behavior. (See Chapter 13 for more details about these regulations and the role of the SCIP.)

Spying may appeal to those who are less inclined to do the work that competitive intelligence actually requires. CI entails a considerable amount of digging and thinking, which is not as glamorous as the Hollywood version of spying.

Americans generally believe in fair competition, and while we recognize that there are those who do not play fair, most people support the notion of obtaining information in a principled manner. Legitimate CI departments and firms limit their searches to publicly available information and ethical conversations.

Are there practitioners who dumpster-dive or hack into company private networks or perform illegal searches? Absolutely. But just as one fraudulent "cure" does not mean that all medicine is quackery, a handful of abuses of the ethical practices do not mean that all competitive intelligence professionals engage in "spying." As if to prove this point, the number of articles about CI that use the word *spy* in the title has significantly declined. It still appears, but considerably less so than 10 years ago. Despite the myth, legitimate CI is not spying and never has been.

Myth #2: Everyone Has Access to CI, So There Is No Advantage to Doing It

Having *access* to CI is *not* the same as actually *conducting* or using CI. After all, while virtually everyone knows the benefits of a healthy diet and exercise, that is not the same as actually engaging in them. In fact, the reality is just the opposite.

Competitive intelligence actually "un-levels" *the playing field*. This is fabulous news! While every company has the ability to get the same information, most don't bother to access it. Therefore, to the extent that a company actually invests the time and effort into checking assumptions, confirming what it knows, and finding what it doesn't know, it gains a significant advantage by actually doing CI—even limited CI.

Further, many companies that actively seek information rarely move from gathering it to actual intelligence. That is, when they do collect this kind of material, it's more likely to be used as data rather than insights; and it's more likely to focus on competitors, which tells them very little about the current needs of the marketplace and customers. Although the same vast quantity of information may be available to anyone who seeks it, not everyone—in fact, very *few* people—can *translate* the results into relevant findings for their particular product or service.

The literature is replete with stories about a number of persons who witnessed the *same event, yet report it differently*. In much the same way, the analyst's assessment brings a different level of understanding than a given executive's might. For example, when I forward articles to clients, they frequently respond that although they've already read that very article, what I highlight and offer commentary on provides a level understanding that they did not originally recognize. My insight, a result of my experience and macro-view and prior knowledge about the topic, has allowed them to see the same topic in an entirely new light.

You can never assume, even when others have the same information you do, that they can (or will) analyze and interpret it in the same way, uncover as much knowledge as you have, or make good decisions based on that knowledge. The opportunity to do more with the same information always rests in your hands.

Small businesses may not think that they are on a level playing field with larger businesses, yet there is no evidence that big businesses are more insightful or know how to turn that information into more useful intelligence. They are often more likely to spend considerable dollars gathering information, but that is not intelligence.

Myth #3: The Most Valuable Information Is Already Known within My Company

This cliché sounds so very much like Robert Fulghum's popular little book, *All I Really Need to Know I Learned in Kindergarten*. It's almost become a mantra within the CI community that 90 percent of what is known or what you need to know already resides within your company. Accordingly, there is a bias for internally generated information.

While there is undoubtedly valuable knowledge that exists within your company, finding the person who has it or mining that data for the desired bits and pieces of the puzzle can be an extremely difficult and haphazard undertaking. And if you do manage to unearth the information within the company, crossing the hurdle of *believing* that information still remains. In general, companies tend to prefer their own insular perspective to outside points of view and will almost always defend *their* knowledge. This attitude fosters a false sense of confidence that impacts crucial decisions, especially those that aren't built on a CI foundation.

Yet if established companies are so knowledgeable about their own industry and customers, can we explain why and how small, new, upstart companies can enter the market, gain customer acceptance, and generate great revenues? How did the Apple iPod penetrate and dominate a market owned by the Sony Walkman (and its competitors)? How did Toyota enter and take over a market owned by GM and Ford? How did Nokia, a manufacturer of *toilet paper*, gain control over the cutthroat world of global telecommunications in as little as 30 years?

These companies came into their markets and became successful because they recognized that the existing businesses did not realize, understand, or provide what customers wanted. This situation occurs repeatedly in every industry. New companies manage to fill a gap that current companies simply don't see. As author George Orwell aptly put it, "To see what is in front of one's nose is a constant struggle."

Believing that 90 percent of necessary information is already within one's company is simplistic, and it does a great disservice by precluding any efforts to seek an external perspective. It's very difficult to recognize change, to see what's new and different. The outside or unknown cannot be seen if you rely solely on looking inward.

Myth #4: Our Executives Are Very Knowledgeable about Our Industry

Executives are quite confident about their knowledge of their own industry. Understandably so. Some may even be arrogant about what they know, but most are, at the very least, quite sure of themselves. After all, they have either been in the industry a long time or are quick studies who have been able to access many resources about their business.

They use trade publications, associations, and newsletters; or they simply schmooze with experts and colleagues from competitive companies. Therefore, it's easy for management to believe they know or have access to much information, if not all of it, about their industry. As a result, they see little if any need to spend money just to confirm what they already know.

But do they really know as much as they *think* they know? As we can attest from our own work in CI, virtually 99 percent of our clients have confirmed that they learned *some* critical information about their industry that they were unaware of prior to reading the results of our CI investigation. The other 1 percent emphatically stated that the results were incorrect because they didn't conform to the supposed "knowledge" (read "executive beliefs") that these executives possessed prior to the research. In all instances of doubt, however, they were ultimately proved wrong.

The new knowledge we brought fell into one of two categories: (1) What they learned contradicted what they knew (which was outdated or never true); (2) it was a signal or indication of change of which they were unaware. Once we made a logical case for the transition from the past to the future, from familiar to new information, which our research indicated was coming, then their minds were more open to the new information.

While many executives do unquestionably know a lot about their industries, they cannot possibly know it all. It is simply not feasible to keep pace with the changes that are taking place in their industries at increasingly higher velocities.

Perhaps more importantly, they are less likely to seek out or know about relevant information from industries indirectly related to theirs, or to macro changes occurring in society or business in general. And as we have hammered repeatedly, the external factors may impact your business more than internal ones.

Furthermore, executives must acknowledge that their staff may not know about, or may not want to be messengers of, bad news. How likely is it that you get the information your staff doesn't want to tell you? It is always better to have a reality check to ensure that what you know still applies.

Myth #5: Information Is Free

The proliferation of information and resources over the past 20 years has convinced many that the information sought can be found at no cost. What, then, is free, and what does *free* truly mean? In the context of copying from a publication such as a library book or an online site, there is the notion of *fair use*, which allows some privilege of use in much the same way as cutting an article from a newspaper and copying it. In that regard, there is a lot of free information. But someone had to create it; someone owns it; someone had to organize it; and none of this was done for free.

There *is* a lot of free information that is embodied in thoughtful, critically acclaimed articles (e.g., *Harvard Business Review*) or studies that can serve as miniature CI investigations. However, even considering the available volume of information, there rarely appears to be the *specific* information that you are looking for. Google the words "garden tool," for example, and you are likely to retrieve close to 14 million hits. But try to find any market specifics about this category, and all I can say is good luck. Yes, there is a lot of information out there, yet you would be fortunate to find a small percentage that relates to your specific needs.

Libraries are widely recognized as good sources of free information. Although libraries contain a wealth of information, even the best business libraries contain just a limited percentage of publicly available business data. The amount of material *not* housed in libraries is, in fact, increasing exponentially. It can often be found in association offices, fringe publications, private newsletters, conference proceedings, and other venues, many of which require paid membership or a fee to access the data.

In the earlier days of the Internet, many reputable sources (including newspapers and trade publications) offered free access to their archives. But they lost revenue on two accounts: Offering free information reduced subscriptions, and it required staff to update and maintain it. When many of these free sources started charging a fee, even a modest one, their hits declined. Very few companies have made the transition successfully from free to fee as has the *Wall Street Journal*. But stay tuned: This is the model that more and more companies are seeking.

As is so often the case, you get what you pay for. While Google is a fabulous source of information, it is not so for business information, as discussed in Chapter 9. The major newspapers, trade publications, and specialized newsletters are rarely cited. These publications may offer free access on their sites, but they won't be found during a Google search. Additionally, a growing amount of information is now available electronically and exclusively from commercial databases such as LexisNexis, Factiva, and others. Note that these sources are fee-based and are not easy to use by those not educated in these systems.

Uncovering specific, current, reliable information requires training and skill. For instance, all of the information that you need to file your business taxes is available from the IRS. Yet, to ensure that there are no mistakes or problems, most businesses hire an experienced tax preparer. The same is true for business information that needs to be focused on a specific question or issue, then organized and properly analyzed: A professional investigator is a better option.

Myth #6: Intelligence Costs Too Much

Ah, that familiar plaint, "It costs too much." Everyone wants a bargain, and why not? The question, however, is not how *much* the intelligence costs, but rather, "How expensive is a blunder in the marketplace?" "What is the cost of getting it wrong?" "How much will it cost to redo it?"

Everything needed to run a business comes with a cost attached. From raw materials to real estate, from computers to coffeemakers, from personnel to paper clips—everything costs money. A more compelling question is, "What is the cost of *not* having the necessary intelligence for your decision?"

The same is true for information, the raw material of intelligence, strategy, and good decisions. Information is the foundation for your choices. A poor foundation will impact what's built on top of it. Sure, the building may not collapse; but is it worth taking that chance? Your business's success results from making good decisions, avoiding mistakes, and minimizing risk—and good intelligence is the key.

The cost (in time or money) of getting the right information has to be appropriate to the purpose to which it will be used. A decision that requires a significant outlay of resources, such as entering a new market, targeting a new customer base, or exploring an acquisition or merger, requires an in-depth investigation with commensurate costs. On the other hand, the background needed for an upcoming first meeting with a client in an unfamiliar industry would probably require only a minimal amount of information, sufficient to enable a basic understanding and allow one to ask appropriate questions. This will obviously have a lower cost.

The range of available information and/or the difficulty of obtaining it are often a mystery to those outside the competitive intelligence profession. It may come as a surprise to learn that competitive intelligence is the *least* expensive part of most business transactions. These include designing features for a product or service not valued by potential customers, creating and printing collateral materials, developing a marketing campaign for an off-target offering, or arranging numerous meetings with a potential M&A firm that is wrong for the company. It's far better to spend on the areas that support *objective* decisions than to base decisions on assumptions and internal beliefs.

When the question of cost arises, ask yourself "What is the cost of bad or incomplete intelligence, a missed opportunity, a bad decision, erroneous assumptions, incomplete data, or being unpleasantly surprised?" Of course, those who believe in myth number 5, that information is free, may have some level of sticker shock when they see that first proposal for professional research.

Sure, information costs. But so do mistakes—even more dearly. When properly used, information is an investment. What business executives need to take into account is not how much good research costs, but how much return it will bring.

Myth #7: There's No Information about Private Companies

It's frustrating when you need to find specific information about a company, but you just can't seem to locate it. And if the subject is a private company, many readily believe there's very little public information.

Actually, there is probably a lot more information available about companies, even those that are privately held, than you might suspect, and this is especially true in the Internet age. That said, the amount and type of information to be had varies widely by company and industry, and directly correlates to:

- The public face presented by the company (i.e., the degree to which it seeks coverage)
- The media interest in that company or industry
- Support from the industry (in how many periodicals are available on the topic, as well as subscriptions or advertising)

Two examples illustrate this point. One of our clients requested information about the production capacity of one of their privately held competitors—not an unusual request, of course, but one that might breach our ethics. However, we went directly to the town newspaper in which the company was located and asked for all the relevant articles it had published in the prior two years. Unbeknownst to our client and to us, the company had recently recovered from a devastating fire and was almost finished rebuilding. The company spokesperson h_____reporter complete details of its operations, including all the lines it was running, the new capacities that the rebuilding had provided, number of employees, plans for the future, and a lot more information that was of great interest to our client.

In another instance, our target company was headquartered in France. There was very little publicity available about it, not surprisingly, as the French are much more closed about their operations. However, the target company was a major account for its overseas bank, and the bank regularly highlighted its major customers in its newsletter. Fortunately for our client, the company's president sat down for a lengthy interview in which he expounded on the company's strategic vision and plans for the next five years, the very details we were seeking. All we had to do was translate, and, voilà, the information was all there.

Even the most private companies will find it very difficult to remain anonymous, despite their best efforts. This is not to say that it's *easy* to uncover the desired information; quite often it is not. And it tends to be even more challenging with small companies and divisions of larger firms. This is where the direct contact method (humint) of competitive intelligence is more useful.

As noted in Chapter 9, one of the best places to find material about private companies is their hometown newspaper. The headquarters or branch city usually is of interest to the local community and is therefore well covered by the local press. These publications appear to be particularly concerned with rumors and how information circling these regional firms may affect the local population. Often, these newspapers provide more detail (more column inches), more data, and more commentary than the primary industry journals. These newspapers can be a gold mine since the company's guard is often down in interviews conducted by "small-town" newspapers because "nobody reads them."

And, as I pointed out in Chapter 9, press coverage of Toyota by the Los Angeles Times, headquartered in Torrance, California, is not as in-depth as is coverage by Torrance's local paper, the *Daily Breeze*, which provides far more coverage, in column inches and frequency. Both are good sources for companies (even private companies) as the focus is different.

Even usually guarded information has a way of sneaking out. In one instance, my company uncovered the financial details on a very successful private food company in an industry publication devoted to information technology. The background on financial and marketing details was included to put the information on technology systems into perspective. Another example involved a privately owned, highly successful, and rapidly growing chain of shoe stores in Texas, which exposed an extraordinary amount of financial, operational, and strategic information in an article devoted to the success of a local business.

Information on private companies tends to crop up in unexpected places. Some privately owned U.S. companies provide SEC-type financial information, even though they're not required to do so. All companies in some countries (such as the United Kingdom) are required to file financial documents that may include information on your area of interest. And the Internet can be our best friend when we are searching for information. Once published, this information never disappears. There are sites where people, including employees, will put details about a company; a growing number of blogs exist solely for that purpose. Of course, information from sources other than the most reliable ones must always be verified.

But make no mistake about it, information about private companies is out there, and it is more likely to be found today than in the past. All you have to do is look, really look—deep—and in unexpected places. The amount of time and effort is proportionate to the importance of finding the information.

Myth #8: Google Is a Great Source for CI

"Everything you need to know about business information is available online, and you can (probably) find it on Google." "If it's not available on Google, it probably doesn't exist." We've heard both of these statements from many business people and even from some of our clients. From our experience, such claims made about Web resources often fail to recognize the significant limitations not only to *what* is available online, but also to *relevant* information.

While it's true that Google and the dozens of other major search engines available contain enormous amounts of information, these web sites generally offer very limited *business* information. They rarely include citations from the major newspapers (*New York Times, Wall Street Journal*), business magazines (*Fortune, The Economist, Business-Week*), trade publications (*Adhesives Age, Supermarket News, Automotive Weekly*), trade associations, or a whole host of other potential business resources discussed elsewhere in this book.

This is not meant to dismiss the value of Google and the competing search engines. They do have their place, and we almost always include them at the start of our own investigations. But many of the entries may not include dates, which are critical for evaluating how current the document is. And sources that are unknown or not mainstream should be regarded as nothing more than opinion, and not even expert opinion.

Google is fine, but it is not the be-all and end-all for business information. The greatest advantages that search engines impart are links to hidden web sites, information that you would not likely find without excessive searching. When we were looking for information on campus card programs, our search engine linked us to valuable details from a major university's department offering this program, which provided additional insights on the purchasing process not likely to be found elsewhere, and the document was public.

I have read far too many blog comments and articles on how to do CI which include statements such as: "I go straight to the company's web site and find almost everything I need there." This statement indicates a serious lack of understanding that most companies' web sites are designed to publicly present the company's biased and incomplete viewpoint. Any company whose competitive intelligence investigation goes beyond searching Google or a company's web site will be far more complete and will provide input for better decisions. Bottom line: Search engines are valuable, but they must be weighed against their limitations.

Myth #9: Every Decision Should Include CI

Good, solid intelligence undoubtedly improves decisions. While we zealously believe in the value of CI, let's be real. Not *every decision* needs in-depth research and analysis. An ideal decision, of course, would include all possible information, all of it accurate, with every possible alternative considered. But is that possible or even necessary in all instances? Good, solid information is beneficial in most decisions, but conducting CI for every situation is an expectation that is neither practical nor realistic. There are circumstances in which a decision must be made immediately; in such an instance, that decision maker will have to rely on his or her experience, knowledge, and judgment. Some decisions are not as critical as others and therefore require no imperative for doing CI.

There are also situations in which the underlying causes are quite basic and may not require CI. For instance, the state of Florida depends on a steadily growing influx of retired people from other states to replace its aging population. When the population began to decline, former governor Jeb Bush created a blue-ribbon committee to study the reasons why and to develop a plan to reverse the trend. The findings were based on a requirement of awareness of generational cohorts— data that the government collects. The oldest generation, the GI generation, born between 1905 and 1924, peaked at 60 million. They were followed by the Silent Generation, those born between 1925 and 1944, which peaked at half that number, 30 million. The replacement rate would necessitate attracting *double* the relocation rate of the Silent Generation just to stay even with the GI generation. But the next generation, the boomers (77 million), are even larger than the GI generation. Readily available data tells Florida which group to target; ergo, no CI is necessary here.

There are occasions when having the necessary information and identifying all the possible alternatives are constrained by other limitations on a project. When decisions must be made by a certain date and time, the effort and time required to get the information may not be worth the benefits. So, while intelligence may offer some advantages when meeting with a potential customer, there may simply not be ample opportunity to do what is needed. In such cases, the information you have, or the surface information that you can get quickly, may well suffice.

One final thought on this myth: While we believe that companies would benefit from making intelligence a more regular component of their decision-making activities, we find it ironic that Americans are more likely to do research when buying a refrigerator, a car, or a TV than when making an important and costly strategic business decision. Any component of your life that requires an investment of money would benefit from some investment of time and research. After all, you will eventually learn it—but later. Better to have it *before* the decision is made.

Myth #10: CI Software Provides Intelligence

Software is very enticing for businesses; it's often seen as a way to save time, money, and staff. Most companies already collect large amounts of information in the course of everyday business, and there is a wide range of software to keep track of that information. Some use ordinary spreadsheets, while others use a collection of databases, many of which don't talk to one another. Still others use a combination of products, including some of the newer customer relationship management (CRM) applications and other knowledge management software. So, where does CI software fit into the CI mix?

These various CI tools and systems allow a company to access, gather, store, and organize business data. In fact, many companies rely on CI software to find every piece of information about their competitors. No wonder, then, that software tools have become sought-after and exciting additions to the quiver of arrows used by businesses in pursuit of success. These tools are viewed as superior to, and easier than using people as resources for needed information. But are they better? Are they sufficient? The myth says that they are, and some companies operate as if those software tools are all they need.

The reality, however, is that software cannot undertake critical thinking, cannot replace common sense and good, old-fashioned problem solving. In other words, intelligence is not software. Intelligence requires human thinking and analysis, the ability to understand meaning and implication, and appreciation for a situation's context. Software has not yet evolved to determine which information is most useful; *that* still requires the human mind.

This is not to denigrate the value of these software tools; do use them to do what they do best. Let software gather and organize information. Let it help narrow the breadth of information collected. But don't lose sight of its limitations. Software can only gather the information that is within its own scope and reach, which excludes information not available electronically. Hard as it is to accept, much business information is offline and software does not cover all sources. The information on which decisions must be made is much more broadly dispersed and inherently more complex than found via software. Therefore, the "intelligence" provided by those tools is, by its very nature, limited.

If you're thinking about using CI software, consider both the advantages and disadvantages.

Advantages of CI Software

- Good for monitoring and keeping up with general and specific information from a very wide array of sources.

- May uncover valuable information that would not be found via conventional channels.
- An efficient way to deal with a large volume of information, more than can be reasonably handled by staff (considering time and cost restraints).
- Good for aggregating a variety of information by categories; therefore, helps to access the specific area of interest.
- May uncover patterns and linkages not visible to staff (a critical benefit available from software that is not necessarily dedicated to CI).
- Efficient for answering frequently asked questions (FAQs).
- Can be very powerful if it builds on other, non-CI software (e.g., sales software).
- May provide a turnkey process of finding, gathering, organizing, and preparing a report (particularly useful for companies that don't have CI staff).
- Helps a company to be more organized by having a CI-dedicated site, whether it's access to the information itself or to those in the company who have the information.
- Enables other company personnel to have access to information without monopolizing a CI person's time.
- Frees up the CI person to work on more sophisticated and difficult inquiries by providing information to everyone in the company.
- Is becoming more sophisticated and useful with every passing year (e.g., the trend toward Software as a Server, or SaaS, networked-based access to leased software rather than outright purchase).

Disadvantages of CI Software

- Software does not analyze, think, or add the perspective of common sense. It cannot solve problems.
- Using software may result in overreliance on its capabilities and results and may preclude employing the direct contact humint approach.
- Input is limited by the scope of the software. Users may not realize or remember that more or better sources are not included and will therefore not reach out to find them.

- The software may require considerable work and significant training to set up. Users must understand the basics of CI, not simply how to use the technology.
- It must be updated regularly, with these updates communicated to users. Information and updates must be sourced and dated.
- Updates require regular maintenance to add new information or categories and delete what is no longer valid.
- There is no "one size fits all." CI requires considerable investigation and research into which software is best for your company. To ensure that it is appropriate for the task and users, it's best to select software *after* determining what it will be used for and who or which departments will be using it.
- CI is generally considered best for repetitive tasks, which the company must identify.
- It may not be as successful as anticipated for those users less comfortable with technology, who may not use it as often as others and who may not bother to input the information they do have.
- CI creates levels of access; therefore your company must decide whether everyone should have access to the same information and how to differentiate which material will be available to specific employees. Will salespeople or others remove or take information when they leave?
- CI presents security issues. Non-customized software may be more vulnerable to outsiders.
- It's not as good for one-off projects, which may not include the appropriate monitors/sources.
- Many of these programs are incompatible or even unworkable for the average employee, making the retrieval and analysis of information that much more difficult in helping to make decisions.

(Thanks to Ellen Naylor and Derek Johnson for their input on these advantages and disadvantages.)

Clearly, there are some good reasons to consider CI software, but it must be used as a *supplement* to competitive intelligence, not as a *replacement* for it.

Myth #11: Data, Information, and Intelligence Are the Same

We explored this concept in depth in Chapter 5. However, we can summarize this crucial point by stating that while data is clearly very important in business, we often neglect to recognize that data *by itself* conveys little meaning. A former college professor of economics had a fondness for pointing out that in 1957 banana consumption around the world increased 10 percent over the prior year. In that same period, he told us, the rate of suicide had increased an astounding 10 percent. Taken at face value and totally without any intelligence context, one could deduce that the consumption of bananas was responsible for those suicides.

The absurdity of this conclusion is obvious, but it does illustrate the point that data alone is not enough and in fact does not even rise to the level of "intelligence." It is only when enough relevant data is brought together, analyzed, and fit into a meaningful picture that the resulting data and information may move up to the level that we can call intelligence.

The importance of relevancy, accuracy, and sufficiency for a given set of data cannot be overstated. Without all of these elements, the input must be viewed with skepticism. Undoubtedly, in the rational world, there can be no connection between the consumption of bananas and the rate of suicide. One of these elements is obviously irrelevant to the other. What is relevant is that data is only a subset of information. Useful, yes, but only a subset.

The next step is an understanding of the difference between information and intelligence. For example, reports on the number of home foreclosures registered during the 2007–2009 housing crisis made it seem that the crisis was far larger than it actually was. This information negatively impacted public confidence and decisions. When default data is related to the overall number of mortgages across the United States and then turned into an actual rate of default, it becomes more useful. This, of course, does not diminish the horror of losing one's home, but it puts the overall situation into perspective. The reality is that only a small percentage, roughly 6 percent, of all mortgages, were in jeopardy in early 2008. This is a seriously trouble-some number and worthy of note, but it is not catastrophic. Nor does it show a complete picture, once we factor in the number of defaults caused by second homes and speculation. The number of defaults is *data*; delving deeper into the components leads to *intelligence*.

In other words, data is a subset of information, and information is a subset of intelligence. You cannot have intelligence without data or information, but you cannot have intelligence with data only. They are clearly not the same, and it's a point that a business must remember when data is the primary input. So when you're in a presentation of dazzling graphs and charts, probe until you get the full picture.

Myth #12: Competitive Intelligence Is a Waste of Time

It is always interesting to find that people who do not perform any CI for their business are quick to opine that CI is a waste of time. Then again, they tend to have the same attitude about other things they do not do for their business, such as strategy, market research, vetting potential hires, employee incentives, marketing communications, and so on.

The value of competitive intelligence is powerful yet easy to dismiss for those who have a particular way of viewing business. CI is an investment in the business, one that produces measurable return on investment (ROI). Business moves fast and changes in unexpected ways. How can you possibly hope to be current if you don't conduct regular research? You don't expect your kids to be successful if they attend classes only occasionally. The same concept holds true in business—to be current, you must be attentive all the time.

The results of CI clearly detail the changing market drivers, new strategic and marketing approaches, alternative uses for your product or service, unknown customers, emerging competitors, different distribution channels, and more.

Several sources cite the fact that nearly half of the firms listed in the 1970s Fortune 100 are no longer in business. Although we cannot attest to all the factors that may have done them in, the bottom line is that each failed to maintain a growth curve necessary for long-term success. And that success requires attracting new customers, retaining existing customers, and keeping up with change. Is CI a waste of time? It is only if you know your industry so well that you haven't made costly mistakes about your customers, the market, or competitive factors.

Myth #13: Competitive Intelligence Is Only for Business-to-Consumer (B2C) Industries

Conducting CI simply means knowing the right information for making the smartest decisions. This applies equally to business-to-consumer (B2C) and business-to-business (B2B), as well as to non-profits.

The purpose of competitive intelligence is to uncover unknown competitive insights and opportunities and discard industry beliefs that are no longer true. It is concerned with looking at the entire competitive landscape—at what drives success in the marketplace, at finding emerging competitors and why they are gaining customers, at uncovering potential pitfalls (e.g., new regulations that may impact the business or industry), and at finding new directions for the industry or customer base.

We get the same results for industries covering business-to-consumer and business-to-business—for industries ranging from exterior building materials to flexible manufacturing to medical equipment to semiconductors, as well as the full range of consumer products and services. In more than 1,000 investigations, the results and the value are strikingly similar.

Myths: The Last Word

Myths exist for every industry and have a life of their own. Accepting these beliefs as truisms leads to poor decisions, increased risk, and diminished chance of success.

If you believe that CI is spying, you may not undertake the important step of finding the information needed in an honest and ethical manner. Act illegally, and the same fate may result. Believe that there's no advantage to doing competitive intelligence because we all have the same information, and you create your own limitations in strategy, and run the risk of being blindsided. Believe that you know it all because the most valuable information is already known within your company, and you'll miss out on all that is out there, especially those external factors and indirect industries that can seriously derail your strategy. If you think CI is too expensive, you'll learn that the cost of bad information or assumptions is far more costly.

If you allow the myths to dictate your actions or inactions, then you have given the power of your company to others. Enough said. Check it out and destroy those myths. Act in your own best interest; your success depends on it.

12

What's in It for Me?

"CI has helped us make more good decisions at Nutra-Sweet and fewer bad ones. It's worth up to $50 million annually—combination of revenues gained and revenues not lost to competitive activity."
—Robert Flynn, former CEO of NutraSweet and a
firm believer in competitive intelligence

Customers are always asking themselves, "What's in it for me?" The same question applies to this book: "What is the benefit of competitive intelligence? If it's so valuable, why don't I know more about it? Why isn't everyone doing it and using it?" We'll save you some time mulling these questions by listing our 15 top "what and why" advantages of competitive intelligence:

1. Provides an accurate and objective view of the marketplace
2. Answers management's questions
3. Produces only good news—even when the news is bad
4. Improves decisions and minimizes risks
5. Avoids surprises
6. Details where your product or service fits and lets you discover underserved customers
7. Helps identify new opportunities before the competition finds them
8. Indicates early warning of competitor moves, thus enabling countermeasures
9. Provides input to generate ideas to respond to change
10. Challenges or verifies assumptions and intuition
11. Helps your company be proactive and decision-ready to respond more effectively to events and opportunities
12. Enables your company to not waste resources competing where you have low chances of success
13. Allows you to set more realistic goals that offer a greater probability of success
14. Offers great ROI, return on investment
15. Results in strategic decisions that are more aggressive, made faster, and with greater confidence, as uncertainty is diminished.

The benefits of a engaging in competitive intelligence are manifold, and we haven't even touched on all of them. By maintaining a higher level of awareness of the competitive landscape and by supporting a sustained state of readiness to make decisions, companies can make those bold moves that address both strategic and tactical goals with confidence.

CI Provides an Accurate and Objective View of the Marketplace

Your company does not operate in a vacuum. Current, objective, and relevant information balances or overcomes the human factor of overconfidence, self-interest, risk aversion, and inability to see the big picture or the near future. Whether or not you conduct competitive intelligence, you will eventually learn the reality of the marketplace.

With CI, you learn it *sooner*, sometimes much sooner, and that gives you a significant advantage. Even if companies decide not to proceed with an action based on CI findings, at the very least they have a heads-up when a competitor ventures into a similar decision. This gives companies time to create countermoves, even if that is to explain or sell the reason why that was a bad idea. Learning sooner offers an option for a company to monitor events until it determines that it is the right time to move. It allows for a well-thought-out decision.

Strategic decisions about the marketplace require the strong underpinnings of solid and current strategic information about that marketplace. This means more than objective and accurate information that tells the story. It requires an intelligence that's deeper than information and leads to meaningful insights and implications. It must include an external view of all the factors that can and will impact your business, including knowledge of industries that are indirectly related to your industry and changes that are occurring there.

Finally, it should include what *isn't* there—what you didn't even consider yet is still important to your decision—considerations related to the economy, demographics, societal thinking, and behavior.

CI Answers Management's Questions

There are multiple bonuses when you conduct competitive intelligence. It identifies questions that should have been asked, but may not have been.

CI is the systematic process of collecting, analyzing, and presenting objective information to answer management's questions. As such, CI not only answers management's questions, it effectively helps management identify and satisfy customer needs and desires and learn new important information they didn't even know to ask about. This includes market drivers, barriers to entry, unknown customers, substitute competitors, and discontinuities.

1. CI brings awareness of what is true today as well as what is no longer true.
2. CI alerts management to what's emerging and what and who to monitor.
   - CI reveals information that executives did not know or information that was known but ignored or underestimated.
   - CI raises one's antenna so that executives can be alert to changing clues.
   - CI cannot plan for unknowns, but the undertaking teaches how to recognize what's new and important.
3. CI eliminates or avoids surprises.
4. CI minimizes risk. The better the decision based on the right information, the less likely that the decision will be wrong or need to be redone.
5. CI provides a view that is likely to be closer to the customer's perspective, which is less subjective than the company's viewpoint and more likely to reveal opportunities.
6. CI is proactive. Whether the company takes action immediately, based on new learning or insight, or monitors what's happening to gain more information, it will act sooner than without CI.

CI Produces Only Good News—Even When the News is Bad

Good news is good news, and bad news is also good news.

The value and benefit of CI is that it provides accurate, current information and analysis that reflects prevailing reality. Information that challenges beliefs is good to know. If you learn that your assumptions are wrong or that you're missing important information, then you have the opportunity to make appropriate changes sooner, and likely with less cost and negative consequences than you otherwise would have. But if they are right, then you're in an even stronger position—knowing that you have confirmation.

When the findings do *not* support the company's assumptions or basis for a new initiative, senior executives may become angry or dismissive of the findings, an understandable reaction. But if they can view results from the perspective that finding out sooner what the company would likely discover later and after significant investment, then it's better to find out what you never considered and why your plans won't work. This is a bonus that results from the negative input.

In addition to saving time and money by not proceeding with an unworkable plan, a good CI undertaking is more useful when it produces a plan B or C—either other approaches or other customers. These other plans may not be as exciting or appealing as the original plan, but they are likely to produce revenue and results. The disappointing news should be accompanied by a sufficient explanation for the company to verify for itself. The CI investigation must connect the dots helping to explain why the expected turn of events was inaccurate.

We've peppered this book with examples that illustrate this very point: Good news or bad news, CI produces reality. And that's the best news, because the best decisions are made on a basis of reality, increasing the success factor.

Reality is objective reality, not what may appear logical or reasonable during meetings and in-depth discussions and chart-filled presentations, all of which reflect internal perspectives.

You can have a brilliant strategy. You can have awesome products and services. But if they don't resonate with today's reality, their chances of success are deeply diminished. Even if you achieve operational excellence and flawless execution, you're still left with outside factors that you can't control. CI uncovers those factors and presents the good news—even when it's bad news.

CI Improves Decisions and Minimizes Risks

The primary purpose of competitive intelligence is to make better decisions by minimizing risk. This applies both to big decisions, such as entering a new industry, expanding the line, or doing a merger (M&A), and small decisions alike. CI enables a company to learn the reality of the marketplace and to move from crisis-driven to opportunity-driven. Large companies, at least until the current economic crisis, have a financial cushion and can afford to make mistakes without going out of business. Small companies don't have that cushion. Businesses learn through experiences such as making bad decisions and losing money that their assumptions were incorrect and/or no longer true. Small companies, without that same monetary cushion, cannot expect the luxury of experience, at least not on a large scale. It's essential, therefore, for them to get it right the first time.

A single mistake can result in loss of a major client, a competitive advantage, an alliance, or . . . of the business itself. The cost of doing your homework is far less than the cost of that mistake. The value that CI provides is an accurate, current, objective view, including indications of the near future, thereby reducing risks and improving decisions. As hockey great Wayne Gretsky said, "I skate to where the puck is going to be, not to where it has been." CI clearly details where the puck is going—not where the company *thinks* it is going or *wants* it to go, but the reality of where it *is* going.

This is the difference between assumptions and information.

- Competitive intelligence helps executives see what is generally not yet seen, known, or understood by the industry. It connects the dots that exist but aren't yet known.
- CI challenges assumptions and gut instincts and beliefs. If they hold up, great. If not, then you have new, important information about a changing world to verify for yourself. Based on more than 30 years of experience, it is clear that executives' assumptions and intuition are generally short of the mark, yet they are very good at rationalizing their losses. Even after 40 years of losing market share, General Motors blamed its troubles on the 2008 failing economy.
- Assumptions and gut instinct tell us what we have believed for a long time. They are also what we *want* to believe, because they are familiar and comfortable. New information requires changed thinking and changed strategy or tactics, and that can be really painful. Further, executives don't know whether the new strategy or tactics will succeed, and they'd rather take their chances with

the devil they know, not the devil they don't know. They assume competitors have probably not changed either, so there's comfort and ready support in maintaining the status quo. It's easy to dismiss new entrants, who have the advantage of being comfortable with new information.

CI Avoids Surprises

Surprise in business is *rarely* good. In fact, it's usually an indication that a change, hitherto unknown to the company, is taking place. Small surprises are fine, since they indicate a change in its earliest stages. Big surprises are not fine. They reveal that a company is unaware.

"Ninety-nine percent of all surprises in business are negative," said Harold Geneen, former CEO of IT&T. Information obtained during a CI investigation alerts the company to small surprises, those critical first sign of change.

In Chapter 7, we used the example of our garden tools client who, after receiving our report, developed a combination spreader/sprayer. The product development cycle took two years, and rather than merely deploy the product into the marketplace based on old information, the company tasked us to reaffirm our earlier findings. The new effort revealed that the market had shifted considerably in the intervening years, and our client quickly adjusted the product prior to launch. The launch then proved successful, and the client wasn't surprised by all the changes.

Kmart surprised the retail world by resurrecting its layaway program. The company brought back this seemingly anachronistic concept before most businesses recognized the recession in the fall of 2008. As a result, this successful program became an instant hit with credit- and cash-strapped customers when sales were declining at other retailers. This was one of Kmart's most successful promotions, partly due to a changed view of layaway—from *paying down* a little each week to *planning ahead* to pay off items (Christmas gifts in December, patio furniture in the spring). Note that Kmart didn't just bring back an old idea; they adapted it to fit changing times.

A company that does not do CI is likely to be reactive, waste resources, and make poor decisions that need to be reconsidered and possibly redone. Our garden tools client not only did its due diligence at the right time for its product development, it then embarked on a post-development due-diligence effort to ensure the company was still on target. As our client discovered, innovation is useful only when it meets customer needs. CI, in this instance, revealed those changing customer preferences, which the distributors knew about and which made them more open to stocking this new product.

Generation Y consumers ("millennials"), born between 1977 and 1994, are a very attractive target. They're almost as large in numbers as the boomers and similar to them in that they are different in meaningful ways from demographic groups that preceded them. They will impact many aspects of life, both business and personal, in the same dramatic way as did boomers. But unless you have studied this group and understand them, your company will yield to competitors who know, for example, that Gen Yers are the biggest users of libraries. Surprised? And you thought this was the *technology* generation!

Contrary to conventional wisdom, Gen Yers are having sex for the first time at a later age; they're more religious than previous generations, more conservative than their older siblings, more socially conscious, and more tolerant. They believe in alternative family structures, are most comfortable in groups, are less materialistic, and they are very close to their parents. Surprised again? There's much more to learn and numerous opportunities that will result from this knowledge. This is too large a group to ignore. Have you considered this group as your customer? Where are some of your opportunities to do so?

Although surprise is often not good in business, it is good when you recognize surprise in its earliest stages, when it offers an opportunity to shift thinking and to consider market changes. If you're not continuously surprised, this is an indication that your radar is turned off.

CI Details Where Your Product or Service Fits and Uncovers Underserved Customers

Every company believes it has a good understanding of its customers—who they are and why they buy. A company needs this understanding so it can continue to offer a product or service that precisely fits those needs. But needs change, and so do the customers. CI offers updates on those changes.

Market opportunities also exist when you identify unserved or underserved markets. This will not only allow market expansion but also pinpoint the reasons that a market might be underserved and thus prevent a mistake.

Keep in mind that effective CI is not just a one-shot deal. The ideal situation is gathering information on an ongoing basis, continually assessing the landscape to ensure that you always keep an eye on your customers, not to mention being vigilant about the movements in the marketplace so you can react appropriately. New customers are discovering you. And to the extent that they're different from what you expect, this offers an opportunity to seek more of these "different" customers.

CI Helps Identify New Opportunities Before the Competition Finds Them

One of the goals of CI is to help identify where the market, industry, and customers are headed, and to do so before the competition catches on. In short, CI's objective is to get the information you need in order to grow your company.

Among the desirable information that CI can offer up are answers to such questions as: Where is the market for your product or service headed? Are there identifiable shifts in customer needs or desires (features, packaging, venues)? How do you capitalize on those? What technologies will affect your industry or your customers? Are there any firms that are likely trendsetters? What shifts in their strategies are making them so?

Identifying these is always important, but when you can do so early in the process, you can be proactive in the marketplace and successfully beat the competition. You are seeking continued success. Some opportunities and trends will move ahead relatively quickly; others will require more confirming evidence. In either case, the company will be able to act, given the reality of the marketplace, sooner than it would have without the CI.

CI Indicates Early Warning of Competitor Moves, Thus Enabling Countermeasures

This is where paying attention to competitors has value. Has a competitor introduced a new feature that is resonating with customers?

Is it selling its product or service in a different way? Is it doing so through a different distribution channel? Is it using a new or different marketing approach? Is it selling to a customer group that doesn't usually buy this product or service? Is it partnering with a totally different business to expand its reach?

Has a competitor figured out something that your company has not? Is it important? It's not unusual for companies to take action that the customer doesn't care about. That is, the competitor thinks it's far more important than does the customer. Just because a competitor makes a move doesn't mean it's a good one or that it's proportionate to the costs involved. Nonetheless, when you know about such a move, you can carefully consider what that means. And if warranted, take action to determine just how valuable that move is and then take counteraction.

Competitors are part of the competitive landscape that must be monitored. If you don't know the answers to the questions at the beginning of this section, then this is one of the benefits from CI that you are missing. While your time is far better spent focusing on your customers and the marketplace than on your competitors, some attention should be paid to competitors' actions, as each competitor has strengths and weaknesses that might present a challenge to your company.

And don't forget that your competitors include substitutes and indirect competitors.

CI Provides Input to Generate Ideas to Respond to Change

A comprehensive competitive intelligence project will often produce a plan B or plan C that generates new ideas to respond to changes in the marketplace, a definite advantage. But what does this have to do with CI?

CI generates ideas. First and foremost, to generate ideas for your business, you have to have information and understanding about a wide range of issues and many businesses besides your own. This is part of what is developed through CI.

When you stop to think about it, most new ideas are either a repackaging of old ideas, a mix of something old with something new, or doing something better or faster. Therefore, one of your CI assignments might be to research the marketplace for ideas and then do some brainstorming to see how these might apply to your business or situation.

Take, for instance, the loyalty programs adopted by the airlines. American Airlines was credited with the first frequent-flyer program, back in the early 1980s. All the other airlines followed shortly thereafter, and the concept soon flowed into the business world in general. Loyalty programs are now so pervasive that you can find their application in restaurants, bookstores, supermarkets, dry cleaners, and many more venues that now offer such "membership" programs.

How can you use CI to generate your own ideas? Look for ideas used by others to successfully grow their businesses. This means doing a continual environmental scan of both your industry and of industries that have the same or a similar customer base. This is why it is important not to limit yourself to learning about things only in your own industry. You need to be able to think out of the box of your own industry and pay attention to success in other industries.

The newest iPod shuffle is smaller than an AA battery or house key, weighs less than one-third of an ounce, and offers many of the same features as Apple's more expensive models. What does that mean for nontechnology companies? Have you considered adding features to your least expensive products or services? Or making your product smaller?

Most businesses focus on their higher-priced models, so consider opportunities to appeal to customers who perhaps can't afford the higher-priced models yet may be enticed by a feature or two. Businesses rarely recognize the customers who want only a basic model, which gives them the limited features they seek and which they view as less likely to have problems.

Though we do not support smoking, we noted that Philip Morris has a new product called Marlboro Intense. The product is shorter in length and therefore offers fewer puffs, to accommodate those who go outside to smoke and don't have the time to finish a full-size cigarette. Lower potency versus longer and milder. Downsizing is not a new idea, of course, but in this instance, Philip Morris adapted the idea of downsizing to accommodate a shift in the amount of time that workers have for smoking.

CI Challenges or Verifies Assumptions and Intuition

But what about that beloved gut feeling, that intuition? Don't these count? Many executives rely more on their gut and intuition than on any external source, and with good reason. After all, they boast, "I wouldn't be in this position if I didn't know what was best." That argument had some merit in the past, when markets and industries changed more slowly or not at all; when new competitors did not enter the market as rapidly; when distribution channels were limited to one or two; and when new significant features were only occasionally added by the competition. Those days are no longer with us. Intuition is no longer as reliable and must now be balanced with solid, sufficient, recent, and relevant facts provided by CI. Not tossed, supplemented.

Unfortunately, we have too often seen how a seemingly "great" product simply does not sell. Just watch QVC or HSN, especially when they're trying out new offerings (and keep in mind that these are the best of products brought to them!) Do you wonder who is buying them and why? It's not enough to be enthusiastic and to believe that prospects will be enthusiastic. It has to be a product or service that the buying public is willing to buy.

When companies are not selling at the level they expect, they often blame price, and rarely do they believe that the customer doesn't want their product or service. Sometimes it is price, but that's rare. Companies don't consider a contradictory perspective, when the low price might actually limit sales.

A client came to us with an improved medical device that cost about 20 percent of competitive products. During our discussions with institutional buyers, we found that the lower price for an improved product was off-putting to them. They suspected that the quality or durability could not exist at this price point. Rather than fight with potential customers to change their perspective, we recommended that our client consider a different strategy: introduce the product at a higher price to get in the door, and then lower it as a negotiating tool or as the product gained acceptance. The bonus is that the higher price would provide a cushion for the company in the early sales process. In a changing environment, assumptions and intuition must *always* be challenged to ensure they still hold true. Allow for the fact that your logic may not be the same as your customer's.

CI Helps Your Company Be Proactive to Respond More Effectively to Events and Opportunities

It's said that timing is everything when investing in the stock market. But is that applicable only to stock market investing? This concept, we believe, is equally relevant to business decisions to enter or leave a market, to acquiring or divesting a new company or division, or to launching a new product.

When the economy is good, timing may be less important. In a recession, many businesses are affected, and a company has to move more cautiously because the customer base, consumer or industrial, is less willing to buy. In an economic crisis, the rules of the game change, and a company has to think much more carefully about what it is doing, and whether and when it should be doing it.

Regardless of the economic environment, a company should always be ready to move. And how can you get ready? Our answer is, of course, by doing CI. Although you cannot anticipate the unknown, CI can provide information that enables you to respond to changes and to respond to them sooner.

For example, male shopping habits have changed over the years in ways that haven't yet been broadly acknowledged and discussed. Men are doing more of their own shopping, and they're more interested in fashion. Online, men shop far more quickly, spending only about one-third the amount of time that women do, and they spend more money. Retailers in the know (e.g., Brooks Brothers and Neiman Marcus) have beefed up their men's sites to address men's different way of shopping. Becoming aware of these shifts provides the insight to make changes before you recognize them from competitors.

In short, CI tells you about changing events and potential opportunities so that you're always ready to move to keep up with your customers. They're moving (that is, changing) and you have to move with them.

CI Enables Your Company to Not Waste Resources Competing Where You Have Low Chances of Success

In addition to assessing your own and your competitions' products or services, you also need to know first and foremost the *customer* needs and wants and whether you can satisfy those needs at the price the customer wants to pay. Doing a proper CI assessment lets you identify those elements that make this market untenable for you, and thus allows you to either mitigate the problem or get out of this business segment and concentrate on one in which you can achieve success.

Executives of one nonprofit client thought that they had an advantage when they decided to distribute their product through a channel not used by any competing products. Fortunately, they were challenged to provide evidence that this was a good decision. Our comprehensive CI analysis revealed the fallacy in their assumptions, and they understood why their method would fail. We were able to show *why* no other companies were using the channel they wanted to use. More important, this example shows why ideas need objective input. Another idea may have been masterful—but not this one.

Successful businesses need to know their products and where they stand in the marketplace. Competitive intelligence provides the path to understanding your place, current or potential. Market share data is not available for most industries (except cars, soda, beer, and a few others whose industries engage in regular surveys) so most companies have no idea of the competitive landscape and their threats or opportunities. As previously mentioned, when one of our clients learned during our CI investigation that the market was ten times larger than they thought, they mounted an aggressive new sales effort.

CI Allows You to Set More Realistic Goals That Offer a Greater Probability of Success

This is a corollary to the preceding section (*not* competing where you have a low chance of success). In the earlier "good news–bad news" section of this chapter, we indicated that "a good CI exercise will often produce a plan B or C—either other approaches or other customers." In a number of projects in varying industries, we have often come up with plan B that provides a more successful route. In the case of a supplier of computer screens, managers were targeting the wrong end of the market; in the case of a medical device, the preferred target market was the wrong one, and we told the client about a different group of customers who were interested; in the case of a financial institution, we advised a rethinking of their market strategy to a more successful outcome.

One of the objectives of CI is to identify other opportunities that can be pursued to success. A generalized market demand for a company's product or service does not necessarily translate into an opportunity for *your* company. Sometimes, it does take a plan B that has achievable goals, and CI can help identify those.

CI Offers Great Return on Investment (ROI)

Unfortunately, we know of no financial ratio that exists to measure return on investment for competitive intelligence. What we do know is that companies need information to make the strategic decisions that lead to success. Strong knowledge of the marketplace and the competitive landscape result in optimal decisions for the company.

Theoretically, the ROI for competitive intelligence, though occasionally measured in increased sales, might be measured more accurately through the avoidance of mistakes. Too many times, we have been hired to conduct CI research *after* our clients did not get the results expected from their decisions. They then wanted to understand what they had missed to begin with. For example:

- One client cut its losses after spending tens of millions of dollars on a business it hoped would succeed but that we showed could not.
- Another avoided getting into the wrong end of the business (expensive versus low-cost products) and saved approximately $2 million.
- One firm opted for purchasing lower-priced equipment that would accomplish the same purpose, thus saving a $150,000 capital investment.
- And then there are the sweet rewards. A new entrant into delicious-tasting chocolate needed to understand which segment (private label, raw materials to other chocolate manufacturers, branded products) of the industry would produce the fastest return on its investment. We laid out all the options that pointed this client in the right direction.

Strategic Decisions are More Aggressive, Made Faster, and With Greater Confidence, as Uncertainty is Diminished

There is little that is more satisfying and rewarding than when you have the power of knowledge behind you. Decisions are more focused, doubts diminished, and the likelihood of success is vastly improved.

The final report and ensuing discussion for a recent project resulted in the company's executives changing a part of their business practice within minutes of reading the report. The information was not new to them; they had simply underestimated its importance to their customers and had ignored it—repeatedly. After reading our report and the different way we presented familiar information, they recognized their assumptions were incorrect and immediately decided to test out this change. We were delighted when the client told us that this one insight alone was worth the price of the research.

The comfort of conventional wisdom cannot be compared to the power of the correct decision. For example, internal decisions about pricing—that sales will be dramatically increased once prices are lowered continue to linger. In every ranking we have ever seen, however, price is not the most important element in selecting a product or service. When price is the dominant decision point, then your product or service has been reduced to a commodity. Customers (B2B or B2C) believe that the lower-priced items are just as good as the higher priced ones. This means your offering has not been differentiated.

A decision to figure out (or go back to the drawing board and develop) those differentiators will produce a better product or service. And your sales and marketing staff will be more successful as uncertainty about your offering is decreased. You're not like the others and you have the CI to provide the evidence.

Due Diligence: Doing Your Homework

When marketing initiatives fail, when the customer isn't buying what you're selling, and when decisions don't produce the desired results, executives suddenly want an explanation and seek out customer feedback to understand what happened. They look back on the carnage and ask, "Why?" But is that really the best time to figure out who threw the proverbial wrench into the works? Why not get educated *before* it happens?

That's what competitive intelligence provides—education, information, elucidation, and understanding of the market—of customers, of promotions, of distribution channels, and of many other factors. CI produces facts and emerging information and insights that are analyzed to produce an objective assessment of the market as it exists today and as it is changing. If you've never done a market assessment, then you're relying on what you know, which is either yesterday's news or your own not-yet-validated assumptions.

And if you haven't done a market assessment in more than a year or two, then you're assuming your industry has not changed or that you already know of all the relevant changes. Can you *really* believe that in these volatile times? If you're that confident, can you detail specifically what has changed and how such changes have affected your company? Can you point to where it has not changed?

Competitive intelligence is doing your homework. It's preparation for thoughtful, careful decisions. This does not mean that companies cannot make good decisions without CI. But in challenging times— recessions, new competitors, changing attitudes, and innovations—the case for CI becomes ever clearer. Relying on past successes (or doing nothing) is less likely to provide the results the company is seeking.

The corollary is that *not* doing CI is a refusal to accept that currency has only temporary value. Nothing is permanent in business, and even less so in the long term. Even the most successful companies have experienced and are experiencing downturns, some after decades of increasing sales. Think eBay, GE, Sears, Polaroid, IBM, and even the venerable Starbucks.

The huge value of competitive intelligence is its inherent ability to make you see what's happening today (reality) and what's emerging and changing—*before* your competitors become aware, when your opportunity is greater. Because so few companies do CI, those who do have an incalculable advantage. Bob Galvin, Motorola CEO, expected "CI to help him and his management team create the future business for his company." (Jan Herring, *The Future of Competitive Intelligence: Driven by Knowledge-Based Competition*)

Finally

It is clear that in today's competitive environment, a business cannot afford to rely on knowledge it gained 20 years ago, 10 years ago, and even last year to ensure its continued competitive advantage. CI is a management discipline that has repeatedly proven its value. Mikey urged us, in the legendary award-winning commercial for Life Cereal, "Try it, you'll like it." Give CI a chance to prove its value to you. You will not be disappointed.

13

Playing by the Rules, SCIP, Resources

Ethics

Let's get this straight right from the start: Competitive intelligence is *not* a cloak-and-dagger, shady activity carried out by Dumpster divers and other unscrupulous people. Those who are actively involved in competitive intelligence are dismayed when our profession is viewed in this light (or whenever spying is the theme of a given movie). Fortunately, this association has diminished over the years, but it still pops up occasionally.

As a practitioner of this discipline for more than 30 years, here is my take, one that is shared by many of my CI colleagues:

- If it involves lying, stealing or trespassing—we don't do it.
- Dumpster diving—we don't do it.
- Paying sources for confidential information—we don't do it.
- Appropriating passwords—we don't do it.
- Encouraging people to violate nondisclosure agreements—we don't do it.
- Using a false identity or pretense to get information—we don't do it.
- Acquiring a company's proprietary information—we don't do it.
- Asking new hires to divulge proprietary information from a previous employer—we don't do it.
- Giving gifts or favors to get proprietary information—we don't do it.
- Receiving proprietary information from an anonymous source—we don't do it.

In fact, all members of our professional association, the Society of Competitive Intelligence Professionals (SCIP), agree to follow the following Code of Ethics, available on the SCIP web site (www.scip.org):

1. To continually strive to increase the recognition and respect of the profession.
2. To comply with all applicable laws, domestic and international.

3. To accurately disclose all relevant information, including one's identity and organization, prior to all interviews.

4. To avoid conflicts of interest in fulfilling one's duties.

5. To provide honest and realistic recommendations and conclusions in the execution of one's duties.

6. To promote this code of ethics within one's company, with third-party contractors, and within the entire profession.

7. To faithfully adhere to and abide by one's company policies, objectives, and guidelines.

In fact, the Economic Espionage Act of 1996 makes the theft or misappropriation of a trade secret a federal crime (www.economicespionage.com/EEA.html). Richard Horowitz, an attorney and SCIP member, wrote a paper for SCIP titled "Competitive Intelligence and the Espionage Act," plus dozens of article available on his web site at: www.rhesq.com.

Our preferred method is to conduct informal, seemingly unstructured conversations, as outlined in Chapter 9 on human intelligence, where the goal is to obtain information that is freely and openly discussed with customers and suppliers. It's similar to eliciting company remarks found in articles or press releases when a company is seeking to get the word out about the company, its products, or its services. This is one of the many ways that companies draw attention to their offerings.

In Chapter 11 we mentioned a client who asked for the marketing strategy of one of its competitors. We said that this information might not be openly available, but if it was, we would procure it. As it happened, the target company was headquartered in a small city in France, and the company's president had given an interview to his banker (for the bank's newsletter), in which he expounded on his five-year strategic marketing plan. All we had to do was translate this published, openly available document—entirely legal and completely ethical.

This is the *only* way that CI should be done.

For further reading on this topic, we recommend *Competitive Intelligence: Navigating the Gray Zone*, published by SCIP's Competitive Intelligence Foundation in 2006. It includes more than 30 examples of actual corporate ethics guidelines and implementation steps. In addition, the book clarifies what constitutes legal and ethical competitive intelligence activities, and offers guidance on developing and implementing ethics policies (www.scip.org/Publications/ProductDetail.cfm?ItemNumber=1209).

Confidentiality

Whether or not a company requests a nondisclosure agreement (NDA), the CI practitioner should consider what information is confidential. This is a combination of common sense and specific guidance from the company. Materials provided by the company, and those developed by the CI company, should be considered proprietary and should not be shared without the company's consent. Members of the team should not discuss the project with anyone outside of the company.

Further, we do not believe it is appropriate to work with other clients in the same subject area (as defined by the scope of the assignment) during your engagement with a particular client or for a period afterward.

Society of Competitive Intelligence Professionals (SCIP)

I've mentioned SCIP a number of times throughout this book (www.scip.org), and in the interest of making a full and honest disclosure, I want to acknowledge that, yes, I am a card-carrying member of this organization and was honored with its Fellows Award. SCIP, a global association of competitive intelligence professionals, conducts workshops, webinars, and annual conferences; publishes numerous papers and a magazine; hosts a job bank; and provides other resources to CI practitioners. Chapters and affiliates serve the local membership; annual conferences are held in the United States and Europe; and a resource directory assists companies in finding external CI professionals.

The monthly issue of *Competitive Intelligence Magazine* offers a variety of articles of interest to CI professionals. A sample issue is available by contacting the organization. The peer-reviewed *Journal of Competitive Intelligence and Management* is no longer published, but remains available in the SCIP archives, as do articles from all SCIP magazines. *SCIP Online*, the organization's electronic newsletter, provides hundreds of useful links biweekly, including articles mentioning CI, sources of data, and software products. In addition, the SCIP web site offers numerous books about CI and related areas of interest, including some mentioned in the next section.

Recommended Reading

CI Books

My CI colleagues recommend several books, as follows:

Ashton, Brad, and Dick Klavans, *Keeping Abreast of Science and Technology*. (Columbus, OH: Battelle Press, 1997)

Bensoussan, Babette E., and Craig S. Fleisher, *Analysis Without Paralysis: 10 Tools to Make Better Strategic Decisions*. (Upper Saddle River, NJ: FT Press, 2008)

Bouthillier, France, and Kathleen Shearer, *Assessing Competitive Intelligence Software: A Guide to Evaluating CI Technology*. (Medford, NJ: Information Today, 2003)

Kahaner, Larry, *Competitive Intelligence: How to Gather, Analyze, and Use Information to Move Your Business to the Top*. (New York, NY: Simon and Schuster, 1996)

Naylor, Ellen, *The Business Intelligence Source*, lists more than 130 CI books on her web site, www.thecisource.com/resources/books.

Nolan, John, *Confidential: Business Secrets—Getting Theirs, Keeping Yours*. (Yardley-Chambers, 1999)

Tyson, Kirk W. M., *The Complete Guide to Competitive Intelligence* (4th ed.). (Sydney: Leading Edge Publications, 1996)

In addition, SCIP's Competitive Intelligence Foundation has commissioned a series of books on specified topics that are available for sale in the SCIP bookstore, including the following titles (www.scip.org/publications):

Conference & Trade Show Intelligence
Starting a CI Function
Competitive Intelligence Ethics: Navigating the Gray Zone
Competitive Technical Intelligence

John McGonagle of The Helicon Group, who reviews CI books for SCIP's *Competitive Intelligence* magazine, considers the following as the best choices. They are listed in chronological order, along with the publisher's web site. McGonagle's reviews are archived in *Competitive Intelligence* at www.scip.org.

Vibert, Conor, *Competitive Intelligence: A Framework for Web-Based Analysis and Decision-Making.* (Cincinnati, OH: South-Western Educational Pub, 2003)

Gilad, Ben, *Early Warning: Using Competitive Intelligence to Anticipate Market Shifts, Control Risk, and Create Powerful Strategies.* (AMACOM, 2003)

Miller, Jerry P., *Millennium Intelligence: Understanding and Conducting Competitive Intelligence in the Digital Age,* Business Intelligence Braintrust. (Medford, NJ: Information Today, 1999)

McGonagle, John J., and Carolyn M. Vella, *Protecting Your Company Against Competitive Intelligence.* (Westport, CT: Quorum Books, 1998)

Meyer, Herbert E., *Real-World Intelligence.* (Friday Harbor, WA: Storm King Press, 1991)

Sawyer, Deborah C., *Smart Services: Competitive Information Strategies, Solution and Success Stories for Service Businesses.* (Medford, NJ: Information Today, 2002)

CI Software Articles

The following articles on CI software originally were published in *Competitive Intelligence* magazine and are available from SCIP:

- Aaron/Naylor
  Knowledge.works (software column). January/February 2002, pp. 57–59.
- Anderson, Tom
  From unstructured text to valuable insights: Leveraging text analytics to meet competitive intelligence needs. January/February 2008, pp. 12–15.

- Beurschgens, Andrew
  Speed dating with software vendors. May/June 2008, pp. 27–30.
- Bukowski, Daniel
  Getting the most from Microsoft Office: Tap into an underutilized asset in your organization. January/February 2008, p. 10.
- Camastro, Eric
  Ten steps to selecting the right CI software. September/October 2008, pp. 50–52.
- Farcot, Raol
  CI software sanity check: Know what technologies are right for you. March/April 2004, pp. 53–54, 59.
- Farcot, Raol
  The right recipe for next generation CI software. May/June 2004, pp. 47–48.
- Farcot, Raoul
  The perfect CI Software—is it a myth? March/April 2005, 8/2, pp. 55–56.
- Fuld, Leonard
  CI software report 2002. May/June 2002, pp. 15–23.
- Himelfarb, Dan
  Mind mapping software to show interrelations across companies, customers and supply chains. January/February 2008, pp. 58–59.
- Naylor/Aaron
  Intellectual property software solutions. November/December 2001, pp. 48–50.
- Powell, Tim
  Skila: CI software for the healthcare industry. April/June 1998, pp. 53–54.

"Intelligence 2.0—People, Process and Technology Systems for Anticipating Industry Change" is a small directory of solutions, plus a series of contributed white papers on best practices from specific vendors (www.aurorawdc.com).

Intelligence Software Report® 2008/2009 is available from www .fuld.com.

CI Courses and Programs

It is discouraging that more colleges or universities, especially institutions with a business concentration, do not offer CI courses. Most don't even offer even *one* course! Accordingly, it is not surprising that future executives and managers have never been exposed to competitive intelligence and are not familiar with this strategic management discipline.

I've therefore provided the following list as a starting point for finding CI courses and programs. They were aggregated by suggestions from several CI professors, notably Professor Jonathan Calof (University of Ottawa) and Professor Sheila Wright (De Montfort University, United Kingdom). This list may not be complete or current, as courses are more attached to the instructor than to the school. That is, when the competitive intelligence instructor leaves the school, the likelihood of another teaching that course is minimal. To my knowledge, Mercyhurst College in Erie, Pennsylvania, is the only university in the United States currently offering a CI degree.

Dr. Calof occasionally updates his list, which can be found at http://intelligence.management.uottawa.ca/intelligence_courses.htm.

- Blekinge Institute of Technology, Sweden
- Boston University, Massachusetts, US
- Cambridge University, United Kingdom
- Cranfield University, United Kingdom
- De Montfort University, United Kingdom
- Ekaterinburg, Russia
- ESADE Spain
- ESCP-EAP, France
- Hebrew University, Ben Gurion University, and Rishon Le'Zion, Israel
- Imperial College, London
- Johns Hopkins Graduate Certificate in Creative Intelligence
- Loughborough University, England
- Maquarie University, Australia
- New Zealand (university unknown)
- Northwest University, South Africa

- Open University, United Kingdom
- Oxford University, United Kingdom
- Rotterdam School of Management, Netherlands
- Sandhurst Military College, United Kingdom
- The Chartered Institute of Marketing, United Kingdom
- The Institut für Competitive Intelligence, Germany
- Thunderbird School of Global Management, Arizona, US
- Universidad de Belgrano
- University of Ottawa
- University of Pittsburgh, US
- University of Pretoria, South Africa, offers an intelligence certificate
- University of South Australia
- University of Technology Sydney, Australia
- University of Windsor, Canada
- Wits Business School, South Africa
- BCIT, Canada, offers a marketing intelligence course

Corporate CI Departments and Titles

The old bard, Shakespeare, got it right when he asked, "What's in a name?" There are dozens of possible titles for people engaged in competitive intelligence, full- or part-time. Companies with active departments that conduct CI use a variety of names, including *competitive intelligence*, *market insights*, and *consumer insights*. The diversity is even broader when you look at the business cards that Jens Thieme, a director on SCIP's board, has collected at several CI conferences, which include the following titles:

Practitioners

- Business Analyst
- Business Developer
- Business Intelligence Analyst
- Business Market Intelligence Manager—Marketing Services, Insight & Planning

- Business Performance Analyst
- CI Support Management Consultant
- Competitive Intelligence Director, NA
- Corporate Development Manager
- Director of Market Intelligence, NE/SW IOT
- Director, Strategic Intelligence—Business Development
- Director, Strategic Planning
- Director, Market Intelligence
- Global Marketing Intelligence Manager
- Head of Market & Competitive Intelligence
- Head of Product Management
- Head, Product Marketing & Product Management
- Head, Competitive Intelligence
- International Business Analyst, Market Intelligence & Planning
- Manager, Business & Market Intelligence
- Manager, Business Intelligence
- Manager, Strategy & Development
- Manager, Marketing Strategy
- Managing Director
- Market Insight & Strategy Specialist
- Market Intelligence Specialist
- Marketing Analyst & Business Intelligence
- Marketing Manager
- Research Specialist, International
- Senior Business Intelligence Analyst
- Senior Director, Business Intelligence
- Senior Global Strategic Competitive Intelligence Manager
- Senior Manager/Strategic Planning
- Senior Manager, Competitive Intelligence
- Senior Project Manager
- Senior VP, Business Development
- Strategic Corporate Development
- Strategic Planning—Competitive Intelligence Manager
- Strategist, Market Intelligence

- Strategist & Market Intelligence Consultant
- Technology Solutions Marketing, Strategic Marketing & Communications
- Vice President, Business Development
- Vice President, Business Intelligence
- VP, Business Intelligence
- VP, Head of Strategy Controlling & Operations—Group Function Corporate Strategy

Consultants

- Corporate Business Development Manager
- Group Director, Strategic Analysis and Intelligence
- Managing Director
- Research Director
- Sales & Marketing Manager
- Senior Business Development Manager
- Senior Consultant
- Senior Manager
- Senior Vice President
- Strategic Account Manager—Technical Insights
- Vice President, Strategic Marketing

We are now at the end of our journey, and we should pause for breath and see how far we've come in our very special look at competitive intelligence.

Have we reached our destination? Is there a next leg to this journey? Have we conveyed the message appropriately? Do you now understand the value of CI? Will you apply the lessons you learned here to your business? Will you and your company undertake some CI activities to learn its value, and will you listen to the findings, regardless of what may be uncovered?

The purpose of this book is to hammer home my passionate belief that there is enormous value to conducting competitive intelligence. There is no doubt that a good CI investigation will provide an advantage to you and your company, by minimizing risk, avoiding surprises, and making smarter decisions.

Yes, this is the end of the book. Embrace the experts who produce good CI reports; they hold up a mirror to reflect the realities of the marketplace, and that can only be a good thing.

"The greatest obstacle to discovery is not ignorance. It's the illusion of knowledge."
—Daniel Boorstein, historian

Acknowledgments

No one ever writes a book alone, and I certainly could not have done so without the support and help from colleagues and friends, some of whom contributed to this effort and many more of whom went out of their way to give me continuing encouragement.

Far more people, over the course of my business life, helped than I can thank here in this brief acknowledgment. It is the cumulative wisdom they willingly shared that allowed me to put my thoughts down on paper. I particularly want to thank my many competitive intelligence/SCIP (Society of Competitive Intelligence Professionals) colleagues—especially Babette Bensoussan, my dear Aussie colleague and author of multiple books, who was always just a phone call away to share her deep understanding of business, competitive intelligence, and strategy.

Dan Himelfarb, my colleague and friend for more than 20 years, has offered continuing friendship and innumerable hours discussing how to make CI more valuable. Thanks to Jan Herring, Ellen Naylor, Arik Johnson, Tim Powell, Sheila Wright, Jonathan Calof, Richard Horowitz, John McGonagle, Bonnie Hohhoff, Steve McIntosh, and August Jackson.

Paula Johnson has been my go-to colleague for honing my message; and Devon Blaine and Paul Edwards supplied critical information about publishing when I started this project. Jane Applegate generously shared the benefits of her experience and provided invaluable exposure for CI and me. The Association for Strategic Planning afforded numerous opportunities to foster a better understanding of the connection between CI and strategy.

My family has always been behind me in this endeavor, and I want to thank my children, Briana and Adam, who take great interest in my projects and who have incorporated some of my thinking and CI practices into their own business careers. My husband, André, who writes a little, has provided objectivity and has constantly challenged me; he still keeps asking, "Who's doing the movie?"

A special thank you to my transhuman friend FM-2030 who taught me to think about the future in an expansive and exciting way. And I am very grateful to John Wiley & Sons for making this book a reality and for the opportunity to share my passion.

About the Author

Seena Sharp is a pioneer in competitive intelligence, having established one of the first competitive intelligence firms in the United States in 1979—Sharp Market Intelligence. The Los Angeles–based firm, which works with companies across the United States, Europe, Asia, and Africa, publishes the popular *SharpInsights*, brief alerts on market changes.

Sharp Market Intelligence provides "market due diligence" and early warning to companies that are evaluating growth opportunities—market entry or expansion, new product launches, strategic planning, mergers and acquisitions, new distribution channels, and business development.

Her company has worked with a broad array of the world's leading businesses, including American Express, Nestlé, Berkshire Hathaway, Hilton, Rubbermaid, Chase Manhattan Bank, Blue Cross, Mitsubishi, American Cancer Society, and many more companies whose names are less familiar.

Brooklyn-born, Sharp earned her credentials in mathematics and a master's degree from New York University. During this time she worked for four corporations in New York City, including BBDO Advertising.

Sharp has authored or been featured in dozens of articles in such publications as *World Trade, Inc., Marketing News, Boardroom Reports, Bloomberg Business, Chief Information Officer Journal, Los Angeles Times, Nation's Business,* as well as in competitive intelligence publications. *Competitive Intelligence Advantage* is her first book.

Passionate about sharing the value of competitive intelligence, she has addressed business groups throughout the United States and Europe, including Harvard Business School's Entrepreneurial Conference, the New York Times Small Business Summit, European Business Information Conference, Strategic Leadership Forum, American Management Association, American Marketing Association, private companies, and universities including Thunderbird, UCLA (University of California Los Angeles), and the University of Wisconsin.

Sharp received the Fellows Award from her professional association, Society of Competitive Intelligence Professionals.

Index